Kangaroo Dreams

A Memoir

Tuan V. Nguyen

Quill Hawk Publishing

ISBN: 978-1-965142-61-5 (Paperback)

ISBN: 978-1-965142-62-2 (Hardback)

Library of Congress LCCN: 2025923376

Book Cover by Ava Wood, Fins and Feathers Designs

Quill Hawk Publishing (Edmond, OK)

For my mother, father, and extended family in Kiên Giang, Bình Định, Australia, and the United States.

In loving memory of my elder brother, who lost his life at sea in the pursuit of freedom.

For all boat people and refugees in the world.

"Each Vietnamese refugee—or indeed any refugee—in the world is a piece of history that needs to be told. They embody misery and suffering, and they force us to confront terrible chaos and evil, but they cherish us for their enrichment to our society."
–Dr. Tuan V. Nguyen

Contents

Preface

Life's trajectory rarely follows a straight line. Mine has been a voyage filled with unexpected turns, heartbreaking loss, and moments of profound rejoicing. This memoir chronicles my journey, from a young refugee seeking freedom to a medical scientist dedicated to research in the field of Osteoporosis.

The daring and perilous escape from Vietnam remains vivid in my memory, marked by the desperation and uncertainty of a future adrift at sea. Yet, amid the hardship, a flicker of hope emerged. A simple comment about a kangaroo, Australia's national emblem, during my immigration interview led me to a land brimming with opportunity. This is the inspiration behind the title of my memoir, Kangaroo Dream.

Australia embraced me with open arms. It became a sanctuary where I could rebuild my life and pursue my passion for knowledge. My life journey in Australia is a story not just of personal fulfilment, but of the remarkable individuals who supported me along the way: mentors who guided me, colleagues who inspired me, and a nation that embraced me as her own.

This memoir was written and published in 2025, marking half a century since the Vietnamese "boat people" settled in Australia and Western countries. This memoir serves not only as a reflection of my personal life journey, but also as a contribution to the collective narrative of refugees around the world. These accounts can help readers, both at home and abroad, understand the reasons behind our departure from our homeland in the past and the emergence of an overseas Vietnamese community that has made, and continues to make, significant contributions to both Vietnam and the world.

While this memoir chronicles my journey, I believe it also mirrors the shared experiences of millions of Vietnamese refugees or "boat people" worldwide who haven't had the opportunity to tell their stories. Like me, they endured hardships in foreign lands, fought to survive in unfamiliar societies, supported their homeland from afar, and rose above adversity. Each refugee, anywhere in the world, is a living history that deserves to be told. They carry the weight of misery and suffering, compelling us to face chaos and evil, yet their resilience and contributions enrich our society. I hope this memoir gives voice to their untold stories.

My journey as a medical scientist feels like an untold story. Unlike many other scientific fields, memoirs by medical researchers are rare. By sharing my stories, I aim to illuminate the fascinating and often challenging journey of medical discovery. This field needs funding support in Australia. A deeper understanding of medical research fosters appreciation for its role in saving lives and improving our overall well-being.

As you delve into these pages, you'll discover both the joys and the struggles, including the years lost to war, the longing for a homeland left behind, and the relentless pursuit of a dream that took root in a foreign land. Ultimately, it's a story of resilience, the enduring human spirit, and the profound impact one can have when given the chance to flourish.

Tuan Van Nguyen

Prologue

The year was 2021, and the crisp October air held a hint of something more... a turning point. Sunlight streamed through my office window. It was the hue of aged honey, casting light upon the mountain of research papers that seemed poised to overwhelm me entirely. Just another day in the relentless trenches of academia.

Then, my phone buzzed, displaying a "No ID" number, the kind typically associated with unsolicited telemarketing pitches. With a groan, I considered letting it go. But a strange premonition, a prickle at the back of my neck, urged me to answer.

"Hello?" I answered, bracing myself for the usual sales spiel.

The voice on the other end was clipped and forma. "I would like to speak to Professor Tuan Nguyen."

I confirmed my identity, a sliver of unease creeping in as the caller introduced himself. "This is Paul Singer from the Office of the Governor-General." My initial skepticism flared as elaborate scams were getting out of hand these days.

"We've been trying to reach you," he continued, a hint of reproach lacing his voice. He referred to emails and calls to the university, all efforts I had entirely overlooked amid the intensity of my research. Feeling embarrassed, I offered stammered apologies.

Then, a totally unexpected news arrived. "Professor," he announced, his voice dropping an octave, "I have some good news for you. You've been nominated for the Order of Australia."

Silence. The weight of the words hung heavy in the air. The Order of Australia, the nation's highest civilian honor, seemed unreal to me. Then, a wave of questions rushed through my mind: Who had nominated me? How did they know about my work?

But the regulations, Mr. Singer explained, maintained strict confidentiality. No names, no details. Just a simple request—acknowledge the nomination and follow the online procedures. As I navigated the website, a section outlining my contributions caught my eye:

For significant service to medical research, to osteoporosis and fracture prevention, and to tertiary education.

Words that reflected years of dedication, a life poured into chasing knowledge to improve lives. Mr. Singer revealed that the list of those awarded the Order of Australia would be announced on a very specific date: January 26, 2022. Australia Day.

Mixed emotions flickered within me. This recognition, on the cusp of a significant anniversary, felt like a twist of fate. January 26th, 1982, was the day I arrived in Australia. Forty years later, on the very same day, the Order of Australia might be conferred upon me. A coincidence? Perhaps. But for me, it felt like a serendipitous link, a culmination of an odyssey that stretched far beyond this moment.

The first person I couldn't wait to share this news with was Professor John Eisman, my former mentor and confidante at the Garvan Institute of Medical Research. As I recounted the phone call, we reminisced about the path we'd traveled together, a shared journey of osteoporosis research filled with triumphs and setbacks. John disclosed a secret, revealing that he had been among those contacted to verify my work, bound by a confidentiality clause that prevented him from sharing the news earlier. "You've come a long way," he said, a familiar warmth in his voice.

My long way began with a perilous sea crossing, continued through the harsh realities of refugee camps, and eventually found solace in the land I now proudly call home: the Lucky Country. This country embraced me, and I had poured my life's work into it.

This prologue is just the beginning—the first chapter of a story that transcends my own. It's a story about countless refugees who, like me, fled conflict and rebuilt their lives, contributing to their adopted home. It's a proof of the resilience of the human spirit, the hope that propels us forward, and the profound changes a new homeland can foster.

Time may blur the edges, but the core remains: a tale of displacement, survival, and the hard-earned sense of home. Join me as I retrace the steps of my journey, weaving together threads of exile, resilience, and the profound embrace of a new life.

Chapter One

The Mekong Flows Through Me

The Mekong Delta has always cradled my life, a fertile land where rice paddies shimmer under the endless sun. Born into a family of farmers, my roots run deep in this rich soil. My father, Nguyễn Ý, hailed from Phước Thành village in Tuy Phước district, a small, quiet place far north in Bình Định province of Central Việt Nam.

I knew little of my paternal grandfather, Nguyễn Chín (or perhaps Chính). His birth and death dates were mysteries swallowed by time. The only echo of him that reached me was through my grandmother's story. Upon hearing news of my father being wounded in the South, she vanished like smoke in the wind, leaving a gaping hole in our family history.

In the 1940s, my father moved south, a young man swept up in the tide of the Việt Minh Army fighting against the French. He rose through the ranks to become an officer until a fierce battle at Cây Trâm commune (near Rạch Sỏi town) took a cruel turn. French forces inflicted a grievous wound, forcing doctors with limited resources to amputate his right arm. War's brutality had marked him deeply. Discharged from the army, he returned to the land. His spirit unbroken, he became a farmer.

My mother's side of the family told a different story. My maternal grandfather, Nguyễn Ngọc Châu (1897-1962), came from Mỹ Chánh village in Phù Mỹ district, also in Bình Định. How he ended up in the south and married my grandmother, Nguyễn Thị Thân (1905-1989), remains a mystery. Whispers of a great-grandmother of Chinese descent add a touch of intrigue to our lineage, an extended family that thrived and grew to nearly 1,000 members. Imagine that—in a village of just 5,000, our extended family made up almost a fifth of the population. We were a village within a village, bound by blood and shared history.

Four children blessed my maternal grandparents. My mother, Nguyễn Thị Thinh, was the eldest, followed by my uncle Trà and aunts Biên and Số. Uncle Trà rose to become a village-level official during the Republic of Vietnam (1954-1975), but was tragically taken in a motorcycle accident in 1968, leaving behind a young family. My grandfather also brought a cousin, Hạng, whom we lovingly called Cậu Hai, meaning Uncle Two. He was a fellow Việt Minh soldier who fought alongside my father against the French. Sadly, he fell in battle in Kiên Giang, leaving behind five more orphaned children.

The winds of war further scattered our family. The branches of our family tree stretched far beyond Bình Định. Two uncles, Uncle Three and Uncle Four, once high-ranking officers in the People's Army of Vietnam, regrouped in the north, retired in the 1980s, and returned to their roots in Phù Mỹ. The separation from a "branch" of our family in Kiên Giang stretched for an agonizing 70 years until a chance encounter on television in 2006 rekindled the connection. Years later, fate offered me a chance to visit both my paternal and maternal hometowns on a work trip to Quy Nhơn. Walking those ancestral lands, I couldn't help but feel the weight of history, the triumphs and tragedies that shaped who I am today.

The veil over my parents' courtship remains thin. Their story, like so many others shaped by war, remains untold. Yet life bloomed amidst the chaos. In 1950, my eldest brother arrived, the first of seven siblings to grace our family. Though fate initially intended for nine, a heartbreaking twist took my eldest sister at birth and a younger brother, Khánh, in a river accident at the tender age of six. We, the remaining children, found solace in the gentle murmur of the Bàn Tân Định riverside village, its lullaby a constant in our lives.

This is my father's birthplace: Phước Thành village, Tuy Phước District, Bình Định Province.

My village wasn't much to look at on a map, just a dot about 25 kilometers from Rạch Giá Town (which is now a full-fledged city). But to us kids, it was the center of the universe. It was prosperous too, not in a fancy way, but in a solid, built-to-last way. The houses were sturdy, and the heart of the village beat in the bustling market. Every day, folks came from all around to trade their goods. It was a symphony of colors and smells—mountains of ripe mangoes next to baskets of fat, wriggling carp, and the earthy scent of fresh vegetables mingling with the sweet perfume of baked goods. Walking to school each morning, I'd weave through the crowd, mesmerized by the vibrant stalls. The market spilled over into little shops lining the streets, selling everything a person could need, from clothes and medicine to a fresh haircut. Our village was like a microcosm of the Mekong Delta itself, a place humming with economic activity, but always bathed in a sense of peacefulness.

Mom and Dad in front of the house they built, and the one that built me.

Our house wasn't much—a small thing nestled right on the riverbank and dwarfed by the towering coconut palms that swayed in the breeze. But from our little porch, the whole village unfolded before my eyes like a beautiful map. The gentle river meandered like a silver ribbon, reflecting the sky, and the village sprawled out on either side. There were neat rows of tiled-roof houses, interspersed with older houses with thatched roofs that whispered of tradition. Beyond the village, the green rice fields stretched out to the horizon, an endless sea of green that swayed in the wind. Behind our house, we had our little paradise—a shady orchard where fruit hung heavy on the branches, and cool, clear ditches teeming with fish. Whenever guests came by, there was no need for fancy preparations. We'd simply head out back, pluck some fresh vegetables, and maybe chase a fish or two for a feast.

Our neighborhood was a wonderful mix of cultures, and many of our kindest neighbors were Khmer families. They always spoiled us with delicious homemade cakes. These sweet treats were a welcome surprise left on our doorstep. My mother, never one to be outdone in the generosity department, would whip up her most mouthwatering creations and invite them over for a shared meal. Village life had a simple rhythm to it. Each morning, after the lively buzz of the market had settled, folks would head out to their fields. Under the golden kiss of the rising sun, silhouettes bent and swayed, a peaceful yet vibrant dance of labor across the landscape. By midday, the heat would become too much to bear, and everyone would drift back home for a well-deserved rest. It was a life lived in harmony with the land, a beautiful simplicity that left a lasting impression on me.

As the sun dipped lower in the late afternoon, casting long shadows across the land, the rice fields transformed once more. They cloaked themselves in a peaceful, idyllic beauty, the air thick with the promise of nightfall. But it was on moonlit nights that the village truly came alive. The scene took on an almost magical quality, bathed in the ethereal glow of the moon. The sprawling branches of the trees provided a natural gathering place for villagers, whose voices intertwined in a melodious chorus of conversation and songs. Laughter would ripple outwards, carried on the gentle breeze, creating a sense of warmth and joy that spread through the entire village. On some nights, the rhythmic pounding of pestles against mortars would fill the air, a traditional soundtrack to the act of threshing rice under the watchful eye of the moon. It felt like a scene straight out of Musician Lam Phương's "Khúc Ca Ngày Mùa," a timeless melody that captured the very essence of our village life:

Behold the vast countryside under the golden moon
The clear moonlight shines through the deserted village
Shines on the soul of the village, many songs of love for life
Shines on the soul of the village,
many songs of love for life

...

Let's dance and sing together as the moon rises
Wishing for two seasons of fragrant rice
Rice brings back many wonderful songs
Rice brings back many wonderful songs ...

Education was just as important in our household as the crops we tended. My father often said, "Knowledge is like a lamp, lighting the way to a brighter future." Our village only had one small elementary school, but it was a place that buzzed with life under the guidance of Mr. Phát, the principal, and his dedicated children, who were all teachers.

Mr. Phát epitomized conservative values such as respect for elders, hard work, honesty, patriotism, humility, discipline, personal honor, and chivalry. He instilled within us these lessons through daily pronouncements like, "Did anyone disrespect their parents today?" This mantra echoed deeply and was a constant reminder of my filial duty.

According to the gossip of the village elders, I was one of the brightest and well-behaved students. Report cards were never a source of worry, as I never dipped below third place in my class. My mother often laughed when she recounted how, as a child, I would pester her with endless questions, one of my favorites being, "When will I learn enough to be president?"

My Father: Wounds of War, Woven in Time

My father, a man of spiritual strength, became a village legend. Despite the missing limb, he carved out a life of purpose. Mr. Ba Ý, a nickname synonymous with him, was well-known throughout the village. Even war couldn't extinguish his spirit. He wielded his sickle with practiced ease, and his penmanship remained a source of pride. Whispers painted a picture of a time after his discharge from the Việt Minh army when suspicion hung heavy. The Ngô Đình Diệm government branded him a "communist planted back" in the South, resulting in his arrest despite minimal evidence. Thankfully, after just six months, he was released due to insufficient proof.

Farming was the rhythm of his days. Sunrises found him tending to his fields, a cup of coffee at the local market his only daily indulgence, except for the jubilant celebrations of Tết. Only then did the fields take a backseat.

His circle of friends was vast, but a singular bond shone brightest - Uncle Tế. Originally from Thái Bình (North Vietnam), he had migrated south in 1945. During my father's imprisonment, a reflection of their deep friendship, Uncle Tế risked everything. Under the cloak of darkness, he rowed a little boat to deliver a hidden bag of rice, which was a beacon of support in a desperate time. Uncle Tế, a man who yearned for peace, echoed that sentiment in the names he bestowed upon his children: Quyết (Resolve), Chiến (Fight), Sinh (Life), Bình (Peace), Tồn (Exist), Tiến (Progress), Yên (Accord), and Lành (Happy). These weren't just names; they embodied his values, a legacy I hold dear. These were the faces I considered siblings, an extension of the family my parents had built.

Uncle Tế's family was like a microcosm of Vietnam. One of his sons, Chiến, had served in the South Vietnamese Army, while another, Sinh, had joined the communists. Yet, they treated each other like blood brothers, without any conflict whatsoever.

In 2004, my father passed away at the age of 81, after a brief illness, leaving a void that time would slowly mend.

My Mother's Quiet Constellation

My mother embodied the spirit of countless Vietnamese mothers, their lives woven from sacrifice and devotion to family. She spent her days tending to the hearth and her family, consistently placing our needs before her own. A vibrant splash of color was absent from her wardrobe; her clothes, whether simple tunics (áo dài) or everyday wear, were a symphony of browns, blacks, and the deepest blues. Even the white blouse she possessed was more of an eggshell whisper than a true white. Makeup was a foreign concept, even on the joyous occasions of my younger sisters' weddings.

Her world revolved around the rhythms of our home, punctuated only by trips to the nearby pagoda or the market in the heart of the village. Venturing further, say to Sài Gòn, was reserved solely for medical emergencies and hospital stays. This reality meant the simple pleasure of sharing a leisurely meal with her children and grandchildren was one she never truly experienced. In the years of my visits back home, I longed to treat her to a restaurant meal—a chance to show her off—but my intentions were always met with a gentle but firm rejection. Reasons varied from the perceived extravagance to the comforting familiarity of a home-cooked meal. As a consequence, my mother, even by the standards of our small town, never truly indulged in a luxurious meal.

Her formal education mirrored that of many rural mothers—a mere five years of schooling, enough to equip her with basic reading and writing skills. However, life's lessons were learned not through textbooks but through the calloused hands guiding a boat oar or the deftness of a hand preparing a nourishing meal. Letters never flowed from her pen, nor did she ever grasp the novelty of a telephone. Yet, a quiet pride in the accomplishments of her children and grandchildren swelled within her. Her words, a constant refrain, still resonate with me: "The most difficult lesson in life is how to live."

During my elementary school years, every academic achievement was celebrated with a trip to the market and a sweet reward—a bowl of bánh tầm bì, with its thick, round rice noodles served with shredded pork skin, fresh herbs, pickled vegetables, and a side of sweetened fish sauce. This treat was as delightful as her love.

I vividly recall my sixth-grade entrance exam, a critical milestone at the time. To take this exam, I had to make the long journey to the town of Rạch Giá, just like many other rural students in my village. That morning, I boarded a wooden boat. She had packed my favorite snack—sticky rice with peanuts and salt, carefully wrapped in banana leaves—and slipped in a few coins for a treat of iced syrup. When I returned, she was there waiting by the riverbank, her eyes filled with concern as she asked how the exam went. I told her about the tricky math problem involving water pipes filling a tank, a puzzle I had encountered during my primary school years. Despite the challenge, I succeeded, earning second place in the province and proudly passing the exam. The memory of that day underscores the support and quiet strength that was the hallmark of my mother.

High school took me to Rạch Giá town, a world away from the familiar rice fields of home. There, I lived with relatives on my mother's side, alongside two of my cousins. News of any small accomplishment would send ripples back to our village. Soon, a familiar figure would appear on the horizon—my mother, arriving by riverboat with a bounty of love in the form of sticky rice, fruits, and sometimes even the rare treat of chicken or duck. These stolen moments together were fleeting, mere whispers amidst the constant churn of the river. A few precious hours, punctuated by stolen glances at the clock, before she had to catch the afternoon boat back home. Back then, the journey was a four-hour odyssey, nothing like the swift thirty-minute Honda rides we take today.

This pride in achievement echoed through the generations. News of a grand-child or niece succeeding would bring a radiant smile to my mother's face. A few years ago, when one of my nieces aced her college entrance exams, the news became a village celebration. "Little Thuận got into college!" my mother would proclaim to anyone who crossed her path, her voice brimming with a joy that warmed the very air. One sweltering summer afternoon, I found my mom on the sofa, meticulously counting something. When I peered closer, I saw a list of her grandchildren, each name marked with a small tick. A contented chuckle escaped her lips as she muttered to herself, "These kids are quite good."

Unlike the common perception in Vietnam, favoritism was a foreign concept in our household. My mother loved each of us with an evenness. Being the youngest son brought no special privileges. In fact, her heart often ached for my older brothers. The second, tragically, vanished while escaping by boat from Việt Nam, leaving a void that time could never fully mend. The third, she would lament, "He's working too hard," her voice filled with quiet worry. This same unconditional love extended to her grandchildren and nieces. Distance, however, played a subtle role. Living near my mother, my nieces and nephews enjoyed a closeness my own children couldn't replicate.

A special place in her heart was reserved for my cousins, particularly the children of Uncle Trà. Perhaps it was a reflection of her deep love for her father, who had only one son. Any gossip or negativity aimed at them was met with her swift disapproval, a fierce protectiveness that never wavered. Even in her final days, when words failed her, a flicker of recognition and affection would light up her eyes whenever my cousins visited her.

My Aunt Tư, my mother's sister-in-law, was another recipient of her love. After Uncle Tư's passing, Aunt decided not to remarry, devoting herself to raising her children with quiet resilience. She recalled her initial nervousness upon joining the family, a feeling that quickly melted away. In all the years since, my mother, Aunt Tư recounted, had never spoken a harsh word, demonstrating the gentle spirit that defined her.

On July 17th, 2008, at the age of seventy-nine, my mother passed away.

As the Western saying goes, "There are many wonders in this world, but the greatest and grandest wonder is still the mother." Losing her was like losing a piece of the very sun that gave my life warmth. Tears, on that day, flowed freely, a natural outpouring of grief for the greatest treasure I had ever known.

Looking back, life before 1975 wasn't one of luxury, but we weren't impoverished either. Through sheer hard work and perseverance, my parents accumulated a wealth of farmland across districts. Our family even possessed three tractors, marvels of engineering imported from France and the United States. I vividly recall a specific green John Deere tractor, a symbol of the partnership between my father and an uncle. These tractors, worth a staggering 1,000 taels of gold each, served countless farmers in the area. The tractors were more than just machines; the income generated by the tractors also funded my brothers' and my education in Rạch Giá and Sài Gòn.

My mother Nguyễn Thị Thinh (1928-July 17, 2008)

My Eldest Brother's Beacon

My parents, though farmers themselves, instilled in all of us a thirst for knowledge. My eldest brother was the shining star, a beacon of academic achievement that cast its light on the entire extended family. He was the village's first torchbearer, the one who aced the National Talent Examination and graduated from university as a chemical engineer. There was another star, a female cousin who also passed the exam, but societal expectations in the 1960s kept her from university. Back then, the national talent exam was a brutal filter, only allowing 10-15% of high school students through, and a mere 5-10% of those chosen for university. Education was a privilege reserved for the elite, and those who breached its gates became local heroes.

My brother wore another hat—that of a teacher. When high school beckoned, I found myself living with him in a boarding house. Those were formative days, etched in my memory with a bittersweet ache. Studying became my lifeblood, fueled by his constant exhortations to "read a lot, books are your weapons." Idleness was met with a swift, "What are you doing? Aiming to be a garbage collector?" I wasn't a dunce, but in his eyes, I perpetually fell short. The quadratic equation became my personal Mt. Everest, and his booming frustration, "With this performance, what future awaits you?" echoed in my ears. Frustration gnawed at me, but defiance remained a foreign language. A flicker of pride in my academic awards, displayed proudly on the coffee table, was met with a dismissive, "Mediocre at best, competing with the blind." Praise was a rare commodity, yet it became clear—his harshness was a twisted form of encouragement, a relentless push to reach for an ever-receding horizon.

The fall of Sài Gòn in 1975 brought changes. My brother, after a brief stint in a state-owned company, abruptly quit. The reasons remained unspoken, but the rigid structure chafed at his spirit. He retreated to the familiar embrace of our grandparents in the countryside. Unlike the calloused hands of my father and me, his were unfamiliar with the feel of a plow. Some called him a "dandy;" his Honda motorbike and "fashionable" attire represented a euphemism for a "bourgeois" lifestyle back then, setting him apart. In the rustic haven of our grandparents' house, he was the favored child, indulging in coffee runs to Rạch Giá with his friends on his trusty Honda. It was on one such trip that our paths crossed.

His demeanor held an unfamiliar urgency. He revealed his plan to flee the country, his voice laced with a question: "Are you coming?" The idealism still clung to me, a stubborn belief in a brighter future. Witnessing the exodus from

Sài Gòn had left me wary. Friends vanishing from work, whispers of jungle camps, and the harrowing tales of those who escaped only to be captured... these were the realities that painted a grim picture. My silence hung heavy in the air. With a sigh, he entrusted his Honda and precious Seiko watch to me, his voice thick with emotion, "Take them. Tell Mom and Dad... I'm leaving."

Little did I know that stolen moment by the roadside would be our final good-bye. It was this very act of kindness, this parting gift, that would later paint me as a bourgeoisie in the eyes of my communist colleagues. The constant jibes and the accusations of a bourgeois lifestyle became not just stupid but unbearable.

My elder brother, Nguyễn Tuấn Khải, who vanished into the unforgiving waves of the South China Sea during his 1981 escape from Vietnam.

The escape route was an unorthodox one—a fishing boat captained by the soon-to-be father-in-law of my brother's fiancée. The man, a seasoned sailor with over three decades at sea, boasted he could navigate back to Rạch Giá blindfolded. This instilled a sliver of hope and a fragile belief in a safe passage.

Twenty souls in total, all from my brother's future wife's family, embarked on that perilous journey at the tail end of 1980. The exact date remains lost in the swirling mists of time.

Silence descended, a heavy cloak that choked life out of hope. The boat, with its human cargo, vanished without a trace. Accident? Storm? Pirates? The sea offered no answers, its vastness a graveyard of secrets. Even a visit from a medium, a figure believed to possess the ability to commune with the dead, yielded no solace. My mother, at the mere mention of my brother's name, would crumble, tears etching deep furrows down her weathered cheeks.

A few months later, my journey to a refugee camp in Thái Lan offered a glimmer of hope, a desperate grasp at finding my brother. Notices plastered on walls, pleas to the Red Cross, outreach to the United Nations and volunteer organizations—each avenue a dead end. Perhaps the sea claimed him, another nameless soul lost in its vast embrace.

He wasn't alone. The United Nations estimated that from 1975 to 1995, close to a million Vietnamese embarked on perilous sea journeys, fleeing a war-torn homeland. Thái Lan, a beacon of hope, witnessed the brunt of this exodus. A study painted a grim picture—over half the boats fell prey to pirates, and a staggering 200,000 to 400,000 vanished, their passengers lost forever at sea, never to reach the promised land.

He became one of the Vietnamese souls claimed by the sea during that desperate exodus. His life was cut short by the yearning for freedom. The sea holds his remains, but the ache in our hearts will forever ripple from his absence.

Chapter Two

Unforgettable Days

The Vietnam of fifty years ago was a world apart from the one we know today. A generation gap has grown between those who lived through the turbulent times of the past and those who were born into a more peaceful time. Many young people born after 1975 know little about Vietnam from half a century ago, despite occasional media references to the "subsidy period" and the hardships of that time. Many young people don't understand why there is such a large Vietnamese community abroad today. My nieces and nephews wonder why their uncles and aunts left Vietnam to settle in foreign countries. Therefore, I thought I'd share a few memories of Vietnam from half a century ago so that we can better understand and empathize with each other.

I grew up during the long war that spanned from 1954 to 1975. The fateful year of 1954, when Vietnam was divided into North and South, was also the year I was born. From 1954 to 1975, Vietnam was split into two: the North, following communist ideology, and the South, adopting a republican system that could be considered, to some extent, democratic. The North, backed by the Soviet Union and China, fought against the South, supported by the United States and its allies, under the banner of "Resist America, Save the Country." But in reality, it was a proxy war, a brutal civil war between brothers, lasting more than two decades.

The peaceful memories of the 1960s that I described above were fleeting, as the atmosphere of war intensified in the late 1960s and early 1970s. My village was informally classified as a "rice and bean" area, meaning that while most of its residents lived in regions under the control of the Republic of Vietnam (RVN) government, some resided in territories governed by the communist guerrillas, commonly known as the Việt Cộng. In certain rural areas, the RVN maintained control during the day, but at night, the communist guerrillas would return to their families to obtain food and medicine. Everyone knew which families had members who were Việt Cộng, but no one spoke of it openly. We all maintained a facade of normalcy. Occasionally, Uncle Ba Tẻ, a close friend of my family, would ask my father to buy medicine for him to deliver to the Việt Cộng in the neighboring villages, where my parents owned a lot of land and tractors.

I saw the RVN army conduct operations in the rice fields behind our house. Sometimes, armored vehicles came. There was rarely any shooting. They'd sometimes stop by our house and ask for a few chickens. I also saw American and South Vietnamese soldiers patrol the river in flat-bottomed wooden boats called sampans. The Americans sometimes swam in the river, likely due to the heat. I'd see a few guerrillas in the village at night; they'd sometimes ask for money or medical supplies. They seemed friendly enough.

Whenever there was a clash between the RVN army and the Việt Cộng, the vast majority of villagers would flee to areas controlled by the RVN. They had understandable concerns about the guerrillas due to their secretive nature and the rumors of their harsh methods for resolving disagreements. I witnessed some terrible deaths. On my way to school many mornings, I'd see bodies floating in the river that villagers or local soldiers had recovered. They wouldn't let us kids get too close, but I'd sneak a peek and see many bodies with their heads smashed in. People said the Việt Cộng accused them of being traitors in the neighboring villages and had been executed with hammers before being thrown into the river. I later saw a hammer like that in a museum in Bến Tre province.

On April 30, 1975, after twenty years of bloody war, Vietnam was reunified. The twenty-year war caused immense losses to the nation. No one knows the exact number of casualties during the war, but it is estimated that around two to four million people, both soldiers and civilians from the North and the South, had died. The North suffered more losses than the South.

The reunification of the country was met with jubilation by many, including me. In the South, people were weary of war and loss, so April 30, 1975, was seen as the end of the conflict and the beginning of national unity, rather than a victory for one side over the other. However, those in power had different plans. They aimed to dismantle the South's relatively advanced economy, suppress its cultural and educational institutions, and replace them with a new ideology modeled after the Soviet Union and China.

However, the events that unfolded after 1975 showed that the revolutionary regime had failed in its mission to build the country. Just five years after reunification, the South, and indeed the whole of Vietnam, was plunged into economic recession, national division, social injustice, and moral decay. Almost all aspects of social life in the South, including arts and culture, were fundamentally and systematically changed. "Systematically" here means that it was deliberate, categorized, and compartmentalized. I witnessed these changes firsthand, from a personal and family perspective.

The new regime's cultural policies were particularly striking. Media outlets were filled with harsh accusations, labeling cultural works from the RVN era as "degenerate" and "poison" from the "American Empire." This led to the banning of thousands of popular songs, including love songs by renowned artists such as Phạm Duy, Trầm Tử Thiêng, Lam Phương, Vũ Thành An, Từ Công Phụng, and Nhật Trường. Unfortunately, their lack of understanding of Western culture further muddied the waters. For instance, Phạm Duy's song "Mùa Thu Chết," inspired by the French poem, "L'Adieu" by Guillaume Apollinaire, was deemed "anti-Autumn Revolution!" These superficial and childish generalizations, published in black-and-white newspapers, caused anyone with even a basic appreciation for art and culture to shake their heads in dismay at the intellectual capabilities of the new regime's cultural administrators.

Before the fall of Sài Gòn in 1975, a vibrant literary landscape flourished. Authors such as Võ Phiến, Dương Nghiễm Mậu, Mai Thảo, Thanh Tâm Tuyền, Tô Thùy Yên, Duyên Anh, and numerous others explored diverse themes and

22

created timeless works. But the new revolutionary regime brought a chilling silence. These writers, once celebrated, were now branded "cultural saboteurs" for the West. Their works, deemed subversive, were banned and vanished from shelves. Even some purely research-based works (such as surveys of 19th-century peasant life) did not escape the label of "cultural poison."

The irony wasn't lost on me. In school, we'd learned about China's ruthless Emperor Qin Shi Huang, who burned books to silence dissent. Little did I know, a similar purge would unfold in my country. Following a propaganda blitz demonizing these authors, book burnings became a horrifying reality. Mountains of books and newspapers—legacies of the Republic of Vietnam era—were piled high in public squares. As flames devoured these pages, cheers erupted from the indoctrinated, while the true guardians of culture could only sigh in despair.

The irony is that after more than forty years of reunification, those literary works have been republished, and those songs deemed "decadent" and "sentimental" are now performed publicly. After more than four decades, bolero songs—once condemned—have suddenly experienced a revival, completely eclipsing the popularity of the "red songs" that glorified the revolution. This shift reflects the naivety and hasty judgments of those in power at the time, who failed to understand the enduring power of art to resonate with the human spirit. It's a tribute to the enduring human desire for stories that transcend ideology and capture the complexities of life—the joy, the sorrow, and the simple beauty of everyday existence. These banned works, previously regarded as dangerous, now serve as monuments to a suppressed past, reminding us of the voices that were considered inappropriate during that turbulent era. Their resurgence feels like a long-awaited victory, a vindication for the artists and readers who cherished them in secret all those years.

The "revolutionaries" also imposed a new type of language in the South. It was still Vietnamese, but a Vietnamese that was being sinicized. In the past, our Vietnamese language had a natural structure, evident in everyday words like "bảo đảm" (ensure), "đơn giản" (simple), "thành hình" (take shape), "khai triển" (develop), and "ít nhiều" (more or less). However, under the new regime, these words were suddenly inverted to "đảm bảo," "giản đơn," "hình thành," "triển khai," and "nhiều ít." The meanings remained more or less the same, but the way of speaking and writing was reversed. Only later, through research, did I discover that all these inversions were common ways of speaking and writing in Chinese.

The new regime embarked on a subtle yet pervasive campaign to erase Southern Vietnamese dialects. Familiar names like Tân Sơn Nhứt Airport were given clunky, bureaucratic titles like "Tân Sơn Nhất Station." Even everyday words like "bùng binh" (traffic circle), ingrained in the Southern vocabulary, were replaced with more "standardized" terms like "vòng xuyến," which left everyone bewildered. The absurdity reached new heights when Từ Dũ maternity hospital was briefly renamed "The Delivery Workshop." This new, sterile linguistic style felt forced and childish, very different from the rich Southern dialect. These changes fostered a sense of alienation among Southerners. Unification began to feel more like occupation by a new power, one that sought to erase our cultural identity.

This cultural purge extended beyond language. Campaigns were launched to enforce a new aesthetic on Southern youth. Long hair, a symbol of rebellion even in the West, was deemed unacceptable. Anyone unfortunate enough to be caught with it risked a public head shaving–a humiliating spectacle designed to break spirits. Fashion wasn't spared either. The once-trendy styles of the 1970s were deemed decadent and slashed off backs right on the street. Even the traditional áo dài, a beautiful symbol of Vietnamese womanhood, was frowned upon in government offices, labeled a relic of the "petty bourgeoisie." It appeared that these tactics were more than just fashion edicts; they were deliberate attempts to dismantle the very fabric of Southern life.

The gulf between North and South wasn't just cultural. The new leadership, particularly those from the North who relocated to the South, often displayed a troubling arrogance. Their self-righteous demeanor felt more akin to new-age colonizers than brotherly compatriots. They viewed Southerners with a patronizing air, labeling Southerners as "losers" who needed guidance, particularly in culture, science, and technology. This condescending attitude fueled resentment and a sense of being talked down upon. It was a sharp contrast to the pre-unification South, where we had a strong sense of national pride and intellectual achievements.

The arrogance of the new administration wasn't just a theory; it manifested in everyday interactions. I vividly recall a day at university when a political commissar named Hải addressed a room full of students, lecturers, and professors. His booming northern accent filled the hall, punctuated by wild gesticulations and spittle flying with every emphatic point. He launched into a tirade about the superiority of the socialist system, painting the Republic of Vietnam regime as a bastion of corruption. In his view, everything from the West was deemed negative, while everything from the Soviet bloc was considered exceptional. Soviet watches, he declared, were superior to their Swiss counterparts.

"Who says Swiss watches are good?" he boomed, not waiting for a response before dismissing it as American propaganda. "Soviet watches," he insisted, "are the epitome of beauty and durability." He seemed to relish using the phrase "American puppet" as a derogatory slur against us in the South. Then came his pronouncements: "The American puppet poisoned you all," he thundered. "They bombarded you with so many newspapers and books to confuse you, so that you couldn't distinguish truth from lies." His solution? A chilling declaration: "We will only provide you with what you need to read."

The true meaning of that statement wouldn't dawn on me for another five years. The only newspapers and books allowed were state-controlled publications that strictly adhered to the official narrative. Foreign news was carefully curated, solely from the socialist bloc—primarily the Soviet Union. I also came across some glowing magazine articles portraying life in North Korea as idyllic. These publications reveled in one-sided information: a world where everything socialist was virtuous and America the embodiment of evil.

The human cost of the upheaval was devastating. Some "winners" seized the homes of former officials, a blatant display of dominance. Many acquaintances simply vanished, later resurfacing with whispers of "re-education camps"–a chilling term, I later learned, borrowed from China and the Soviet Union, that masked the reality of imprisonment. These camps weren't solely for military personnel and government officials of the former RVN regime, though they were a primary target. Artists, scholars, business professionals–anyone deemed a potential threat to the new order–found themselves swept up in this brutal purge. The duration of these imprisonments varied wildly, from a few agonizing weeks to a soul-crushing decade.

My father-in-law, who passed away many years ago, endured ten harrowing years in a reeducation camp. Like many others during that tumultuous period, his story remained shrouded in silence, as he was deeply reluctant to discuss the trauma he experienced. What little we know about his ordeal comes from the sparse details he shared with family, painting a picture of unbelievable hardship.

Before his arrest, my father-in-law served as an economic advisor and analyst for the United States Agency for International Development (USAID) in Vietnam. His work involved providing critical economic insights during a time of intense conflict, supporting efforts to stabilize and develop the region. However, after 1975, his association with USAID made him a target, as the new regime often suspected USAID personnel of being CIA operatives. While my family and I had already fled Vietnam as refugees, he was apprehended and sent to one of the notorious reeducation camps, vanishing without a trace. For a time, we were left in agonizing uncertainty, unaware of his whereabouts or condition—a fate shared by countless families torn apart during that chaotic era.

In the camp, my father-in-law faced harsh conditions. He recounted that the initial days were particularly grueling, marked by intense interrogations and torture as the authorities sought to extract information from him. Despite their efforts, he maintained that he was merely an economic analyst, with no sensitive intelligence to offer. Unable to glean anything further, the camp authorities reassigned him to hard labor in the rice fields, where he toiled under harsh conditions alongside other prisoners. The physical demands of this work, coupled with the psychological toll of captivity, tested his endurance.

However, my father-in-law's intellect and unique skills eventually led to a change in his role within the camp. The authorities discovered that he was fluent in the Hán language (classical Chinese), a rare and valuable skill. Recognizing his expertise, they tasked him with teaching Chinese to the camp's cadres, the officials overseeing the prisoners. This shift likely offered him some reprieve from the grueling physical labor, though it did not erase the oppressive reality of his imprisonment. His ability to adapt to these circumstances speaks to his resilience and resourcefulness in the face of adversity.

My father-in-law endured ten long years of imprisonment without ever being formally charged with a crime. The lack of due process was a hallmark of these camps, where individuals were often detained indefinitely based on their past affiliations or perceived threats to the new regime. When he was finally released, he emerged physically and emotionally scarred, carrying the weight of his experiences in silence.

After his release, our relatives in Australia worked tirelessly to sponsor his immigration, reuniting him with family in a new country far from the land of his suffering. He resettled in Australia, where he sought to rebuild his life, but the memories of the camp remained a heavy burden. Despite the opportunities for return, he never set foot in Vietnam again, an indication of the deep wounds left by his decade of imprisonment. Until his passing, he carried the quiet strength of a survivor, though he rarely spoke of the pain he endured, leaving us with only fragments of his remarkable story.

According to the Vietnamese authorities' admissions to Amnesty International, by 1980, over 100 re-education camps dotted the landscape. These official figures, however, painted a sanitized picture. Reports in 1980 suggested well over a million South Vietnamese citizens had been imprisoned, if only briefly. Additionally, 40,000 individuals remained detained without ever facing a trial. By 1988, a Vietnamese deputy foreign minister acknowledged the imprisonment of 100,000 former RVN personnel, while international sources believed the true number to be closer to 200,000.

The human cost of these camps was horrific. Tens of thousands perished within those walls. The precise figures are lost to the fog of war. International organizations estimate over 10,000 deaths, but the true number likely lies much higher. Some succumbed to the crushing mental pressure, driven to suicide by relentless torture and the utter hopelessness of their situation. Others died from the backbreaking labor, from the gnawing hunger and thirst, from illnesses left untreated, or from the brutality inflicted by their captors. Tragically, even prominent figures weren't spared. Scholar Hồ Hữu Tường, despite having no ties to the RVN, found himself imprisoned. Denied proper medical care, his health deteriorated rapidly. Released after two years, he returned home a broken man, dying shortly thereafter. The Ba Sao camp alone bears silent testament to this tragedy; a stele now stands erect to commemorate over 600 souls who perished between 1975 and 1988.

For many released prisoners, life offered little reprieve. They saw only a future devoid of hope, a life under a regime that offered no path forward. Escape became their sole option, driving them to embark on a dangerous journey, either across the border or the sea, in pursuit of freedom. Even their children, no matter how diligently they studied, were condemned to a life with limited opportunities. The new regime implemented a discriminatory policy called "backgroundism," systematically excluding the children of former RVN officials and military personnel from opportunities for higher education. Favoritism ran rampant, with children of party officials categorized into privileged groups for university admissions regardless of their academic merit.

Conversely, students from "undesirable" backgrounds, regardless of their academic competence, were barred from pursuing higher education. This policy choked off the potential of countless talented Southern youth, condemning them to a life of limited prospects and discrimination in their own land. The dreams of university and a path to a brighter future were cruelly snatched away. Millions in Sài Gòn were forcibly relocated to isolated areas euphemistically called "New Economic Zones." These were little more than forced labor camps disguised as economic ventures. Disease and backbreaking labor claimed thousands of lives.

Social Upheaval

South Vietnam was neither a rich nor a poor country. According to an analysis report by the CIA, the average per capita income in the South in 1973 was $120, lower than other countries like Thái Lan (around $200) and South Korea ($285). However, in reality, I found that life in the countryside of the Mekong Delta was quite comfortable. Almost every household had at least one acre of rice fields and owned riverboats, radios, and even televisions. Some households had motorcycles (Honda) as their means of transportation. I had never seen people in the countryside go hungry or lack clothing. The lives of most people in the Mekong Delta, including my extended family, were reasonably comfortable. Following reunification, life became extremely difficult. By 1976, the country had largely controlled most economic activities under a socialist model, effectively banning free enterprise. Farmers were forced to sell their rice to the state at very low prices, preventing them from freely consuming or selling their own produce. The money that the farmers held in their hands did not reflect the effort they put into their fields. In fact, the farmers did not have much land to cultivate, because their land was put into organizations called 'Cooperatives,' where no one worked or wanted to work. My parents permanently lost hundreds of hectares of land to the Cooperatives.

Part of the new economy was the "Rationing System," sometimes also called the "Subsidy System," that had been in place since 1957 in the North. The authorities applied this rationing system to the entire South. According to this rationing policy, all sources of food and essential necessities were distributed through ration cards issued to each family. They had specific standards for each social class. A normal citizen was entitled to 150 grams of meat per month (equivalent to the average daily meat consumption of an adult today), but government officials were entitled to 300 to 500 grams per month, depending on their rank. Rice was also distributed according to the rationing system, and the standards by class were very clear.

The most brutal cut, however, was the economic strangulation with stagnant wages and dwindling rations—a family surviving on one meal of rice, another of watery porridge. Doctors, with years of study, couldn't afford a decent meal. People began selling the remnants of their past lives and bartering for survival. The government turned a blind eye, content with a populace too hungry to rebel.

Hunger, a stranger until 1975, became a constant companion. Families ate, but not well, just to survive. Teachers fainted in classrooms; their students hollow-eyed with hunger. Those who ventured into business, failed, and were reduced to scavenging in heaps of refuse for scraps to sell. The very sight of plastic bags, washed in grimy water to be reused, became a symbol of our degradation.

Living became a grim struggle for basic hygiene. Even professors, once accustomed to a certain standard, shrugged when questioned about the filth in their quarters. There were no soap, lime, or rags. Cleanliness became a privilege. Who could blame them for succumbing to the squalor, when fetching water itself was a monumental chore?

The grime crept in slowly, a silent thief stealing the pride from our homes. Cobwebs became macabre chandeliers in neglected corners, and dust motes danced in the wan sunlight filtering through grimy windows. Just a few years ago, these homes gleamed, but now they mirrored the hollowness that had settled in our hearts.

Begging wasn't something we were accustomed to. But then, neither were emaciated figures sprawled on sidewalks, their pleas lost in the din of a city struggling to survive. Hunger gnawed at everyone, stripping away people's dignity as they scrambled for scraps.

The "revolutionary spirit" our northern brothers once possessed evaporated with each visit south. Gifts, once a token of affection, became an expectation. A friend of mine, his face flushed with anger, vowed to never welcome another relative from the North after a particularly brazen demand.

Corruption seeped into every crevice of society, a grotesque parody of socialist ideals. Even death wasn't spared. Funeral homes, once places of dignified farewells, became dens of extortion. The cost of a decent burial became an unimaginable burden, forcing families to barter and beg. Doctors, once revered healers, morphed into hustlers, exploiting the sick with exorbitant fees and bogus prescriptions.

While South Vietnamese society before 1975 wasn't without its injustices, the inequality was far less severe than what followed. This disparity stemmed from a system of favoritism. Healthcare was stratified, with dozens of patient tiers dictating room quality, treatment, and medication access. Catholics faced significant barriers in government, law enforcement, and the military, holding them back from leadership positions.

Social hierarchy extended even to death. Obituaries reflected class divisions, with ordinary citizens receiving minimal space in newspapers while high-ranking officials were eulogized with extensive write-ups and flowery language–a practice echoing regimes in Soviet Union and China.

The most glaring injustice was the wage system. Starting salaries for doctors and teachers were barely enough for necessities. No other country seemed to have such a skewed system. To survive, people resorted to selling belongings, relying on family, or finding alternate income sources–a reality the government appeared to ignore. While not to the extent of the Soviet Union's famines, the situation pushed soldiers and civil servants towards desperation, a factor contributing to the desire for escape and freedom.

This pervasive inequality bred frustration. Here was a society supposedly built on equality, yet rife with greed and exploitation. The government's paltry wages left its people vulnerable–a glaring contradiction to the revolutionary ideals of building a socialist society with "socialist people." It became clear that a system built on eroded morals and a declining human spirit could offer little true progress.

Five years. A mere blink in the grand scheme of history. The South I knew, flawed as it was, had vanished. In its place was a society suffocating under the weight of a new ideology... a hollow victory leaving nothing but a gnawing emptiness and the bitter aftertaste of betrayal. The new Marxism–Leninism had fractured the foundation of our society, ripped apart families, and turned men and women into mere shadows of their former selves. The economic failure was evident; a tangible manifestation of the rot had set in. As I looked around at the desolate landscape of our lives, I couldn't help but question whether the early revolutionaries, even in their most ambitious visions, could have foreseen this bleak reality.

New Hegemony

After the victory, many Southerners were branded as "Nguy," a term steeped in condescension, aimed at undermining their dignity and echoing colonial attitudes now wielded by those asserting moral superiority. "You are Nguy," they would declare, "therefore your opinions hold no value." This stigmatizing term has since become a profound obstacle to national reconciliation, further entrenching divisions within the country.

I quickly discovered that their understanding of the South was as shallow as their pride. We in the South weren't a utopia, but we had built a life with higher standards, a freer flow of ideas, and a connection to the outside world. They mocked our "morality," a product of a full stomach, a society less driven by petty jealousies and denunciations. Life here wasn't perfect, but it wasn't a race to the bottom.

The veneer of revolutionary zeal soon tarnished. These men, honed by decades under the socialist system, lacked the most basic skills. They were so rude, uneducated, and ironically, pathologically arrogant. We, the vanquished, began to see not just arrogance, but a deep insecurity. Most of them didn't understand English or French, so they were unable to read textbooks, scientific papers, and manuals written in those languages. In the hospital, some of the new cadres struggled to write proper Vietnamese, and many were unable to spell the names of medicines in English or French. Yet, if a Southern doctor wrote the name of a medicine in English, he would be criticized for being a "US-puppet remnant!" Their lack of scientific knowledge became a source of both frustration and amusement. Being "Nguy," suddenly took on a perverse pride—a badge of competence in a sea of ignorance.

Disillusionment deepened as we witnessed the cracks within their ranks. North pitted against South, and the South ostracized within the very land they called home. Meetings echoed with chants of "Unity, Great Unity!" but outside those walls, distrust festered. Whispers of a familiar darkness—factionalism and nepotism—crept in. "First self, second position," they'd say... a cynical mantra for self-preservation.

Personal Cracks

Still, the early 1975 was a time of youthful idealism for me. Graduation day arrived, and I embarked on the next chapter, not with the youthful idealism I'd once envisioned, but with a quiet determination. My assignment: Rạch Giá–my hometown, a coastal haven now grappling with a new reality. The bustling port city of my childhood was quieter; the once vibrant streets subdued. But life, in its stubborn way, endured. The Planning Department, its resources strained, welcomed me as a research officer. Here, amidst charts and data, the fight would be waged not with guns, but with meticulous research.

I believed that the brutal war was over, the country was united, and our task was to rebuild a nation ravaged by conflict. With enthusiasm, I immersed myself in research and teaching, travelling the length and breadth of Vietnam, from the southernmost tip of Cà Mau to the northernmost gate of Nam Quân, from the fertile Red River Delta to the idyllic island of Phú Quốc. It was only by traversing the entire country that I truly appreciated the beauty, grandeur, and vastness of Việt Nam in peacetime. These journeys also revealed the devastating impact of war: the country was still scarred, its people still suffering, still in despair. Everywhere I went, I documented my experiences in the form of reports, essays, and even poetry for radio and newspapers. My love for my homeland and the idealism of youth fueled my tireless work.

Yet, amidst the rebuilding, a new tide of change began to sweep in, one that carried unfamiliar currents. It was during this period of transformation that I, like countless others, started to grapple with the realities of a reshaped society.

The year was 1978. Việt Nam had just officially reunified, a nation stitched back together after decades of war. I, a young man from the South, found myself on a business trip to Hà Nội, a city shrouded in mystery. We (my boss and his son, a driver, and myself) piled into a Ford Falcon, a symbol of luxury back then, and embarked on the long journey north.

The 17th parallel, once a dividing line, now felt like a portal to another world. Poverty clung to the landscape like a shroud. We stopped in Thanh Hóa, my boss' hometown. It was a place where families shared a single pot of rice, barely enough for five. The post office? A ramshackle hut with a thatched roof. In Thái Bình, a gaggle of children chased after our car, their faces pressed against the fumes, a sight that still stings. They'd never seen anything like this metal beast before.

This wasn't the prosperous North our leaders promised. Hà Nội itself was completely different from the vibrant Sài Gòn. My boarding house, near the Long

Biên bridge, overlooked deserted streets. The only signs of life were the occasional Russian cars or a lone cyclist. Here, in the heart of the city, French colonial villas stood like faded dreams, their grandeur lost beneath layers of neglect. Years later, when I returned for work, I stayed on the same street, a bustling avenue now, unrecognizable from that first encounter.

The people too, bore the marks of hardship. Men sported mismatched uniforms, a constant reminder of war. Women, a far cry from the poet's "fragrant graceful figures," wore worn black pants and white shirts, their hair in severe, samurai-like styles. The city felt muted; its vibrancy replaced by a quiet resilience.

My heart had ached for a glimpse of Long Giang Pagoda, the setting for a cherished novel, *Butterfly Dreaming Fairy*. The book promised an idyllic scene–an ancient pagoda perched on a hill, bathed in emerald green. But in Hà Nội, no one recognized the name. Temples, it seemed, were of little consequence. The driver, eager for a detour, took a chance on a similar-sounding pagoda, Long Hàm. Disappointment washed over me as we approached the small, moss-covered structure, devoid of the magic I'd envisioned. No monks resided there; only the wary stares of neighbors.

It was then I learned of the "heaven and earth shaking" period–the Land Reform. Temples became casualties, their souls shattered alongside statues thrown into rivers. This explained the emptiness I felt... the missing spirit so ingrained in the South's pagodas.

The trip solidified a growing disillusionment. The North, far from the utopia promised, was mired in poverty. Our leaders' words now rang hollow, mere propaganda or lie. As I returned to the South, a different kind of hardship awaited: economic woes, forced collectivization, and a suffocating new way of life. The reality painted a grim picture. Corruption thrived, social scores dictated lives, and fear became a constant companion.

The changes, swift and sweeping, had brought us not to a brighter future, but to a place of profound loss. Even idealism, once a shield for me, began to crumble under the weight of reality.

The introduction of "Collective Farming" further squeezed our livelihood. Our family lost vast swathes of land that had painstakingly accumulated over years of backbreaking labor by my parents. Even our three tractors were taken away, deemed necessary contributions to the collective. These economic upheavals were a complete contrast to the relative prosperity we enjoyed under the RVN regime. Families, once living comfortably like ours, were now equally destitute–a forced equalization.

I found myself struggling to adapt to new and dramatic changes. Accustomed to the relative freedom of the South, I chafed under the new regulations and restrictions. Back in my university days, "thought crime" felt like something out of a bad science fiction novel. You know, the kind with telescreens in your living room and jackbooted government agents reading your mind. It was a plot device in George Orwell's *1984*, a chilling vision of a totalitarian future. Punish you for what you think? Absurd! I couldn't wrap my head around a government that is afraid of its own citizens.

Under the new regime, my youthful idealism clashed head-on with harsh reality. One day, during a meeting about collectivization, I spoke out against the policy. I naively pointed out how it had devastated my family's farm. The room went dead quiet. My voice echoed in the tense silence.

Later that week, I was called into a private meeting. Across the table sat a group of stern-faced party officials. Their words were a cold slap of reality. They criticized my "anti-revolutionary" views, warning me that such "thought crime" would hinder my career. There it was–the very word I scoffed at back in university, used with chilling seriousness.

That day, the line between fiction and reality blurred. The nightmare of George Orwell's *1984* wasn't so far-fetched after all.

My enthusiasm was often met with suspicion, sometimes even hostility. We, the young graduates from Sài Gòn's universities, would gather at cafes, our conversations light and carefree. Little did we know, these gatherings were being monitored. One day, my close friend, Dr. PDL, and I were hauled in for questioning. The authorities wanted to know who led these "meetings" (as they called them) and what subversive topics we discussed. They even questioned our kind Aunt Hai, the cafe owner who always let us "sign for our coffee." After enduring a period of intense scrutiny, criticism, self-criticism, and isolation, I realized my future was bleak. Before I could get fired from my job, I resigned and found myself unemployed.

Seeking solace, I retreated to the familiar comforts of my rural home, a place my grandparents always described as idyllic–close to the market and the river. Teaching, a profession I enjoyed, crossed my mind. But the job prospects seemed bleak, so I shelved the idea. As the saying goes, "A troubled mind finds no joy in its surroundings." Often, I'd be overwhelmed by melancholy and resentment, feeling like I was born in the wrong time. In those moments, my mother would offer comfort and a pragmatic solution. "Leave it alone, son," she'd say. "Thinking about trouble only brings more trouble. Look at you, so thin and frail. It worries me." Then, she'd try to set me up, presenting a list of eligible village girls with glowing descriptions: "She's smart and from a well-respected family;" "She's a teacher and a close friend of ours;" "She's the daughter of Uncle A, a very decent and kind man." Most of these girls I hadn't even met! But maybe my mother was right. Perhaps I should have abandoned this "wandering life" and embraced the tranquillity of rural life. With my natural optimism, I threw myself into farming. (Though in truth, I didn't have much land left. Over 90% of what my parents had saved had become part of the collective.)

But as the saying goes, "Man proposes, God disposes." Before I could fully embrace my new life as a farmer, I found myself swept up in a daring venture–a perilous escape by sea, alongside my brother and a group of friends facing similar circumstances.

The thought of leaving behind my family, community, and everything I knew had never even crossed my mind. For days, I was consumed by worry and anxiety, becoming so withdrawn that my mother kept asking, "What's on your mind?"

I thought Vietnamese society, at the time, was shrouded in fear and mistrust. There was no genuine connection, not even among friends. Close confidantes turned into fierce accusers at work. Neighbors became informers, and friends or family reported a careless word. Even within families, people betrayed each other. Everyone was constantly scrutinized and compared over trivial details–food, jewellery, scraps of clothing, bicycles. Trust evaporated and was replaced by suspicion. A minor mistake could hinder your progress. It was a society ruled by fear, and a climate of fear was maintained to ensure obedience. Fear burrowed deeper with each passing day. We were also becoming a society of masks, echoing Andrei Sakharov's words. I couldn't live in such a stifling society.

A Vietnamese author, whose name escapes me now but whose words resonated deeply, wrote something that perfectly captured the suffocating despair that had settled over South Việt Nam: "If there is a country where her people have had to reject their own land, reject the place where they buried each other's umbilical cords, I think, that country has little hope left." That was Việt Nam in the early 1980s, a nation stripped of its hope, its people forced to turn their backs on the land that had nurtured them for generations. It was a time of profound sorrow and uncertainty.

Of course, Việt Nam is now a different country, transformed into a vibrant country, teeming with life and opportunity. The hardships of the past are now distant memories. But as I watch the young people of today revel in their modern comforts, I can't help but think of the hardship suffered by their parents and grandparents. It's a history that should never be forgotten.

Six years. For six years, I had clung to the vestiges of a life that no longer existed. Six years, I choked on the dust of shattered dreams. But finally, the weight of despair became unbearable. I had to leave. Freedom, even if it meant facing the wrath of the sea or a prison cell, was a price I was willing to pay.

Rạch Giá, my once vibrant hometown, had morphed into a desolate departure station. Every interaction felt like a final farewell. A simple handshake with an acquaintance lingered a beat too long, a silent plea to hold onto the fading warmth of connection. Family reunions were punctuated by a single, urgent question: "When will you leave?" The most common blessing, a hollow echo in the stifling air, was, "Have a safe journey."

The news of my planned escape reached my mother like a physical blow. Tears welled in her eyes, but she choked them back, uttering no words of protest. My father, a man hardened by brutal battles, sat cloaked in heavy silence. My younger sisters, too young to understand, stared at me with wide, curious eyes, yet a faint tremor seemed to run through them, as if they somehow sensed the momentous event about to unfold.

Chapter Three

Crossing the Sea

The day I left my peaceful village remains vividly etched in my memory. As the scorching midday sun began to wane, casting a gentler glow, our group of five decided to embark on our journey. Our small boat, rowed steadily by a friendly Khmer neighbor, followed the ebb tide of the river, adorned with water lilies, towards the open sea. A soft breeze rustled through the palm fronds lining the riverbank, creating a soothing rhythm that harmonized with the serene tropical afternoon. I was lulled into a state of reverie, unaware of the harsh realities that awaited us.

After a night's journey, our boat reached the mouth of the river, merging with the lively scene of small fishing boats casting their nets for shrimp in the early morning light. Our presence immediately caught the attention of the fishermen. One of them, a young shrimp catcher, alerted his companions with a booming voice, "Damn it, they're trying to escape!"

At that time, attempting to cross the border illegally was a serious offense, punishable by imprisonment or even death at the hands of the public security force. Prepared for such encounters, one of our group members tossed the fisherman two maces of gold as a bribe to secure his silence. The fisherman eyed the gold, grinned, revealing a row of gleaming teeth, and said, "Bon voyage!"

It was April 16, 1981.

Once out at sea, we boarded a larger, weathered wooden riverboat with chipped blue paint. It was constructed by my brother and his friends a month prior. The boat was approximately fifteen meters long and 6 meters wide, equipped with two engines commonly used for river transportation. It was stocked with ample fuel, dry rations, and drinking water, sufficient for a two-week voyage. Firearms were also onboard, as some experienced members advised that weapons were necessary to defend against potential pirates.

Our group consisted of twenty-five individuals, including three children. My family consisted of my brother, my younger sister, my cousin Dong, and me. Apart from my family, there were three neighbors, a few former officers of the Army of the Republic of Vietnam recently released from re-education camps, some merchants, a few unemployed individuals like me, and a friend I affectionately called Brother Ba—a journalist from Hà Nội who had arrived in the South about two years prior. None of us possessed any seafaring experience. My brother served as our captain.

As we boarded the boat, we were utterly clueless about our destination. One person suggested Thái Lan (Thailand), and the group unanimously agreed to set sail. However, the direction remained a mystery, as no one had prepared any navigational tools, like a compass. Our common goal was simply to venture out, to escape Vietnamese waters, and to harbor the hope of encountering a cargo ship that would rescue us. It was an escape in its truest form.

Our sea voyage was far from smooth sailing, but it wasn't as tragic as the experiences of many other compatriots. We embarked in March, a month known for its calm seas. The saying, "Waves of March, even old women can sail," reflected the tranquil conditions we anticipated. However, this tranquility proved to be a cruel deception of nature.

By the second night, the sea, like a fickle lover, revealed its wrath. Before the first wave struck, the sky turned a menacing shade of gray. The initial wave jolted me awake, drenching my clothes. My brother and the helmsmen shouted, "Prepare for the waves!" Oh God, the sight of a wave towering over our boat left me paralyzed. The young men and I grabbed buckets and frantically scooped water out of the boat. But the relentless, tumultuous waves, surging from the ocean's depths, threatened to engulf our vessel. Every creak of the boat echoed like a death knell. I thought I might perish in this uncharted territory.

Cold dread, sharp and unwelcome, coiled around my heart, squeezing out the naive optimism of the previous night. Spray erupted skyward, momentarily eclipsing the starless void above. The wind, a mournful dirge howling through the rigging, became a chilling counterpoint to the thunderous symphony of the storm. Panic flickered in the wide, pale eyes of the young men and me as we scrambled for buckets, desperately attempting to bail out the water that poured relentlessly into the boat. Like an enraged beast unleashed, the sea seemed determined to engulf us whole. Every creak of the vessel echoed like a death knell in the storm's fury. Here, on this watery battleground, a profound sense of vulnerability washed over us all—a grim reminder of life's fragility in the face of nature's raw power. The air vibrated with unspoken fear; the women's tears glistened in their eyes, and the men were etched with silent anxiety. As for me, I braced myself for the unknown, a chilling premonition settling in my gut.

Yet, as if by a miracle, the sea suddenly fell silent. As dawn broke, streaks of orange and pink painted the horizon. Upon checking, we found all twenty-five of us still intact. Overjoyed, we felt like we had narrowly escaped death, a fragile promise of life rekindled. Exhausted but alive, we embarked on the third day with a newfound appreciation for the sun's warmth.

The flag of the Republic of Vietnam, emblazoned above the small boat, was a desperate message in a churning sea. It wasn't just a flag; it was a declaration of our identity and a plea for recognition as citizens fleeing the turmoil that had engulfed our homeland. As we bobbed on the unforgiving waves, leaving Vietnamese waters behind, numerous cargo ships materialized on the horizon. With each vessel that came into view, hope flared anew. We frantically waved and shouted; our voices hoarse with desperation. But our pleas seemed to vanish into the vast emptiness. Like phantoms, we were ignored, left invisible on the precipice of oblivion. The indifference of these passing giants stung more than the salt spray, a chilling confirmation of our precarious situation.

One afternoon on the third day, we encountered another ordeal–pirates. They were Thai fishermen exploiting the plight of Vietnamese refugees for their own gain. Just as hope began to flicker, a hazy boat emerged on the horizon. As it drew closer, we realized it was a Thai fishing vessel. Initially, they seemed friendly, inquiring about our needs. But then, they brandished long knives and stormed our boat, creating a cacophony of screams and the glint of stolen jewelry. Our meager possessions, the remnants of our abandoned lives, vanished into their calloused hands. They plundered our gold reserves, even snatching my glasses, mistaking the gold frame for real gold.

Amidst the chaos, an unexpected act of kindness surfaced. Perhaps sensing the despair etched on our faces, the pirates pointed us towards the Thai coast. They towed our boat for about one hour, then gestured towards the horizon, indicating the Thai shoreline. With a final glance, they turned their engine and sped away into the open sea. It took us over three more hours to make out the shore. As we navigated from the open sea towards the coast, we passed hundreds of boats fishing or squidding, yet none paid any attention to us.

Reaching Thái Lan: Fishing Village Budi

The Thai coastline, a hazy silhouette against the shimmering water, emerged from the midday haze. A sense of relief, a sweet elixir, washed over me. We docked on the smooth pebble beach of a small fishing village called Budi (or Budee). I later learned that Budi was a fishing village in the Pattani province of Thái Lan, bordering Mã Lai (Malaysia).

Exhausted, battered, but alive, we collapsed onto the sandy beach. We had survived the tempestuous seas, the wrath of nature, and the greed of pirates. We were refugees, stripped of our possessions and our homeland, but we were also survivors, carrying the hope for a new beginning.

Thus, after three days and three nights, the compass-less boat from Rạch Giá, Việt Nam, had drifted all the way to southern Thái Lan. It was nothing short of a miracle that we had survived. Reaching Thái Lan was not the end of the journey but a new beginning. The memories of the sea voyage would forever be imprinted in my heart, a constant reminder of the price of freedom. The vast sea, once a symbol of terror, now held a strange beauty: it was an underwater tomb for fear and a path to an unwritten future.

As we stepped ashore, the villagers rushed out to see us, but they didn't know what to do with us. Looking at their weathered eyes and faces, I saw them greet us with a cautious welcome. Our boat was the first group of Vietnamese to arrive at this fishing village. The language barrier forced us to communicate through body language, eye contact, and smiles. When the boat docked, there was still plenty of food on board: dried rice, sugar, salt, and several barrels of drinking water. We didn't know what to do with these things, so we gave them all to the villagers. Some asked for the two still-functioning diesel engines, which we also gave away. Once we were on land and free, what need did we have for these things? That was what we thought, so we gave away whatever anyone asked for. Thinking back on it, we refugees were quite generous! But it was thanks to this generosity that we gained the favor of the locals.

The locals mostly wore sarongs, a typical attire in southern Thái Lan. Judging by their eyes and way of life, they were very gentle and simple people. We didn't see anyone taking advantage of us. I later learned that this was the Thai-Malay border area, and there were many Muslims living here. At that time, I didn't know if the people we met were Buddhists or Muslims, but back then we didn't care; the most important thing was to reach the shores of freedom, and that was the luckiest thing in the world. I guessed they were Muslims because they didn't eat pork. They also didn't eat dead chickens, even if the chicken had only died a few minutes ago! Whenever there was a dead chicken, they would bring it to us. So, even though we were refugees, we sometimes had a feast!

Our first night in the village was an experience that still brings a chuckle to my mind. Young men from the village (and perhaps neighboring villages) came in droves, not to offer assistance, but to simply... stare. They did nothing but squat, smoke cigarettes, and watch with amusement as we huddled in the concrete courtyard. Some of us lay on the ground, others sat, and still others smoked and chatted. As night fell, a few remained, still smoking and watching.

Our group of young men felt a bit uneasy, so we decided to devise a self-defense plan. Among us were former ARVN officers, fishermen, and scholars like myself. Under the guidance of the officers, we divided ourselves into watch shifts, guarding our "refugee territory" and secretly keeping "toys" ready for any trouble.

This is Budi (Thailand) where I landed in April 1981. Photo by Kevin Bao Huynh (Nail Super Store, IL, USA), a former refugee who also landed in Budi in the 1980s.

As night deepened, the villagers provided us with mosquito nets for sleep. The young men slept on the outer perimeter, while the women and children slept inside. We had our first night's sleep on the land of freedom, the sound of the waves lulling us, the sky clear, the breeze cool. Soon, everyone was fast asleep.

Around midnight, I felt a hand brushing against my leg. I was still awake, so I pretended to be asleep to see what this hand was up to. Just as I was about to react, the other young men shouted, "There's a thief!" I grabbed the hand that was groping me, and we easily apprehended the culprit. We took a closer look and realized they were the same young men who had been smoking and watching us earlier. It seemed they wanted to touch the women, but they didn't expect us to

43

have a defense strategy. We didn't know what to do with them, and they just kept giggling. The officer in charge of our group decided that these young men seemed harmless, so we let them go. It seemed like the villagers had never seen foreigners before, so they were very curious.

We stayed in Budi for about a week when a fishing boat from Việt Nam also docked there. This boat had only about ten young men. They were said to work for a fishing cooperative and had taken the opportunity to escape Việt Nam. This group also came from Rạch Giá but they had set off from U Minh, a rural district of Cà Mau province in the Mekong Delta region. They were dirt poor, possessing almost no belongings. These young men were very skilled at fishing, so having them join our group felt like gaining an "armed force" to better deal with any challenges that might arise.

A few days later, another boat arrived in Budi. This one was larger, carrying over forty people from Cà Mau. This boat was "wealthier" than the previous two, even though it had been robbed by pirates twice. Their journey was quite arduous, taking almost a week to reach Budi. This new boat had children and more "economic elements" on board. Among them was a man I called "Uncle Lieutenant Colonel," with whom I later became close. I called him "Uncle Lieutenant Colonel" because he was a retired air force lieutenant colonel who had been imprisoned for a few years after 1975, released, and was now seeking to escape the country. He was from Bình Định (my father's hometown), as poor as I was (wearing only shorts and a shirt), and he often told funny stories. He had studied in the United States, so he was very fluent in English, and he became the interpreter for all three groups of boat people.

Our days in Budi were quite leisurely, filled with hard-to-forget memories. Some of us went to work as construction workers in nearby towns, and we were even paid fairly. It was only when we ventured outside the village that we realized how much wealthier and more developed Thái Lanwas than Việt Nam. Even this remote village had asphalt roads. Every household had a car, and motorcycles were mainly used for leisure. The women remarked that even their fish sauce bottles and plastic bags were prettier and cleaner than those in Việt Nam. Seeing this, we all shook our heads for Việt Nam, wondering when it would ever catch up to Thái Lan.

One day, as we were going through the refugee registration process, a United Nations (UN) official interviewed each of us, and we had to fill out a blue form. The form asked for personal information, information about our parents, and the reason for leaving Việt Nam. Most of us were not fluent in English at the administrative level, and only Uncle Lieutenant Colonel could explain the boxes in that complex form. So, he naturally became the group leader and sat next to the UN officials to interpret.

He wore shorts, sometimes shirtless, sometimes just a faded T-shirt, a cigarette in his hand, listening to the information and translating it for the UN officials. He rarely looked to see if they were writing it correctly, but just spoke like a... boss giving orders. At that time, looking at Uncle Lieutenant Colonel's style, I admired him immensely. He spoke English very naturally, and with an attitude that was confident to the point of... arrogance. I still remember one day when he was translating for a Thai official, and the official complimented him on his good English; he turned to us and said with a smile:

"I speak English with a fish sauce accent, yet this 'mọi' says I speak English well!"

I still remember the word moi that my teachers in Việt Nam had instilled in me. At that time, Việt Nam viewed neighboring countries like Thái Lan, Mã Lai, Lào (Laos), Campuchia (Cambodia), etc. as less civilized nations (i.e. mọi). Now I heard Uncle Lieutenant Colonel using that word! I thought to myself, we call them mọi but why are they so much more advanced than us, so much richer than us for decades, and polite to us as well? Yet the Vietnamese were arrogant. As a temporary resident in their country, Uncle Lieutenant Colonel appeared to look down on the local officials... for nothing, although he didn't show it, only through the way he spoke to us.

Farewell to Budi

After about four weeks in Budi, we were told to move to another camp. Budi was just a temporary place to do the paperwork, and we had to go to a camp with enough staff for the authorities to assess and determine our refugee status. So, the most peaceful days of our refugee life were over, and the parting day came. Any parting is sad, and parting with Budi was no exception. After approximately four weeks in this peaceful fishing village, having gotten to know quite a few kind people, everyone felt a lump in their throat as they boarded the bus to leave the village. On the day of departure, a few villagers came to wave us goodbye. Looking at the waving arms and gentle smiles, I was deeply moved. It turned out that human kindness could sometimes be even stronger there than in our own homeland.

To this day, writing these lines, I have not yet had the opportunity to return to Budi to thank the villagers who took me and many other compatriots in during the 1980s. I know that some compatriots, after becoming successful refugees in America, have returned to Budi to trace their roots and thank the villagers. One of them is Mr. Kevin Bảo Huỳnh, owner of The Nail Superstore in Illinois. In an email to me on March 14, 2024, he sent many photos of the village of Budi. Looking at these photos, I was filled with nostalgia for the early days when I first set foot in Thái Lan, beginning my journey as a refugee.

Chapter Four

A Kangaroo's Ticket to Australia

We boarded two large buses, leaving Budi behind. After a day's journey, we arrived at the Songkhla Refugee Camp–well-known among refugees. Songkhla, named after a Thai prince, is a province in southern Thái Lan. Songkhla Refugee Camp was a substantial settlement; when I arrived, it housed over 5,000 people. At its peak, it was said to accommodate up to 10,000 refugees. Situated along the coast, it offered a stunning view with the sea in front and a mountain range behind, all encircled by barbed wire. If I remember correctly, the width of the camp was only about fifty to eighty meters, and it took only fifteen minutes to walk its length. Refugees were not allowed to leave the camp without permission.

On my first day at Songkhla camp, I thought I had wandered into a city in Việt Nam. Where did all these people come from? The population density here must be among the highest in the world! Looking at the way they dressed, there were more poor people than rich people, and this was understandable. The vast majority of people who entered the camp had been robbed at sea, so they had nothing left. However, there were also many lucky trips, so people still had gold and money when they arrived. There was a group who had been here for a long

47

time (over six months) and were supported by relatives abroad, so they had a fairly decent life. Some people even had money to open shops right in the camp. Stalls selling fried rice, noodle soup, phở, and coffee lined both sides of the narrow road, thriving in the camp where people, with little else to do, indulged in cigarettes and coffee. Cool-looking young men with shoulder-length hair, reminiscent of gangster movie characters, puffed on Samit or 555 cigarettes over cups of black coffee. Inside the shops, loudspeakers blasted a mix of sentimental golden music, thumping rock, majestic military tunes, and anti-communist songs at full volume, making the ears of anyone nearby ache. The streets were filled with men and women, adorned with bright makeup, glittering gold, and expensive European and American fashion clothes, parading as if attending a festival. Despite being called a refugee camp, it was, in fact, a vibrant microcosm of Vietnamese society.

The air was thick with a blend of dialects, laughter, and the hum of daily life, creating a unique symphony that was both overwhelming and oddly comforting. The melancholic melodies of Nguyệt Ánh and Việt Dũng, two fellow refugees who rose to fame as composers, would sometimes weave through the throngs of people in the crowded alleys. Their songs, brimming with a deep yearning for a homeland left behind, struck a profound chord within me. Back then, the act of leaving Việt Namfelt like a permanent severing of ties. The lyrics echoed this profound sense of longing:

> *The sun there is warm, but how can it compare*
> *To the warm sun of my homeland?*

Or

> *When will I return to Vietnam,*
> *To visit golden rice fields,*
> *to visit boats by the riverbank?*

These words, laced with poetry and a profound longing for home, have stayed with me ever since, echoing in my heart like a bittersweet refrain.

The boisterous energy of the camp couldn't completely mask the cracks in its facade. I saw the living cost of our exodus. Men, their clothes hanging off their gaunt frames like ill-fitting shrouds, shuffled by, muttering to themselves. Their eyes, once filled with life, were now hollowed out, haunted by memories best left undisturbed. One moment, a burst of laughter might erupt, a fleeting flicker of normalcy, only to be extinguished by a gut-wrenching sob the next. Their pain was a palpable thing, a heavy weight in the air, even without understanding their tragedies. The depth of their scars needed no explanation. Stories of pirate attacks and the massacre of entire ships at sea washed over me like a cold wave. These chilling tales were confirmed by the horrific discovery of eleven young Vietnamese women, their bodies bound together, washed ashore on Tha Sala beach.

Songhla Refugee Camp in the 1980s. Photo by John Launder, an Australian volunteer in the camp during the 1980s.

Victims of unspeakable cruelty, they were a powerful reminder of the horrors that had driven us from our homeland. Their deaths weren't isolated incidents. Hundreds of mass graves, filled with the remains of refugees, were discovered across Southeast Asia.

The world knew about large-scale tragedies like the Holocaust and the Killing Fields – but the plight of Vietnamese boat people in the South China Sea remained largely unheard. Later, when I found myself in Sydney, I felt compelled to share these stories. Determined to break the silence, I participated in a writing competition with an essay titled *Killing Sea*. Winning an award brought a small victory in the face of such immense tragedy.

It wasn't surprising, then, that Du Tử Lê, a fellow refugee and a famous poet whose words had become a balm for our collective ache, expressed his final wish as a yearning to return to the sea:

When I die, take me to the sea.
The reverse flow will carry my body away
Across the sea lies my homeland.
The ancient bamboo groves remain evergreen

...

When I die, take me to the sea
And along the way, remember to sing the national anthem
Oh, it's been so long since anyone has sung it (the song now
is like a ghost)
When I die, that sadness will also end
Life in exile will be complete with the soul.

The organization of the Songkhla camp was unlike anything I'd imagined. It resembled a government, complete with a power structure mirroring the one we'd left behind in South Vietnam. Thai officials oversaw things on the surface, but Vietnamese refugees, many former military officers or government officials, held the real power. They recreated a hierarchy within the camp, with a camp commander, a "Security Committee," and an "Information and Culture Committee." On my very first day, I was confronted with the harsh realities of this new life. A young man, accused of being a communist, was yanked from the line and brutally beaten. The crowd, instead of helping, became a bloodthirsty chorus, urging on the attackers. My initial surge of anger was met with a cold dose of reality from my older cousin. He warned me of the dangers of intervening and the ever-present threat of violence within the camp itself. This brutal baptism by fire left an indelible scar on my soul.

The shock of the previous incident barely had time to settle before we were ushered into a stifling auditorium. Vietnamese officials, their faces etched with authority, stood guard. The heavy doors clanged shut, trapping us in a human cage. We were told this was an orientation, but it quickly turned into a twisted game of fear and manipulation. A stern official, his voice dripping with a chilling northern accent, demanded that we confess any ties to the communist regime.

Even the corruption that had plagued South Vietnam seemed to have followed us. According to my cousin, who had already worked at the distribution center, the basic supplies we were supposed to receive from the UN Refugee Agency were mysteriously "sold out." Embezzlement and bribery thrived even amidst a sea of suffering.

The official's interrogation tactics mirrored those of the very regime we'd fled. Confusion and fear swirled within me. Panic surged as I noticed my cousin frantically shaking his head from near a window. It was a silent message... a desperate plea for me to keep quiet. In that moment, I learned the first lesson in survival—the art of the well-timed lie. Standing there, amidst the fear and uncertainty, a painful question gnawed at me: Why would we, a people seeking refuge, turn on each other? It was a wound that refused to heal.

A Kangaroo's Ticket to Australia

The oppressive atmosphere in the camp cast a heavy shadow over everyone. The dream of resettlement in a third country burned bright, a flickering hope that fueled our days. Every time the voice of Khánh Ly, another refugee and famed singer, filled the air with the melancholic melody of "Biển Nhớ" (Trịnh Công Sơn's iconic farewell song), a pang of sorrow twisted in my gut. The lyrics, "Tomorrow I'll leave, the sea will remember my name and call me back..."' truly touched me, mirroring the question that gnawed at me constantly: when would my turn come, and where would fate lead me? Back then, America was the golden ticket, the coveted destination for everyone, me included.

Then, one day, fortune seemed to finally smile upon me. Periodically, representatives from the embassies in Bangkok, which we called "missions," would descend upon the camp. These representatives, from countries like the US, Australia, Canada, and France, all interested in resettling refugees, would conduct interviews and process applications, offering a chance to escape the limbo of the camp.

Three months into the suffocating routine of Songkhla camp, a glimmer of hope flickered. The announcement crackled over the loudspeaker: an Australian embassy mission had arrived. Australia was notoriously tough to get into, demanding not just the usual criteria of skills, education, and English proficiency, but also an essay explaining why you craved a life Down Under.

At that point, any country seemed like paradise compared to the squalor of the camp. My desire wasn't for Australia specifically, but for escape. The problem? My English was abysmal – French was my strong suit. Uncle Lieutenant Colonel, with his girlfriend in tow, had already moved on to another camp, chasing their American dream. My pleas for help with the essay fell on deaf ears. Some claimed they were too busy, others demanded payment, and a few even resorted to a stinging rebuke: "Why didn't you learn English back in Vietnam?"

That day, amidst the despair, a seed of independence sprouted. I wouldn't be a pawn anymore and wouldn't depend on others, especially educated Vietnamese. With newfound determination, I trudged to the camp library. Armed with a battered dictionary, I spent an entire day translating my essay word-for-word, clumsily conjugating verbs and peppering in the occasional French word when English eluded me. The result was a Frankensteinian creation, but it was mine.

Days later, a miracle – my name boomed over the loudspeaker, summoning me for an interview with the Australian mission. Amazement washed over me. Refugee camp lore was rife with stories of ruthless interviews, rejections handed out on whims. The American mission, in particular, held a notorious reputation. There was "Gà Đá" (Fighting Rooster), a Vietnam veteran with a rooster tattoo and a volatile temper. Legend had it that his approval hinged on the most bizarre of criteria—a simple pulling hand with him during the interview. Such anecdotes, bordering on the comical, were a dime a dozen in the camp, indicative of the randomness and despair that colored our lives.

With a mix of anticipation and trepidation, I stepped into the interview room with the watchful eyes of my fellow refugees following my every move. The Australian embassy official, a towering figure with a bushy beard, scrutinized my application and inquired through the interpreter, "Who wrote this essay?"

"I did," I replied, my voice barely above a whisper.

A hint of amusement played on his lips as he countered, "Have you ever learned English before?"

"No, sir," I admitted sheepishly.

"And what brings you to seek resettlement in Australia?"

"I want to study," I answered, my heart pounding in my chest.

"How can you study with this kind of English?"

His words struck a chord of doubt within me, but I clung to a glimmer of hope.

"If not through studies, then perhaps through farming," I suggested.

"Even farming requires capital, my friend," he retorted, his comment sending a wave of confusion through me. In my rural upbringing, farming was a livelihood that demanded nothing more than sweat and determination. Could even pursuing education be an unattainable dream?

Disheartened, I braced myself for the inevitable rejection. But the official's voice took an unexpected turn.

"Apart from these reasons, is there anything else that compels you to come to Australia?"

A memory from my childhood surfaced, a vivid image of a kangaroo, its majestic form etched into my mind. With a newfound spark of determination, I confessed, "I simply want to see a ... kangaroo!"

The officer's eyes widened in surprise, followed by an eruption of laughter. He extended his hand, his grip firm and reassuring, and with a resounding stamp on my application, he declared through the interpreter, "Alright, you're in! Get over to the other desk for the next steps!"

I was stunned and speechless with gratitude. Before I could utter a word of thanks, he waved me towards another counter where the next stage of the process awaited. Thank you, kind Australian gentleman! I will never forget your kindness.

The story of my journey to Australia began with this peculiar conversation, a moment etched into my memory with vivid clarity. I can still recall every word spoken, every nuance of his expression, the reassuring gesture of his hand, and the overwhelming sense of elation that washed over me.

News of my acceptance to Australia spread like wildfire through the camp. Returning to my humble abode, I proudly announced, "Guys! I'm going to Australia!" My friends erupted in cheers, and we celebrated this momentous occasion with a round of coffee, toasting the new chapter ahead.

Phanat Nikom and the Refugee Fragments

After three months at Songkhla, a bittersweet cocktail of hope and apprehension washed over me when I arrived at Phanat Nikhom. The verdant Vietnamese countryside I knew was replaced by a harsh landscape—a seemingly endless sea of brown sand dotted with skeletal trees. Unlike Songkhla's homogenous Vietnamese population, Phanat Nikhom was a microcosm of Southeast Asia's refugee crisis. Laotians, Cambodians, and Vietnamese each occupied designated areas–the Vietnamese being the largest and, according to whispers, the most troublesome. Yet, amidst the hardship, a surprising number of South Vietnamese luminaries—former military officials, artists, and scholars—found themselves united by their displacement, highlighting the war's reach.

Our living conditions represented a marginal improvement over Songkhla. Gone were the flimsy, leaky tents. Here, we were housed in fibro and iron dwellings—a far cry from home but undeniably more substantial. However, the term "proper" felt like a cruel joke when applied to these crowded structures, often crammed with ten to fifteen people. Still, compared to the rickety tents, they felt luxurious.

Life in Phanat Nikhom was a relentless struggle. Unlike Songkhla's readily available water source, here, every drop counted. Water was trucked in daily and doled out with the strictest rationing. Each refugee was allocated twenty liters of water per day. Food rations provided by Thai contractors were a constant source of frustration. The rice was frequently mushy, and the scorching heat, coupled with suspected corruption, often led to spoiled ingredients. A particularly bony chicken dish earned the grim nickname "grenade chicken"—all bones and no meat. Yet, our resourceful and spirited women transformed even these meager offerings into nourishing meals. Every day, young men would collect the rations, women would cook, and families, sometimes a dozen strong, would gather around a shared meal. Despite the hardship, these moments of togetherness brought a flicker of joy amidst the struggle.

Laughter and tears were intricately woven into the fabric of our lives in this strange new world. Broken families, forbidden romances, and the constant fight for survival painted our daily realities. A love affair between a monk and a woman caused a scandal, serving as a reminder of our precarious situation as refugees. However, love, like a stubborn weed, refused to be contained. Next door, an elderly captain's flirtation with a young college student blossomed into a full-blown romance, defying societal disapproval based on age differences. Their story, like countless others, became a cherished part of the camp's lore, symbolizing the enduring power of love even in the most desperate circumstances.

Years later, fate brought me back to Phanat Nikhom on a business trip to Thái Lan. The transformation was astounding. Gone was the refugee camp, replaced by a bustling town with houses springing up everywhere and verdant greenery where once there was only arid sand. There was no trace of our former life here. Phanat Nikhom had moved on, reminding us of the impermanence of even the most seemingly permanent situations. The camp, a sea of corrugated iron that once housed our hopes and struggles, had become a distant memory, replaced by a symbol of the relentless march of time.

Phanat Nikhom Refugee Camp, 1984. Photo by John Launder, an Australian volunteer in the camp during the 1980s.

Learning English in the Refugee Camp

The settlement was a hive of activity. Volunteer groups from across the globe—Americans, Canadians, Australians—buzzed with purpose, offering a lifeline to the displaced. Religious organizations mingled with NGOs, each tackling a specific need. Some taught English, others offered libraries or cultural guidance. Even evangelism had its place. Remarkably, harmony reigned. These groups, aware of the camp's multilingual makeup, carved out distinct roles, avoiding overlap. English classes were readily available, staffed by a surprising number of Vietnamese refugees—reflecting the strength of our pre-war education system.

For me, the camp marked a turning point. The opportunity to study English ignited a spark within me. Initially, I joined a volunteer-run class. However, their focus was heavily on practicality—common phrases for job hunting, with little emphasis on grammatical structure. "How are you?" and "I am fine, thank you." It felt robotic. After a week, the monotony began to gnaw at me. I craved a foundation, not rote memorization. Later, I understood—their goal was basic communication, not academic prowess.

A stroke of luck soon followed. I landed a job at the library run by the Assembly of God, a Protestant organization. Mr. Sok, a Cambodian refugee with the air of a former official, presided over the modest collection. His fluent French and English hinted at his past life, perhaps in education. Every morning, he entered with a warm greeting, radiating leadership despite his quiet demeanor. This role proved to be a goldmine for learning. My daily tasks revolved around organizing books and magazines. The library, though small, boasted a global selection: a thousand volumes, from foreign donations and the Vietnamese community in the US. While Vietnamese, English, and French filled my days, the job itself lacked stimulation. After completing my tasks, vast stretches of time stretched before me. But then, an ingenious idea struck—I could use this downtime to study! A quiet corner became my haven.

My approach was slow and deliberate. Every morning, I salvaged the newspaper wrappers from the vegetable deliveries and flattened them into makeshift reading material. These were Thai-English newspapers, such as The Nation and The Bangkok Post. Familiar nouns from Asian news articles sparked my curiosity. Dictionary in hand, I delved into each word – pronunciation, origin, usage. Days could pass dissecting a single word. This laborious method, however, built a sturdy foundation. The Longman Dictionary became a cherished companion–a reminder of those dedicated mornings.

Building from the ground up was arduous, but it was a world better than haphazard memorization. I meticulously documented grammar rules, whispering pronunciations to myself like a self-absorbed scholar. Within months, my notebook had transformed into a self-made English grammar book. Confidence blossomed, though conversation practice remained elusive.

The importance of a study buddy became increasingly evident. An, a fellow refugee from Huế, became my partner in crime. He championed the single-word approach, believing a vocabulary of 2,500 words could unlock fluency (though in reality, understanding context multiplied that number tenfold).

A Classroom in the Phanat Nikhom Refugee Camp. Photo by John Launder.

Every afternoon, we'd engage in vocabulary quizzes, a constant game of one-upmanship. Laughter filled the air as we learned from one another, cementing new words in our memories. Here, I must confess a childish escapade. An and I, emboldened by our perceived English prowess, hatched a plan to "teach a lesson" to our Cambodian supervisor. We suspected him of condescension, fueled by his superior English (or so we thought). Our strategy? Ambushing him with obscure vocabulary, relishing his stumbles. "How can you be our boss with such poor English?" we'd taunt. Our supervisor, years older and wiser, simply smiled. "Keep studying, young men," he chuckled.

Looking back, our behavior was childish and arrogant. We carried the vestiges of Việt Namwith us, unaware of how our actions might be perceived. Knowing more vocabulary wasn't about superiority; it was about a deeper understanding.

This simple lesson, delivered with kindness by our Cambodian supervisor, resonated deeply.

Bangkok and Beyond

Six months in Phanat Nikhom felt like an eternity. The news that the United Nations Intergovernmental Committee for Migration would resettle our group of fifty-four refugees in Australia sparked a wave of excitement. Australia! A land far removed from the harsh realities of the camp. Our journey began with a bus ride, leaving the confines of the camp behind and hurtling towards Bangkok.

After a year spent in refugee camps, Bangkok hit me like a sensory explosion. A country bumpkin visiting the city for the first time, I marveled at the crisscrossing highways, the towering buildings, and the bustling streets. Bangkok dwarfed Sài Gòn (the "Pearl of the Far East"), which suddenly felt provincial in comparison.

Our arrival in Bangkok wasn't a direct path to freedom. Instead, we were transferred to the Immigration Detention Center (IDC) – a city center facility housing a mix of foreigners, presumably those who'd crossed legal boundaries. The place felt a bit gloomy, perhaps due to the rain, but a sliver of hope shone through in the form of sunlight filtering through the windows.

Our group filled a large room, buzzing with anticipation for the flight to Australia. For two days, we were fed decent, clean meals–a welcome change from the camp fare.

Finally, the day arrived. A bus whisked us to a breathtaking sight: Bangkok airport. Spacious and luxurious, it was a world away from anything I'd ever seen. Shops glowed under bright lights, and everyone around us –passengers, even the police officers – exuded an air of elegance and courtesy. We, on the other hand, stood out in our simple clothes–a reminder of our journey. A picture of our group at that moment would have stood in striking contrast to the polished world around us.

Despite the initial awkwardness, a wave of conflicting emotions washed over me. The Thai government's indifference towards the plight of Vietnamese refugees had left a bitter taste in my mouth. Yet, they had provided shelter during our most desperate times. Saying goodbye to Thái Lan, even this small glimpse of civilization, brought a pang of sadness. Every goodbye is bittersweet, but this one held the promise of a new beginning.

A member of the Intergovernmental Committee for Migration guided us onto the plane. This colossal Boeing 747, a marvel compared to the cramped propellers I remembered from Tân Sơn Nhất, dwarfed everything around it. We were ushered to the back; the curious and sympathetic gazes of fellow passengers spoke volumes about our unique circumstances.

Fortunate enough to snag a window seat, I felt like I was peering into a portal to a world unseen. As the plane taxied down the runway, the bustling airport scene shrank beneath us—a vivid reminder of the contrast with the endless brown of the camp that had been my reality. Inside the cabin, a strange calm settled. Passengers puffed on cigarettes, exuding an air of nonchalance I ached to possess. But my mind was a whirlwind, focused on a single word: Australia. It whispered promises of freedom, opportunity, a life that stretched far beyond the suffocating confines of the refugee camp. A nervous excitement bubbled within me, a potent cocktail that overshadowed any trepidation about the unknown future that awaited.

Chapter Five

First Days in the Land Down Under

The plane's descent jolted me awake. Peering out the window, a city emerged from the clouds—Sydney, Australia. A kaleidoscope of emotions swirled within me: excitement, anticipation, and a hint of apprehension. The flight attendant's announcement echoed through the cabin. "Welcome to Sydney, Australia!"

It was January 26, 1982—Australia Day, a fortuitous coincidence that added a touch of serendipity to my arrival.

Stepping off the plane, a wall of heat hit me. The scorching sun announced it was summer Down Under. The casual attire of those welcoming loved ones—shorts and t-shirts—felt a world apart from the clothes we'd worn in the camps. Sydney airport lacked the glamour of Bangkok, but it whispered promises of a different kind.

We were herded onto a bus, a behemoth in my eyes then. No skyscrapers greeted us, just rows of clean, red-brick houses with manicured lawns. The lush green trees flanking Henry Lawson Drive, named after a famous Australian poet, were a welcome sight after the relentless brown of the refugee camps. Despite the lack of urban grandeur, Sydney radiated a quiet beauty.

Our destination was Cabramatta Hostel, a large two-story complex nestled on a hilltop. This would be our temporary home, a place to learn English and Australian culture before venturing out on our own. Cabramatta, situated in Sydney's southwestern suburbs, was known as a "working-class" area, quite different from the lively energy of Vietnamese cities. Back then, it was almost semi-rural with quiet streets and sparse traffic—a far cry from the bustling markets of home.

The hostel housed refugees and immigrants from across the globe—Vietnamese, Cambodians, Laotians, Chinese, Russians, Poles, Hungarians—a melting pot of cultures all seeking a new beginning. Here, I stayed for three months, adjusting to a life far removed from anything I'd known.

The biggest cultural clash came at mealtimes. The hostel's large kitchen, resembling a huge three-bedroom house in size, served breakfast, lunch, and dinner. Western fare—toast, eggs, bacon—dominated the menu, a complete contrast to the rice, noodles, and pho that formed the bedrock of my Vietnamese diet. It took a year to adjust, but eventually, I found myself enjoying this new breakfast routine.

Lunch and dinner proved even more "disastrous" at first. Beef, lamb, and chicken dominated, with pork a rare treat. The rice was cooked to a mushy consistency, unfamiliar to our Vietnamese palates. Meat dishes were doused in milk, with a lingering fishy undertone that took some getting used to. On days when lamb or beef was served, the diners were predominantly Caucasian, whereas chicken days attracted more Asian diners. On evenings featuring lamb, many opted for instant noodles instead. The hostel administration, however, was quick to adapt. Asian chefs, often refugees, introduced us to rice and chicken prepared in a familiar, flavorful way, sometimes even seasoned with fish sauce—a taste of home amidst the new.

KFC and McDonald's, iconic symbols of American cuisine, held a particular allure. A friend, who arrived earlier, surprised me with a feast from the fast-food chain: golden fried chicken and apples, just like in the movies. Excitement turned to disappointment with the first bite. This chicken lacked the familiar flavor, the five-spice aroma, the texture I craved. It was a strange experience, a reminder that the foods of my homeland held a unique place in my heart.

Years later, my palate would adjust, but that first encounter with KFC remained a vivid memory, a symbol of the cultural clashes and adaptations that marked my new life in Australia. My life was far from perfect, but it was filled with the promise of freedom, opportunity, and a future far removed from the hardships of the past.

First Encounter with St. Vinnies

The first day in Australia was a whirlwind of paperwork, unfamiliar faces, and a strange mix of hope and uncertainty. My pockets were as empty as the future stretched before me. I had zero cents and two outfits–remnants of a life left behind.

Then, a glimmer of kindness. Thirty crisp Australian dollars, not from the government, but from the outstretched hands of the St. Vincent de Paul Society. It wasn't much, but it was a lifeline in a sea of unknowns. This wasn't just money; it was a promise of a fresh start.

They also handed me a voucher... a passport to a new wardrobe. Naive in my newcomer's enthusiasm, I pictured rows of brightly coloured, never-been-worn clothes waiting just for me. But this wasn't a flashy department store; it was a St. Vinnies thrift shop for those down on their luck. The kind staff, sensing my initial disappointment, explained with gentle smiles, "These are pre-loved clothes, but they're still good." Pre-loved. I liked that term. It felt warmer and more generous than the plain "used" I'd been expecting.

Following their guidance, I stood before the racks, a world of possibilities spread out. The rules were simple: three outfits, each consisting of pants and shirts paired together, and a single pair of shoes. Sandals, my trusty companions on the long journey here, were deemed a touch too "proletarian" for my new life. I browsed carefully, my fingers tracing the textures of unfamiliar fabrics. A navy blue button-down shirt, crisp and clean, felt luxurious against my skin. A pair of beige chinos held a promise of adventures, both urban and outdoorsy. Each piece I picked was a tiny victory, a step towards building a new identity.

Those three outfits, carefully folded and tucked away, became more than just clothes. They were tangible reminders of that first day, a symbol of the kindness that greeted me on foreign shores. The shoes, well, those eventually wore down, but the outfits–the navy shirt, the beige chinos, and their companions–I kept. My clothes and shoes became souvenirs of a fresh start, symbols of the generosity of strangers, and a lasting connection to the name St. Vincent, which would become an integral part of my Australian life.

Little did I know then that the connection wouldn't stop there. Years later, I found myself working at St. Vincent's Hospital, dedicating nearly three decades to research there. And, in a beautiful twist of fate, I later became a regular donor to the very St. Vincent de Paul Society that had first extended a helping hand to a wide-eyed newcomer with empty pockets and a heart full of hope.

English Lessons of Freedom

With clothes in hand, it was time for English lessons. I enrolled in an English class in those early days. The classroom was filled with a vibrant mix of accents, a chorus of voices from across the globe attempting to navigate this strange new language. Vietnamese voices, laced with the melodic lilt of my mother tongue, surrounded me—a comforting familiarity. Yet, amongst the cacophony, I struggled to understand the fractured English of the Eastern Europeans, their words tumbling out in a way that left me bewildered. Even the Asian immigrants, with their own unique intonations, seemed miles ahead in their grasp of this foreign tongue.

Discouragement threatened to bloom, but then, during conversations with refugees from Poland, Hungary, and Czechoslovakia, the fog started to lift. Their fears mirrored those harbored by the Vietnamese—a constant wariness of the public security force, a life lived in hushed tones, a hesitancy to share their stories. Despite the distance separating our origins, we were bound by the shared experience of fleeing a communist past.

Treasured memories: my classmate from Poland on the left, and on the right, the wonderful teacher whose name escapes me but whose impact never will.

Our wonderful teacher, a woman unafraid to challenge authority, scoffed at our anxieties. "Australia is not a police state. There's no 'public security' here," she declared, waving a newspaper brimming with headlines critical of the government. Pointing to a picture of Prime Minister Malcolm Fraser, she added with a mischievous grin, "Next election, this guy's out!" I was stunned. She openly criticized the prime minister! My jaw dropped at the audacity and the open criticism. It was a striking difference from the world I'd left behind.

The focus here wasn't on lofty academic pursuits, but on practical application—equipping us with the tools to navigate the job market and integrate into society. Conversation trumped grammar drills, and the teacher, with her infectious humor, made the process a joy. She seemed to appreciate my eagerness and thirst for knowledge, which translated into a barrage of questions. I recall a writing assignment that was a thank-you letter. Fueled by a memory from a

Reader's Digest magazine in the refugee camp, I concluded with a flourish: As always, with affection.

The teacher, after reading it aloud, drew me aside with a raised eyebrow. "Those words," she said gently, "are only for... lovers." Another lesson learned, another layer of cultural nuance absorbed. Yet, a nagging sense of frustration began to simmer.

The repetitive dialogues—"How are you?" and "I am fine, thank you"—felt like a slow trudge through familiar territory. Convinced I could learn faster on my own, I made the difficult decision to leave the class after a week. The teacher, her face showing a hint of disappointment, surprised me with a parting prophecy. "In a few years," she declared, "there'll be a huge celebration for 200 years of Australia. Meet me at the Harbour Bridge!" I chuckled, recognizing the playful absurdity. How could we, two fleeting moments in each other's lives, possibly reunite amidst a national celebration?

But even now, the memory of that spirited teacher remains vivid—witty, compassionate, and a symbol of the welcoming spirit I encountered in this new land. The image of her, a beacon of hope on my journey of assimilation, continues to warm me decades later.

My First Street English Lessons: Dymock and Oxford

Fueled by newfound determination, I decided to take the reins of my English education. Ditching the classroom for self-study, I needed an English-English dictionary—a bridge between the familiar and the unknown. Back in the refugee camp, a trusty Longman dictionary had been my constant companion. Here, it seemed like a natural starting point. But the teacher, bless her heart, had other plans.

"Oxford Dictionary," she declared, her voice echoing in the classroom. "It's the most comprehensive."

The problem? Finding one. Apparently, only a handful of bookstores in the city centre stocked them, and Cabramatta, my suburban haven, was decidedly

devoid of such establishments. Armed with this knowledge and a touch of trepidation, I embarked on my first solo expedition into downtown Sydney.

My very first train journey felt like an odyssey. I was overwhelmed as I emerged
from the Town Hall station. Towering buildings, a far cry from the low-rise landscape of Cabramatta, loomed over me. I couldn't help but think of a wide-eyed
recruit in Sài Gòn, gawking at the city skyline and instinctively knocking off their
conical hat–a nervous reflex in a world so different.

The grand sandstone facade of the Victoria Building stopped me in my tracks.
It was magnificent in the truest sense of the word, standing in clear contrast to
the utilitarian structures lining the street. The city pulsed with frenetic energy;
people hurried by, their faces etched with purpose. My destination, the elusive
Dymock bookstore mentioned by my teacher, seemed lost in this urban jungle.

My struggle began with pronunciation. "Dai-Moc," I'd mumble to each person I stopped for directions. Kind faces would furrow in confusion. My mispro-
nunciation, a product of my Vietnamese tongue, was an invisible wall. Finally, an
elderly gentleman stopped. He listened patiently, then asked me to spell it out.
A wave of relief washed over me as he exclaimed, "Ah, Di-Mic!" His directions,
thankfully simple, led me to the haven of books.

Dymock's, with its three floors overflowing with books, was a world unto itself.
Confidence, misplaced as it turned out, surged through me as I boldly declared,
"I'd like an Ox-Fod dictionary, please." The "Ox-Fod" pronunciation, mirroring
the "Ford" car from back home, felt natural. The blank stare of the bookseller,
however, was not. Reduced to scribbling the word on a piece of paper, I watched
with amusement as recognition dawned. "Ah, Oxford!"

That dictionary became my constant companion in my early struggles. Even
today, forty years later, it occupies a place of honor on my bookshelf–a reminder
of that first foray into the city and the humbling lesson in the complexities
of the English language. French, with its logical structure, had seemed almost
intuitive in comparison. Here, the written word was a mischievous trickster,
defying easy pronunciation. Words like allowance, kibosh, and niche, and names
like Beauchamp and Worcester, became daily challenges–proofsof the chasm
between textbook English and the nuances of everyday speech. It was a realization

that would send me on a lifelong journey, constantly refining my grasp on this ever-evolving language.

Working as a Kitchen Hand: Crying Over Onions

After a few weeks in the hostel, I started looking for work. The newspaper, with its heavily inked classifieds, became my daily ritual. Armed with a red pen, I'd circle every job advertisement that seemed remotely within reach. Sometimes, I ventured out with a group of fellow refugees, a motley crew with varying degrees of English. But more often than not, I was a lone figure, working through the intricate world of employment interviews.

Back then, the language barrier was a brutal gatekeeper. Those with a decent grasp of English could aim for sorting mail at the post office, a seemingly glamorous position compared to the factory work that awaited those like me, struggling to string together a coherent sentence. Every interview was an exercise in disappointment. The polite inquiries about my "experience" were a constant reminder of my blank resume. Here, in this land of opportunity, experience was everything. Nobody wanted to invest time and resources in training someone who might not even last a week.

Dejected after yet another failed interview at an electrical company, I trudged homeward, the weight of each rejection settling like lead in my stomach. Then, a flash of ochre caught my eye—the Belmore Hotel, its unusual architecture an anomaly amidst the city's beige uniformity. It was a sign, I decided, a beacon of hope in a sea of doubt.

Back home, with renewed determination, I scanned the newspaper ads. This time, an entry jumped out: "Kitchen Hand - St Vincent's Hospital." A kitchen? Now, that was something I could handle. Unlike the sterile factories, the idea of a bustling kitchen, filled with the aroma of simmering broths and the rhythmic clang of pots, held a strange allure. With newfound confidence, I discarded the Belmore Hotel's fictional three-year stint and marched head on towards St. Vincent's.

The interview with Georgina Ramsey, the no-nonsense kitchen manager, was a blur. Her questions about my background were met with a bold "Yes," a desperate gamble fueled by the fear of another rejection. Her initial skepticism quickly melted into a wry smile. Perhaps she saw my raw determination and quiet desperation in my eyes. "Start tomorrow," she said, her voice laced with a hint of amusement.

That first day was filled with an overwhelming barrage of sensory overload. Mountains of stainless-steel pots gleamed under the harsh fluorescent lights. The dishwashing machine, a colossal metal beast, devoured piles of plates and cutlery in a mesmerizing, never-ending cycle. My initial task—washing pots—morphed into something far less strenuous. Instead of battling greasy pans, I became the overlord of an endless parade of pots and dishes, feeding them into the maw of the industrial dishwasher.

Onions, however, were a different story. Two colossal sacks of them loomed menacingly. As I peeled the first bulb, tears welled up in my eyes, not just from the onion's potency but also from the daunting scale of the task ahead. Gerry, the ever-observant "Kiwi" supervisor, mistook my tears for homesickness. "Are you alright?" he'd ask, a gentle concern in his voice.

Over time, I developed an onion-taming technique, a small victory in the face of countless culinary challenges. The days were a set of repetitive tasks—chopping vegetables, stocking the pantry, and keeping the kitchen meticulously organized. There were moments of quiet camaraderie with fellow refugees, a shared understanding woven through the cracks of our limited English.

Then there was the phone... the bane of my existence. Deliveries and orders were placed by phone, and the thought of answering this menacing instrument filled me with dread. But the kind Greek storekeeper, sensing my fear, became my patient tutor, coaxing me into the world of telephone conversations. Slowly, the jumble of sounds started to coalesce into recognizable words, and the fear receded.

The shadow of the Belmore Hotel, however, loomed large. Guilt weighed on me with every passing day. Finally, after weeks of internal turmoil, I confessed my fabricated kitchen experience to Georgina. To my surprise, she chuckled. "We knew," she said, her voice devoid of accusation. "But you seemed eager, and frankly, we needed the help." She spoke of the many refugees in the kitchen, men and women with degrees from distant lands, all starting anew in this lucky country.

Six months later, a promotion arrived—–Assistant Chef. A crisp white uniform, a tall chef's hat, and the privilege of working alongside the head chef, a man with a repertoire of culinary techniques that opened my eyes to a whole new world of flavors. The work was demanding, the pressure immense. Two unannounced inspections a week kept us on our toes, the fear of hefty fines a constant motivator.

Yet, amidst the chaos, I learned the importance of cleanliness and organization, the delicate balance of flavors, intricacies of French sauces and Italian risottos. The kitchen, once a place of fear, became a source of pride. I reveled in the rhythmic dance of chopping vegetables, the satisfaction of creating a perfect glaze, the quiet pleasure of presenting a well-plated meal.

Trying My Hand at The Regent

The lure of a fuller paycheck, a siren song amidst the clatter of pots at St. Vincent's, tugged at my resolve. Back home, the needs of my family pressed on me. Though remittances weren't explicitly requested, the unspoken understanding loomed large. Medical bills, unexpected expenses, the constant struggle for basic necessities—these formed a silent chorus, urging me to find ways to send more.

The answer shimmered across the harbor, a beacon of luxury amidst the city's skyline—The Regent Hotel (now Shangri-La Hotel). Freshly opened at Circular Quay, a stone's throw from the iconic Harbour Bridge, it was a five-star oasis in the bustling city. The rumors swirled—impeccable salaries, almost double what I earned at the hospital. The temptation was irresistible.

The interview process was as unique as the hotel itself. Gone were the standard questions; instead, they ushered me into the heart of the kitchen, a stage bathed in the harsh glow of industrial lights. Their eyes, keen and assessing, followed my every move—the way I handled utensils, the cadence of my chopping, the silent dance with food safety protocols. My "wealth of experience" from St. Vincent's kitchen, honed through countless onion-laced battles and perfectly executed dish maneuvers, must have convinced them. A curt nod, a handshake, and I was in.

Stepping into the bustling kitchen, I was greeted by a chorus of surprised gasps. Faces from the refugee camp in Thái Lan, showing a blend of disbelief and amusement, materialized amongst the organized chaos. There was Trang, my younger companion, the one who had shared that perilous boat journey. Clad in his dishwashing uniform, he looked at me, a question mark visible on his brow. "When did you become a cook assistant?" he asked. My response, a mischievous grin and a mumbled, "Just three months ago," left him bewildered.

The camaraderie, however, was short-lived. The double duty of night shifts at The Regent proved too much. The exhaustion, a relentless wave washing over me, forced a decision. With a heavy heart, I said goodbye to the world of fine dining, the precisely arranged platters, and the international symphony of accents that filled the kitchen.

But the experience left an indelible mark. It was a crash course in the art of five-star service, the pressure of a fast-paced environment where every dish was a miniature masterpiece. I met chefs from distant lands, their culinary skills a mesmerizing display of technique and artistry. The Regent, for that brief period, became a portal to a world far removed from the frugal reality of most refugees.

My Sydney Start

A few months in at St Vincent's, a restlessness bloomed in my chest. It wasn't the work itself. The camaraderie in that steamy kitchen felt a world away from the loneliness I'd known in Thái Lan. But Sydney, for all its sunshine and space, felt big and unwieldy on foot. The truth was, I craved the freedom of four wheels.

Kitchen-hand wages weren't exactly banker's hours, that much was clear. A godsend compared to back home, sure, but after rent and groceries, there wasn't exactly loose change jingling in my pockets. Still, every week, I'd peel off a wad of cash, a crisp AUD 150. It wasn't much, but it was a start. Enough, I dared to believe, to buy a taste of freedom on four wheels.

My friend, Sáu Lợi, another refugee from Thái Lan who'd landed in Sydney a few months before me, became my partner-in-crime for car shopping. We crisscrossed Sydney in his newly bought Mitsubishi Magna, but each showroom was a disappointment. Then, a glint of sunshine in Parramatta: a 1977 Toyota Corona, a mere five years old, gleamed under the harsh fluorescent lights. It purred like a kitten on the test drive. At AUD 7000, it was a steal, but a cruel steal for my AUD 5000 budget.

Sáu Lợi , ever the pragmatist, stepped in. "Haggle, friend," he advised, a glint in his eye. "Don't buy a rusty lemon you'll sink money into later." His words mirrored the resourcefulness that had brought us here. Together, we battled the salesman, our broken English a symphony of hopeful pleas. He budged a thousand, leaving us still adrift in a sea of red. Sáu Lợi surprised me then, offering to bridge the gap. "Think of it as an investment," he said. "Freedom on four wheels."

And freedom it was. The first drive-in my car was a revelation. Sydney sprawled beneath a cerulean sky, the sun warm on my face. It was a world away from the motorbike that had been my lifeline back in Vietnam. This was independence, the ability to explore at my own pace.

The Corona proved to be a loyal companion. Week after week, it hummed along, fueled by cheap gas (can you believe a liter was only twenty five to thirty cents back then) and a shared sense of adventure. It became an extension of myself, a symbol of the new life I was building.

For seventeen glorious years, the Corona served me well. It saw countless sunrises over Bondi Beach, late-night shifts at the restaurant, university night classes, and weekend picnics in the Royal National Park. Only when the chassis declared defeat, deemed unsafe by a concerned mechanic, did it finally retire. Even then, the engine, the legendary 17-RC made in Japan, still purred like a champ.

Looking back, those first days in Australia were a heady mix of struggle and possibility. The cost of living was a dream compared to today. And yes, maybe we Vietnamese did love a good car, a symbol of the life we were carving out for ourselves. Perhaps it did raise eyebrows, whispers of government handouts swirling around us. But little did they know, it was our resilience, our determination to create a better life, that fueled our desire for a shiny set of wheels.

A Brush with the Law

The freedom of my new car was intoxicating. Gone were the days of crowded buses and rigid schedules. I juggled work at St. Vincent's Hospital with night classes, navigating Sydney's streets with the confidence of a seasoned driver. Back then, traffic was a gentle murmur, a far cry from the congested symphony it is today.

Then, disaster struck. One crisp morning, as I navigated the narrow, cobbled streets of Newtown, a figure emerged from a doorway. A woman, unsteady on her feet and reeking of stale beer, stumbled towards my car. I slammed on the brakes, heart pounding, as she landed with a thud on the hood. Thankfully, the slow crawl of city traffic meant the impact was negligible.

Shaken, I stepped out to find the woman uninjured, but belligerent. The police arrived, their presence a surreal counterpoint to the early morning bustle. A simple accident that can easily be resolved, I thought. But a cruel twist awaited. The woman, of Aboriginal descent, accused me of negligence.

My temporary driver's license hung in the balance. Court. The word itself conjured images of intimidating judges and stoic lawyers. Reality, however, was a peculiar blend. The courtroom buzzed with a nervous energy, a motley crew of people united by a brush with the law. Shorts and t-shirts mingled with formal suits. The air was thick with a nervous chatter that seemed out of place in this solemn setting.

My turn arrived. The judge, a man with a kind face and a twinkle in his eye, confirmed my name. My limited English became painfully evident. Each answer was a hesitant dance, accompanied by apologetic smiles. When the charge of negligence was read, I countered with my truth—the woman's lack of injuries was evidence of the minimal impact.

My broken English, however, proved more effective than my argument. The judge, realizing the communication barrier, let out a hearty laugh. "This man needs a lawyer for a fair trial," he declared and postponed the case.

A public defender, a godsend in my predicament, was assigned for my next appearance. However, fate intervened again. A commitment at the Regent Hotel clashed with the court date. Faced with a tough decision, I opted for work.

The court, in my absence, found me negligent. My license was confiscated for a year, a harsh penalty for a minor accident. Yet, a glimmer of hope remained. I successfully petitioned to drive a limited route, allowing me to maintain my work and studies.

A year later, my license was back in my hands, a hard-won victory. The experience, though unnerving, served as a baptism by brake. It taught me the importance of not just navigating the roads, but also the complexities of a new system, a lesson that has served me well in the four decades since, keeping me accident and courtroom-free.

A New Beginning: Our Sydney Wedding

The rumble of the new car beneath my fingers was a comforting thrum, a promise of stability. The dream of a family, once a distant flicker, now burned bright. It was at a training workshop in Vietnam, a world away from the chaos of escape, that I met Gấm. Love, as unexpected as a monsoon squall, swept us off our feet, a life raft in the churning sea of displacement.

Australia wasn't just a new land, it was a blank canvas. Gấm and I, refugees bound by love and the scars etched on our souls, approached it with a mix of trepidation and exhilaration. We had promised forever under the familiar gaze of our homeland, a whispered vow amidst the fear. But escape had scattered those dreams, leaving us reunited on foreign soil. Sydney, then, became the stage for the real thing.

In 1982, with love as our biggest treasure, we tied the knot with simple $50 rings.

It was October 16th, 1982. The air, crisp with the tang of spring, held the promise of a new beginning. Forget the extravagance of fairytales, the opulence that graced magazine covers. This was our reality, a combination of resilience and the quiet hum of joy. We weren't wealthy refugees, but survivors with hearts brimming with the audacity of starting anew. Lavish wasn't a language we spoke. Sincerity was our currency.

Our guests, a hundred strong, mirrored our own journeys. The Vietnamese newcomers carried faces that echoed shared struggles and dreams spoken in hushed tones. They were family, not by blood, but by the unyielding bond of shared experience.

My fearless brother, the one who had braved the perilous riverboat journey to ferry us away from Rạch Giá, stood as my officiant. Gấm's elder brother, Trung, who'd arrived two years before, stood by her side. It wasn't a ceremony of grand pronouncements, but of quiet promises reflected in our gazes.

One wedding ring and a simple pair of AUD 100 earrings were the symbols of our commitment. Yet, the depth of our love and the resolve in our eyes, spoke volumes more than any material possession. This wasn't just a celebration of a day, it was a vow whispered into the future. We'd face the challenges hand-in-hand, carve out a happiness that would defy the odds, a love story that would span not just a day, but a lifetime. And for the next forty years, we did, brushstroke by brushstroke, painting a life together on this new and uncharted canvas.

Brick by Brick: Building a Dream in Yagoona

The cramped quarters of our two-bedroom apartment in Campsie were starting to feel like a borrowed dream. Gấm and I, newlyweds with a thirst for space, craved a backyard—a patch of earth to truly call our own–where vegetables wouldn't have to battle elbows. Owning a home in Australia–then, as now–held the weight of a beautiful aspiration.

Two years of diligently saving yielded over AUD 25,000, a war chest for our suburban crusade. Weekends were spent scouring the streets, keeping our eyes peeled for a haven that whispered possibility. Then, in Yagoona, a vision emerged: a charming red brick house with three bedrooms, beckoning us with its solidity. The price tag of AUD 75,000 felt like a summit, but after some friendly haggling, we conquered it, bringing the cost down to AUD 72,000.

The next hurdle loomed: the mortgage. My income, then around AUD 300, and Gắm's, AUD 210, were our war paint. The Commonwealth Bank scrutinized our numbers, the cost of living versus what remained. Finally, they offered a lifeline—AUD 50,000, a generous sum in those days. But the interest rate, 13.5%, was a beast, far different from today's rates. Still, with monthly payments of AUD 483 over twenty years, the dream felt attainable.

One crisp autumn morning in 1985, the keys jingled in our hands. Stepping into that house in Yagoona, a wave of emotions washed over us—the joy of a new beginning, the hope etched into every corner. The air held a clean, autumnal crispness, the perfect backdrop for the fresh canvas of our lives.

Owning a home wasn't just about settlement; it was a plunge into responsibility. Though the loan stretched over two decades, a burning desire to be debt-free fueled us. We poured every ounce of effort into work, and on December 21, 1990, a mere five years later, the final mortgage payment was made. The dream of homeownership, a symbol of our new life in Australia, had solidified.

Our ambition, however, wasn't a one-shot deal. With the arrival of our son, a new kind of space became paramount. In 1991, we embarked on another chapter, a grander four-bedroom, two-story house in Georges Hall.

This time, the loan was steeper—over AUD 100,000, but our income had grown too. With the same dedication, the mortgage was vanquished within five years. This house, to this day, remains the anchor of our family's story. Buying our first home wasn't just a real estate transaction; it was a monumental step in our journey, reflecting our determination and commitment to building a life in the new country that had welcomed us. Brick by brick, we built not just a house, but a foundation for our future.

Our first home in Yagoona, 1985.

Chapter Six

A Calculated Leap

A year and a half had passed, with the rhythm of St. Vincent's kitchen becoming a familiar comfort. Yet, a disquietude stirred within me. The repetitive tasks, while providing a sense of security, no longer sparked the same curiosity. Mrs. Ramsey's words, a gentle nudge towards a future filled with more, echoed in my mind. "There's always room for growth," she said, her weathered face crinkling with a knowing smile. It was time to heed her advice.

The opportunity arrived, shimmering like a mirage in the desert, in the form of a job opening at Royal North Shore Hospital in North Sydney. The title of Assistant in the Biochemistry Laboratory held the promise of something more, a step away from the familiar clatter of pots and pans. Here, the tools of the trade wouldn't be knives and spatulas, but vials and test tubes. My role, while seemingly straightforward—collecting tissue and blood samples—felt imbued with a new level of importance.

I thirsted for knowledge. The intricacies of blood work and the process of extracting plasma from whole blood were mysteries I yearned to learn. Spare moments were spent diligently studying, the textbook a passport to this new world.

Then, one serendipitous afternoon, I found Dr. Ackerman, the head of the lab, wrestling with a complex calculation. Curiosity, a persistent companion, propelled me forward. A furtive glance revealed him grappling with standard deviation, a concept I recognized from my university studies. However, Dr. Ackerman's method, while textbook-perfect, seemed cumbersome and time-consuming.

The urge to offer a solution, tempered by respect for authority, battled within me. Finally, gathering my courage, I hesitantly voiced my observation. Dr. Ackerman's response, a dismissive, "This is a complicated task, young man," stung. The implication, clear and cutting, was that someone in my position wouldn't understand such intellectual matters.

But the spark of defiance wouldn't be extinguished. "If I can't calculate it in two minutes, you can fire me," I challenged, the words tumbling out before I could stop them. Dr. Ackerman, surprised by my audacity, conceded. What followed was a blur of efficient calculations, a simple modification to his formula, shaving off precious minutes. The result, achieved within a minute flat, hung heavy in the air.

Dr. Ackerman's astonishment was palpable. "Where did you learn this?' he inquired, the skepticism replaced by a flicker of admiration.

"In Vietnam," I replied.

"Smart people like you should go back to university to advance your careers."

Those words, like a seed planted in fertile soil, inspired a dedicated pursuit of knowledge. The halls of Macquarie University, Sydney University, and UNSW Sydney became my new paths of learning.

Fresh off two years at Royal North Shore Hospital, I first embarked on a new adventure at Macquarie University. It was 1985, and amidst my studies, I landed a lucky break: a position at the Planning, Evaluation and Development Unit (PEDU) of the New South Wales Department of Health. Despite the official name, the PEDU was the beating heart of epidemiology and disease surveillance for the state. Their mission: research, planning, and advising the NSW Minister for Health. What surprised me most? The entire operation was conducted with just twenty people!

The unit was structured into four sections: surveillance epidemiology, data management, data analysis, and planning. At the helm was a physician with dual specialties in neurology and epidemiology. Dr. Marilyn Rob, the head of the data analysis section, recruited me as her assistant.

The PEDU became the true starting point for my journey in epidemiology. Dr. Rob was an exceptional supervisor, always encouraging and supporting any initiatives I took. However, my role wasn't directly involved in data analysis. Instead, I became the bridge between the researchers and the computers. I coordinated with a team of programmers to meticulously 'organize" the data, which meant ensuring easy access and export for statistical analysis—a seemingly simple task that turned out to be incredibly time-consuming.

Imagine reconciling mountains of medical records with their digital counterparts! Each study involved hundreds of patients, and my job was this crucial first step. Accuracy was paramount—a single error meant starting over from scratch. Over time, I realized a new truth: 90% of the analysis and reporting process was dedicated solely to making the data usable!

Back then, the PEDU boasted a Digital Equipment Corporation (DEC) minicomputer and a fleet of microcomputers from the International Business Machines (IBM) Corporation. These weren't exactly user-friendly machines; they required dedicated computer specialists. A South Korean programmer, Byung Lee, and a Vietnamese refugee-turned-computer scientist, Khoa Le, managed the DEC minicomputers. Khoa, being young and raised in Australia, spoke fluent English, unlike me. We each had our own IBM microcomputers running on the MS-DOS operating system (think pre-history of Windows!). Everything was done by typing commands directly into the console.

Now, here was the kicker: I knew absolutely nothing about computers. No one had ever shown me the ropes. But in this environment, computer illiteracy meant a dead end. So, I took matters into my own hands. Every night, I would bring home those hefty MS-DOS and dBASE III database user manuals and devour them. I meticulously jotted down all the essential commands I needed to memorize. MS-DOS, with its limited set of 30 commands, wasn't too bad. But dBASE III, with its talk of *fields, variables, and observations*, was a whole new language.

Thankfully, with some guidance from Byung Lee and Khoa Le, I grasped the basics pretty quickly. Within a month, I was building decent databases—a skill that would prove invaluable later at the Garvan Institute.

This newfound knowledge emboldened me to delve into the world of computer programming. BASIC was my first foray, followed by FORTRAN (short for Formula Translation System, a favorite among math geeks). Once again, I became my own teacher, tackling basic computational tasks using FORTRAN. Whenever I hit a roadblock, Khoa and Byung lent a hand. It was through FORTRAN that I truly began to appreciate the complexity of epidemiological and statistical formulas and models. I always tell my students, "A strong foundation is crucial. Superficial knowledge isn't enough to grasp the intricacies of a subject."

Empowered by my newfound computer and programming skills, I felt I could contribute more than just the basic tasks assigned to me. I started observing Marilyn and her colleagues as they developed models for epidemiological analysis. Fueled by curiosity, I began venturing to the university library to borrow specialized textbooks. I spent nights teaching myself and conducting my own studies on the side. However, I kept this a secret from Dr. Rob, not wanting to seem overambitious.

One day, brimming with confidence, I presented my work to her. I proudly displayed my analytical tables, showcasing techniques like chi-square tests, linear regression, and logistic regression. Dr. Rob's initial surprise quickly turned to amusement. "Who taught you how to do this?" she inquired, a hint of a smile playing on her lips.

"I learned from textbooks in the library," I confessed.

Her eyes widened further. "And who wrote the programs to run the analyses?"

With a newfound confidence, I replied, "I did."

Astonishment filled her face. "You deserve a better position!" she exclaimed. She then provided valuable feedback, pointing out areas for improvement and guiding me on how to interpret the results. At that moment, Dr. Rob became my first true mentor in epidemiology.

In the photo, I am with Dr. Marilyn Rob at the Planning, Evaluation, and Development Unit in the mid-1980s.

Beyond her guidance, a genuine bond blossomed between us. Dr. Rob was originally from South Africa and worked as a business manager for IBM Australia. Her husband was Dutch. They had two children, Lawrence and Katherine. Years later, my wife and I became close with the Rob family, celebrating New Year's Eve at their home like an extended family. I considered Dr. Rob an older sister, even naming my firstborn son Laurence (with a slightly different spelling)—a gesture that delighted her.

After a fulfilling three years at the PEDU, I decided to pursue a doctoral degree. An opportunity arose at the University of Sydney, where I landed a position as an Associate Lecturer. This role allowed me to enroll in a doctoral program while also gaining valuable teaching experience. My initial assignment was to assist a world-renowned professor in epidemiology. The professor, a firm believer in quantitative research, appreciated my "measurement-oriented" approach. He encouraged me to pursue a doctoral degree... advice I readily embraced.

My doctoral research focused on utilizing Markov models to describe the transitions between different stages of a disease. Imagine a patient with a particular illness: they could progress from a mild stage to moderate, then severe, and potentially even to death. My challenge was to model these transitions and identify the factors influencing each step. This very methodology, remarkably, became the subject of a paper I published in the prestigious journal *eLife* in 2023.

My tenure at the University of Sydney was an era where university professors held immense authority. Each department typically had only one full professor, with the remainder being associate professors or lecturers. These full professors held the key to a student's future, as their approval was often required to secure prestigious post-doctoral internships.

A vivid memory from that time is entering the University of Sydney canteen on my first day. When the professor, who was also the department head, walked in, everyone, including students and faculty, stood to greet him, despite his friendly demeanor. He never asked for such a greeting. However, this act of respect, ingrained in the hierarchical structure of Australian universities at the time, differed significantly from the more informal environments I experience now.

This structure was evident throughout the university. Professors were revered figures, their expertise and experience commanding immense respect. Associate Professors, while not as senior as full professors, were still highly respected for their academic achievements and contributions to their fields. They often served as bridges between professors and lecturers, facilitating communication and collaboration within departments.

Lecturers shouldered the responsibility of delivering lectures, conducting tutorials, and assessing student work. They played a crucial role in imparting knowledge and nurturing the next generation of researchers and academics.

Finally, tutors, typically graduate students like me or early-career researchers, provided additional support to students. They offered one-on-one assistance and facilitated small group discussions, serving as valuable resources for students seeking clarification on concepts or extra practice with coursework.

This hierarchical structure, though sometimes perceived as rigid, offered a clear chain of command and fostered a culture of respect for academic expertise. It also provided a framework for professional development, with individuals aspiring to progress through the ranks and contribute to the advancement of their respective fields.

While my time at the University of Sydney was brief, it proved to be a valuable stepping stone. It provided me with a deeper understanding of the academic landscape in Australia, exposed me to a different teaching environment, and equipped me with the skills and knowledge to pursue my doctoral research. It was also during this time that I was "persuaded" to join the Garvan Institute of Medical Research, marking the beginning of a new and exciting chapter in my scientific career.

Chapter Seven

Building Bones Career

The Garvan Institute of Medical Research wasn't just my workplace; it became an extension of myself. Within its vibrant halls, I lived some of the most important moments of my scientific career. Here, I delved deep into osteoporosis research, forging a path I never envisioned at the University of Sydney.

Sydney University offered a comfortable life: a respected academic environment and a stable income. However, a restlessness began to take root. Conversations with colleagues about more lucrative opportunities, fueled by the university's modest salaries, eroded my initial contentment. Having recently purchased a home, the burden of the mortgage further emphasized the urgency for change. With newfound determination, I scoured the employment pages, a silent plea for a better fit.

Then, it appeared–an advertisement from the Garvan Institute, a beacon of promise. They were seeking researchers for the Dubbo Osteoporosis Epidemiology Study (DOES), a project that was getting underway. Leading the project was Professor John Eisman, an endocrinologist who'd returned from a prestigious postdoctoral fellowship in the US. A true prodigy, he entered the University of Sydney at the astonishing age of sixteen or seventeen. His intellect was as awe-inspiring as his drive. Colleagues cautioned me that working alongside him wouldn't be for the faint of heart. He is dedicated to excellence and refuses to accept mediocrity. However, the prospect of learning from such a brilliant mind, of honing my skills under his relentless pursuit of perfection, was an opportunity too valuable to pass up.

The interview was an intimidating gauntlet. Professor John Eisman, Professor Philip Sambrook, and Dr. Paul Kelly formed a panel across from me. Professor Eisman, their designated drill sergeant, meticulously dissected my Sydney University research. When stochastic process theory (my project at the time) came up, his brow furrowed. "What in the world is that?" he enquired.

Sensing the tension, I quipped, "Think of it as predicting a professor's mood swings—with slightly better math." Professor Eisman chuckled, muttering that he wanted to predict his own.

The next day, Professor Eisman's call shattered the suspense. The team was on board, offering me the epidemiologist role for the DOES project. However, the initial salary fell short of my expectations. Disappointed, I turned it down. Professor Eisman, a great persuader, called again the very next day. This time, the offer had been significantly improved, boasting a competitive salary and a generous superannuation package. The financials now aligned perfectly, and the thrill of the unknown beckoned. With a deep breath, I accepted.

That decision, a seemingly minor shift, ultimately altered the course of my life. It propelled me into the vibrant world of medical sciences, where passion, collaboration, and a relentless pursuit of knowledge became my guiding stars. The rest, as they say, is history. But it all began with a chance encounter and a leap of faith, a pivotal moment that led me to the Garvan and the heart of my scientific calling.

The Garvan Institute, I soon realized, is part of St. Vincent's Hospital, where I'd once washed dishes. So, nearly ten years later, I found myself returning to the very place where my life in Australia began.

The Garvan Institute's genesis can be traced back to 1963, when it emerged as a small research unit within St. Vincent's Hospital, dedicated to unraveling the mysteries of endocrinology and metabolism. This modest endeavor was the brainchild of the Sisters of Charity, the hospital's founders, who envisioned a center of excellence to advance medical knowledge. Their vision was fueled by the generous contributions of Helen Mills, who honored her father, James Patrick Garvan, a prominent politician and businessman from New South Wales, by naming the Institute in his memory.

As the Garvan Institute's reputation grew, so did its financial needs. To address this challenge, the institute's leadership established the Garvan Research Foundation in 1981. This strategic move aimed to attract philanthropic support, enabling the institute to pursue its groundbreaking research unhindered. The foundation's efforts proved fruitful, raising a substantial $110,000 in its inaugural year–a remarkable sum for the time.

The institute's growing stature was further solidified in 1982 when it received its first program grant from the National Health and Medical Research Council (NHMRC) for diabetes research. This recognition cemented the institute's position as a frontrunner in medical innovation. A year later, a formal affiliation with the University of New South Wales (now known as UNSW Sydney) was established, further strengthening the institute's academic credentials.

The year 1984 marked a pivotal moment in the Garvan Institute's history. The New South Wales Parliament passed the Garvan Institute of Medical Research Act, granting the institute autonomous status as a non-profit research entity. This newfound independence empowered the institute to chart its own course, setting the stage for future breakthroughs. The institute's reputation continued to rise, culminating in its designation as one of Australia's five "centres of excellence research" in 1986. This prestigious recognition, coupled with additional infrastructure funding from the NSW Government, paved the way for the institute's expansion into a state-of-the-art research facility.

In 1990, following the retirement of Professor Les Lazarus, Professor John Shine took over as the head of the Garvan Institute. Professor Shine, a luminary in the world of DNA research, was renowned for his discovery of the Shine-Delgarno sequence, a critical element in gene regulation. His arrival marked a new era for the institute, ushering in the age of molecular biology. Under Professor Shine's leadership, the Garvan Institute flourished, attracting substantial funding from the NHMRC and the Garvan Research Foundation. This financial support enabled the institute to expand its research scope and recruit top-tier scientists.

I joined the Garvan Institute during this transformative era. The year I joined the Institute, 1991, was also a year of immense sorrow for the St. Vincent's community. Dr. Victor Chang, a pioneering heart surgeon who performed the first successful heart transplant in Australia (and arguably the world), was tragically assassinated on his way to work. His untimely passing sent shockwaves through the nation, leaving a deep void in the medical field. In his honor, St. Vincent's Hospital established the Victor Chang Cardiac Research Institute (VCCRI). Apart from VCCRI, esteemed research institutions like the Kirby Institute and the AIDS Research Center, spearheaded by the trailblazing HIV researcher Professor David Cooper, flourished within this bastion of knowledge.

During a visit, Prime Minister Julia Gillard aptly christened this corner of Sydney as the "highest density of intellectuals in Australia." And how right she was! In close proximity to Victoria and Liverpool Streets dwelled numerous professors, distinguished physicians, and the site where Australia's, if not the world's, first successful heart transplant took place (following the historic South African operation). Just as the Vietnamese proverb suggests, *"Near the inkwell, you turn black; near the lamp, you become* bright." Working within the *"St. Vincent's Republic"* (as I called it) felt akin to being enveloped in that illuminating glow.

The Garvan of those days was a far cry from its current architectural grandeur. Cramped within a four-story building, my workspace shared a wall with a rodent research lab. Occasionally, a wayward mouse might waltz across my desk, adding an unwelcome touch of charm to the bustling environment.

Despite its quirks, the Garvan buzzed with activity. Roughly 300 scientists and doctors formed a vibrant community, divided into four research divisions: neuroscience, endocrinology, oncology, and bone & mineral. Each division was headed by a distinguished professor, whom we jokingly referred to as "kings" (though whispers suggested otherwise) due to them presiding over research programs, budgets, and student progress.

The Garvan Institute of Medical Research.

The Dubbo Osteoporosis Epidemiology Study

The Bone and Mineral Research Division and my initial focus revolved largely around DOES... The Dubbo Study. While the name itself may not be glamorous, it holds immense significance in the world of osteoporosis research. The study originated in 1988 under the leadership of Professors Leon Simons and John McCallum, initially titled *The Dubbo Study of the Health of the Elderly*. This comprehensive investigation aimed to understand healthy aging from both bio-medical and social science perspectives. In 1989, with the help of Professors Simons and McCallum, my mentor, Professor John Eisman, gained access to these valuable Dubbo resources and launched a new, more specific study: the "Dubbo Osteoporosis Epidemiology Study," dedicated solely to bone health research.

In the 1990s, I was a busy bee in the Garvan Institute's lab.

For over three decades, the Dubbo Study has been steadily making its mark on the world of osteoporosis research. DOES stands out for its sheer scale and longevity, meticulously monitoring the bone health of over 4,000 men and women, all aged 60 and above. Maintaining such a large-scale study over three decades is no easy feat. It requires commitment from the research team, led by the indomitable Professor Eisman, who has tirelessly championed DOES, piloting the ever-present challenge of securing adequate funding to keep the study running. His dedication has ensured the continuation of this groundbreaking research, paving the way for a deeper understanding of osteoporosis and its impact on aging individuals.

During that early period, in addition to Professor Eisman, who captained our study team, I was part of a wonderful team that included Professor Philip Sambrook, a rheumatologist who later became one of my mentors, and Dr. Paul Kelly, an outstanding endocrinologist. Professor Stephen Lord contributed to fall assessments, while Sister Janet Watters infused our work with heart and soul. Shortly after, Dr. Graeme Jones joined the study as a PhD student and would later become a Professor of Rheumatology.

In retrospect, the Dubbo Study wasn't just a research project; it was a shared adventure. Thousands of men and women—teachers, farmers, shop-keepers, families and a small team of researchers—embarked on a journey together. We were all united by a common thread: the silent threat of osteo-porosis. There were countless mornings spent in the little clinic, the hum of conversation punctuated by the rhythmic click of clipboards, all coordinated by Sister Janet Watters. They shared stories, not just of their medical history, but of lives lived—the joys, the struggles, and the resilience that seemed to echo in the very air we breathed. The butcher with a booming laugh, his grip surprisingly strong despite his advancing years; the librarian with a spine as straight as the shelves she tended; the young girl, barely a teenager, whose worried eyes spoke volumes about a family history etched in fragile bones. Each encounter became a brushstroke on the canvas of understanding, a piece of the puzzle we were determined to solve.

The initial data deluge threatened to drown me. One of my many tasks was to crack the code hidden within the data. For months, I became one with spread-sheets, meticulously searching for connections between bone density, lifestyle choices, and the ever-present enemy: fractures. It was a slow, painstaking process, but every discovery sent a jolt of excitement through me.

One afternoon, hunched over my screen, a peculiar pattern emerged. Fractures weren't solely confined to those with low bone density, but also struck individuals with seemingly healthy scores. A knot of nervousness formed in my stomach as I presented this at the next team meeting. Professor Eisman listened intently, a contemplative frown creasing his face.

"Intriguing observation," he finally said. "Perhaps bone density isn't the sole culprit. Maybe factors like muscle weakness or balance issues contribute to falls and fractures." His words ignited a spark and a flurry of new ideas. I then began incorporating muscle strength tests and balance assessments into participant visits.

This pivotal moment served as a clear reminder: science thrives on the unexpected and on challenging assumptions. The following years were marked by a flurry of activities. Our groundbreaking paper, revealing the surprisingly elevated fracture risk in men with osteoporosis, challenged established beliefs and garnered major media attention. DOES was thrust into the spotlight, with Professor Eisman becoming a regular on talk shows, fielding questions on bone health and prevention.

Each team meeting fueled my burgeoning passion for bone health. What began as a simple question–how to predict and prevent fractures–blossomed into a lifelong quest. This seemingly straightforward inquiry propelled me down a path of groundbreaking research, paradigm shifts, and ultimately, the creation of empowering tools for both patients and doctors in the fight against osteoporosis.

Little did I know, the Dubbo data would be the crucible for one of my earliest triumphs. Sifting through the Dubbo data, a revelation struck. The numbers whispered an important truth: women faced the risk of hip fracture as high as, and sometimes even higher than, breast cancer. This insight, published in the esteemed *British Medical Journal,* challenged the medical community.

After a conversation with Professor Philip Sambrook, my sights shifted to the neglected frontier of men's bone health. Through scrupulous studies, we meticulously chipped away at the unknown, identifying key risk factors for fractures and osteoporosis in this understudied population. These studies, hailed as pioneering, paved the way for a more holistic understanding of bone health for all.

But my curiosity propelled me further. The enigmatic world of osteoporosis genetics beckoned. Joining forces with a team chasing the elusive "osteoporosis gene,"—the vitamin D receptor gene"—was a pivotal moment. Yet, this was merely the first step on a thrilling journey. Our research group, fueled by a shared passion, unearthed a treasure trove of genes influencing fracture risk. This tireless pursuit culminated in the "Osteogenomic Profile," a genetic fingerprint that significantly enhanced our ability to predict fractures. It wasn't just about deciphering the genetic code of bone health; it was ushering in a new era of personalized medicine, where treatment plans could be tailored to an individual's unique genetic makeup.

2017 at the Garvan Institute lab—where curiosity met cutting-edge science, one experiment at a time.

However, my journey wasn't confined to the microscopic world of genes. I was a rebel, a relentless questioner of established dogma. Through rigorous studies, I challenged the long-held belief that fat mass dictated bone density, proving that lean mass played a far more critical role. This shift paved the way for more effective preventative measures. Similarly, our work on the link between fractures and mortality, as well as the accelerated bone loss in the elderly, further reshaped our understanding of osteoporosis and its devastating consequences. Additionally, alongside my brilliant students, we crafted the first algorithm for repeat bone density measurement"—a practical tool that continues to shape clinical practice today.

Still, research wasn't enough. I craved tangible tools that could translate scientific discoveries into the lives of patients. Thus, the Garvan Fracture Risk Calculator, my brainchild forged from over two decades of relentless research, was born. This culmination of countless trials and errors wasn't just a number; it was a personalized roadmap to preventing fractures.

DOES became a treasure trove, not just for osteoporosis research, but for understanding aging in general. The research papers were poured out and published in top-tier medical journals. Our work has been cited tens of thousands of times, shaping the way osteoporosis is diagnosed, understood, and treated around the world. It was exhilarating to be a part of something so groundbreaking, something that was truly changing the lives of millions.

But beyond the numbers, there was the human element. Seeing the dedication of the Dubbo residents, who faithfully returned year after year, gave the study a special weight. They were the unsung heroes, contributing to a legacy that would extend far beyond their own lifetimes.

Sister Janet Watters, of course, remained the anchor. She dealt with my data scrutiny with grace, her dedication never faltering. She knew the participants by their favorite colors, the names of their grandchildren, and their anxieties about upcoming scans. She was more than a nurse; she was a confidante, a friend, and a pillar of support in a world grappling with the uncertainties of aging bones.

It wasn't all smooth sailing. Funding was a constant tightrope walk. Grant applications became a familiar battle cry, each rejection a punch to the gut. The specter of the study shutting down loomed large on several occasions. Budget meetings were marathons of negotiation, and late nights were spent frantically scribbling new proposals. Yet, amidst the funding anxieties, a remarkable thing happened. Industry partners and philanthropy (Amgen Australia, Merck Sharp and Dohme, Sanofi-Aventis, Novartis, Bupa Health Foundation, and the Ernest Heine Family Foundation), recognizing the potential of our research, became unexpected allies. They stepped in with crucial support, ensuring the study wouldn't become another casualty of financial constraints. Through it all, the core team remained the unyielding heart of the project. Driven by a shared passion that burned brighter than any budget shortfall, we persevered. We were united not just by scientific curiosity but by a deep commitment to unraveling the mysteries of osteoporosis and making a real difference in people's lives.

The names Dubbo and Garvan are forever intertwined for me. DOES was the embodiment of Garvan's dedication writ large. For me personally, it became the launchpad for a significant portion of my life's work. By 2023, over 350 papers carried the Garvan badge, reflecting the success of the research that emerged from our collaborative efforts. Cited ~33,000 times, this number still ignites a sense of accomplishment. Our research wasn't gathering dust on shelves; it was sparking conversations, influencing others, and putting the Garvan Institute on the global map. These achievements were further solidified by five studies receiving the prestigious "highly cited" designation by Clarivate . In 2020, I was listed among Garvan's top five researchers based on research impact. This recognition was further compounded by ScholarGPS' scientometric group ranking me among the world's top 0.05% most cited scientists. Humbling doesn't even begin to describe it.

However, all the accolades paled in comparison to a simple, yet thought-provoking question posed by a research director: "If we hadn't been here, at the Garvan Institute, would you have achieved this?" My answer came readily. While some milestones might have been reached independently, there's no doubt that the Garvan Institute played a vital role. It fostered a vibrant community of brilliant minds, provided invaluable resources, and continuously pushed us to excel. The Garvan Institute, or for that matter, the Dubbo Study, wasn't just a place to work; it was a place where scientific excellence thrived.

Eureka! (Maybe Not)

The early 1990s pulsed with excitement in the hallowed halls of the Garvan Institute. Our Bone and Mineral Research Division, fueled by an insatiable curiosity, was on a relentless quest to unravel the genetic code of osteoporosis. One particular project, fixed in my memory for its dramatic twists and turns, became a pivotal lesson—a cautionary tale disguised as a potential breakthrough.

Bone mineral density (BMD), the cornerstone of osteoporosis diagnosis and fracture prediction, varies inexplicably from person to person. My colleagues' and I's twin studies had already hinted at a genetic influence, and my research pointed to a staggering eighty percent contribution from our genes. The question loomed large: which genes were the culprits?

Unraveling this mystery held immense promise. Identifying genes linked to the disease could unlock the secrets of osteoporosis, paving the way for novel therapies and personalized prevention strategies. However, this was a pre-genomic era, a time before the dazzling power of high-throughput analysis. Back then, gene discovery was more art than science—a meticulous dance of educated guesswork.

Our focus centered on the intricate dialogue between bone-building osteoblasts and bone-degrading osteoclasts. Osteocalcin, a protein secreted by osteoclasts, acted as a telltale sign of their activity. A logical leap led us to the vitamin D receptor gene (VDR)—a key player in osteocalcin production. This became our hypothesis: if VDR influences osteocalcin, it might also influence BMD.

Fueled by this hypothesis, the lab buzzed with activity. Dr. Nigel Morrison, a brilliant molecular biologist, spearheaded the development of a novel method to identify variations within the VDR gene. Armed with this tool, we embarked on a large-scale genetic epidemiology study, meticulously analyzing the genomes of thousands of individuals.

At this juncture, a talented young researcher and PhD student named JC Qi joined our team. His exceptional blend of clinical acumen and laboratory prowess made him an invaluable asset. Tasked with analyzing the VDR gene variants in hundreds of twins and over two thousand unrelated individuals, JC dove headfirst into the project. Burning the midnight oil with dedication, he completed the analysis in a record-breaking five months.

The statistical analysis, expertly conducted by Dr. Nigel Morrison, revealed an astonishing correlation. Individuals with a specific VDR variant exhibited significantly higher BMD, suggesting a definitive link. The excitement was palpable, bolstered by similar findings in the twin cohort. We were convinced we had stumbled upon a groundbreaking discovery, a major leap forward in the fight against osteoporosis.

A nagging unease, however, bothered me. The results, while undeniably impressive, seemed almost too good to be true. In science, excessively dramatic outcomes often raise red flags, hinting at potential biases or unforeseen errors. The figure that particularly troubled me was the seventy-five percent explanation of BMD variation attributed to the VDR gene variants. We knew hundreds of genes played a role, and for a single factor to explain such a large proportion seemed improbable.

When I voiced my concerns during a lab meeting, the reception was frosty. My skepticism, a dampener on the celebratory mood, wasn't met with open arms. Hesitant to challenge the overwhelming majority, I let the matter rest.

The international osteoporosis conference in the US crackled with anticipation. Our research, seemingly on the cusp of a breakthrough, ignited excitement among our peers. As a team, we felt like frontrunners in the global race to identify the key genes behind osteoporosis. Postdoctoral researchers from prestigious institutions across the US, Europe, and Japan flocked to our lab, eager to join the chase. We had established ourselves as a force to be reckoned with in the field.

Riding this wave of success, our supervisor urged us to translate our findings into a scientific manuscript for immediate publication. The fear of being scooped by another lab added a layer of urgency. Every morning, we were greeted by his relentless query, "How far along are you?" Nights blurred into days as we poured our energy into the manuscript. Finally, a draft was presented, a culmination of tireless work. Our supervisor, ever the perfectionist, meticulously dissected the draft, demanding further analysis to solidify its impact. His grand ambition: publication in *Nature*, the holy grail of scientific journals. Building on our previous publications in Science and PNAS, he envisioned our work gracing the esteemed pages of *Nature*.

The initial draft of the manuscript listed JC, the hardworking research student who had dedicated countless hours to the project, as the first author, with his supervisor, Dr. Nigel Morrison, as the second author. However, after several revisions, the order was reversed, making Dr. Morrison the first author, reflecting his important contribution. Authorship credit in scientific work is always a sensitive issue that people often avoid discussing.

Armed with determination, our supervisor sent the manuscript off to *Nature*. Three agonizing months later, a rejection letter landed with a thud. The suggestion: consider *Nature Genetics*, a sister journal. Furious, our supervisor refused to accept defeat. He consulted senior colleagues, his mind ablaze with strategies. Two days later, in a bold move, he called the editor-in-chief of *Nature*. The details of this conversation remain a mystery, but somehow, *Nature* agreed to reconsider, sending our work to a new set of reviewers.

This time, fate seemed to smile upon us. After another three-month wait, we received a response: revisions were required to address questions raised by five new reviewers. While three offered praise, the remaining two, though not overtly critical, cast shadows of doubt. Further experiments and data analysis were demanded. Nearly 30% of the manuscript was rewritten—a herculean effort fueled by the burning desire for publication. Three months later, the revised manuscript was back in *Nature's* hands.

The review process seemed to be moving at a fast pace this time. Within a month, reviews arrived, again requesting additional analysis and minor edits. We complied, a dance of revisions that continued for two more months. Finally, the moment we had all been yearning for—acceptance!

News of *Nature's* acceptance rippled through the lab. My supervisor, his face beaming, announced our victory, brandishing the acceptance letter. A celebratory champagne toast capped this momentous occasion. On January 20th, 1994, our paper, titled "Prediction of bone density from vitamin D receptor alleles," proudly graced the cover of *Nature*, alongside a laudatory editorial by Professor

Greg Mundy, heralding a new era in osteoporosis genetics research. Another celebratory dinner, this time at a fancy restaurant, marked this milestone.

However, the glow of celebration dimmed a month later with a letter from a scientist in Melbourne. His "Letter to the Editor" questioned the distribution of VDR gene variants in our paper, noting that it deviated from the expected Hardy-Weinberg equilibrium. The letter also echoed the concern I had raised during the initial lab meeting about the excessively large effect size of the VDR gene.

This prompted me to request the raw data from Dr. Morrison for a reanalysis. My analysis confirmed the scientist's observation: the distribution of VDR gene variants indeed deviated from the expected. The culprit? A potential error in the gene analysis itself. An error that could invalidate our entire conclusion. This was a grave matter, a blemish not just on our research group's reputation, but also on the Garvan Institute's.

The Garvan Institute wasted no time in launching a thorough investigation. A review panel, comprising esteemed professors from around the world, scrutinized every aspect of our research. Interviews, lab notebooks, computer codes, gels, and images... nothing escaped their meticulous examination. Even the possibility of data fabrication was explored, with computers being locked down and analyzed. After two long months, the investigation concluded that there was no data fabrication. The computer data synced with the lab notebooks.

However, a crucial detail emerged. The research student, JC, who was battling an illness during the analysis period, had come into the lab instead of recuperating at home. His presence resulted in the inadvertent contamination of over fifty blood samples. This contamination, in turn, skewed the PCR results, leading to a deviation in the distribution of VDR alleles. Thankfully, removing the contaminated samples rectified the distribution, and the association between the VDR gene and BMD remained valid. A collective sigh of relief swept through the lab.

The review panel recommended that we write a letter to *Nature*, acknowledging the findings and submitting the panel's report. We readily complied. The corrected letter appeared in *Nature* on May 1st, 1997, a reminder of the scientific process's rigor and self-correction.

Despite the initial setback, our research opened a new avenue in osteoporosis research. I penned commentaries and even embarked on a research collaboration with Professor Larry Riggs at the Mayo Clinic on an independent study of the VDR gene. Numerous research groups worldwide have attempted to replicate our findings, with mixed results. Ultimately, a meta-analysis established the true, albeit more modest, association between the VDR gene and BMD.

This scientific odyssey, with its exhilarating highs and sobering lows, served as a potent lesson. The pursuit of knowledge demands not just meticulous research but also the humility to acknowledge and rectify errors. The journey to scientific discovery is rarely linear and often paved with unexpected twists and turns. Ultimately, it's the dedication to truth and the relentless pursuit of understanding that propel scientific progress forward.

A Bond Forged in Science

I often reflect on my time at the Garvan Institute, where I was immersed in the world of bone health and endocrinology. Surrounded by brilliant minds, each with their unique focus—clinical trials, epidemiology, or basic research—I felt a profound sense of intellectual stimulation. Names like Gabrielle Howard, Jonathan Hayes, Mark Harris, Andrew Randell, Jacqueline Center, and Graeme Jones were like chapters in my personal scientific journey.

I was fortunate to be both a student and a mentor. Having a head start in research, I could guide my peers from experimental design to data interpretation. There was a certain satisfaction in watching them blossom into independent scientists. Yet, I was constantly learning from them as well, their fresh perspectives often challenging my own assumptions.

My collaboration with Dr. Gabrielle Howard was particularly memorable. Her fascination with ultrasound in osteoporosis sparked my interest in exploring the genetic component of this disease. Together, we delved into the complex world of twin studies, requiring specialized knowledge in population genetics and statistical methods. Our partnership resulted in a series of groundbreaking publications, culminating in Dr. Howard's award-winning PhD thesis.

It was in Dr. Howard's thesis acknowledgment that I discovered an unexpected connection. It turned out that her family had sponsored a Vietnamese refugee named Thanh Nguyen many years ago. Coincidentally, Thanh had married a Vietnamese woman and named their children after Dr. Howard's siblings. She was amazed to find another "Nguyen" who had become such a significant influence in her life.

Reflecting on this serendipitous encounter, I couldn't help but feel a sense of cosmic alignment. The notion of karma—of sowing and reaping—seemed particularly apt. In helping Dr. Howard, I had unknowingly fulfilled a debt of gratitude that her family had incurred decades earlier. This experience reinforced my belief in the interconnectedness of all things and the enduring power of human connection.

I wasn't confined to helping just my lab mates with their research; my colleagues at the Garvan Institute also sought my expertise. From basic descriptive statistics to complex modeling that significantly enhanced the scientific value of their research, I was always happy to contribute. My skills and experience in data analysis were in high demand. Even when they faced challenges with peer reviewers, they would turn to me for guidance. I interacted with almost every professor at the Garvan Institute, and they all benefited from my dedicated support. As a result, I earned the trust and respect of all my colleagues, from students to professors.

I also had the opportunity to elevate the scientific capabilities of entire institutions and hospitals within St. Vincent's campus. Throughout the mid-2010s, I organized monthly seminars and workshops for young researchers and doctors. However, many professors also attended to further their knowledge. Initially, each session had about fifty attendees, but later sessions attracted over one hundred, filling the entire room. Professor Robert Sutherland, the Director of the Cancer Research Program at the Garvan Institute, emailed me, saying, "I don't know what teaching method you used, but all the PhD students and postdoc fellows are raving about you. Congratulations on making such an important contribution."

Truth be told, I've never had any formal training in pedagogy, so I don't have any special methods. I believe that every lecture is a story. I often use storytelling to introduce students to dry scientific topics. For instance, when teaching screening methods, I'd tell the story of a famous American bank robber. Or, to explain regression analysis, I'd recount the life of Francis Galton and his idea of measuring intelligence. These stories added color and interest to my lectures. Later, when I returned to teach in Vietnam, I continued to use this storytelling approach.

A Part of Garvan History

In 2013, the Garvan Institute celebrated its 50th anniversary (1963-2013) with a commemorative publication titled *Pathway to Excellence: 50 Years of the Garvan Institute*. This publication chronicled the Institute's remarkable journey, from its humble beginnings as a small clinical research unit at St. Vincent's Hospital to its current status as an internationally renowned medical research center attracting top scientists from around the world. I was honored to be featured in the publication alongside my work.

Reflecting on a conversation with journalist Phil English, I shared how my journey began in the shadow of displacement—fleeing Vietnam as a refugee, stepping onto Australian soil with scant possessions but a flicker of possibility. That fragile start unexpectedly bloomed into expertise in the hidden mechanics of osteoporosis and fractures, blending epidemiology with the intricate dance of genes.

Fresh from my PhD, an enviable professorship awaited in America, a crossroads my wife and I pondered deeply before declining, hearts pulling us back to Australia's familiar shores. It was a pivot that carried me to the Garvan Institute over 20 years past, where John Eisman, ever the artful convincer, drew me into his fold. Friends still marvel at my steadfastness in one lab: "Doesn't it stale after so long?" I laugh and counter that stagnation is the myth; each week unleashes novel puzzles and triumphs, fueling an enduring spark.

Garvan's spirit—boldly chasing the grand unknowns—has been my north star. Among my deepest gratitude is the Dubbo Osteoporosis Epidemiology Study, a quarter-century chronicle of lives and bones that birthed more than a dozen doctoral journeys. Yet I hold no illusion that knowledge hoarded in ivory towers suffices. Sustained by public coffers, our pursuits owe a debt to the ordinary soul, bridging the lab to lives through actionable safeguards.

That's why my team forged a straightforward fracture forecast, threading together essentials like age, sex, skeletal strength, tumble tally, and fracture scars. Far from dusty archives, we democratized it: a no-cost digital gauge at fractureriskcalculator.com, empowering users to peer into their own vulnerabilities and act.

These days, my zeal ignites around bespoke healing, a pursuit Garvan nurtures with fervor. It's a revelation that so many who shatter have unremarkable bone scans; the stealthy saboteurs lurk elsewhere, withered sinews, treacherous terrains, or chromosomal time bombs. Now, we're layering DNA's blueprint into our forecasts, surfing the torrent of affordable genomics: from the 1990s' steep toll of $1,000-plus for 500 scant signals per soul, to today's bounty of 500,000 for a fraction under that sum. Armed with computational wizardry and statistical precision, we're poised to sculpt this deluge into personal armors, diagnostics, defenses, therapies etched to one's unique code. This isn't mere inquiry; it's reshaping destinies, genome by genome.

My experience at the Garvan Institute of Medical Research was nothing short of transformative. It fostered an unparalleled environment for scientific exploration and collaboration. The Dubbo Osteoporosis Epidemiology Study, a cornerstone of my research, yielded significant breakthroughs in our understanding of osteoporosis and bone health. This wasn't a solo effort; it was truly "our work." Our discoveries not only enriched scientific knowledge but also led to the development of practical tools, such as the Garvan Fracture Risk Calculator, which has a global impact on patient care. The Garvan Institute's vibrant community and commitment to excellence were instrumental to my achievements. The supportive and collaborative atmosphere nurtured my research and allowed me to make meaningful contributions to the field of osteoporosis. This experience underscores the critical role a nurturing and innovative research environment plays in scientific progress.

PROFESSOR TUAN NGUYEN
PROFILE

FROM DIFFICULT beginnings, having arrived in Australia from Vietnam as a refugee, Professor Tuan Nguyen has become a world expert on the epidemiology and genetics of osteoporosis and bone fracture. And despite landing a professorship in the U.S. directly from his PhD studies, Nguyen and his wife decided to return to Australia.

It was here that Professor John Eisman – described by Nguyen as a "very good persuader" – convinced him to join the Garvan Institute. That was more than 20 years ago. "People ask me: 'How can you work in the same place for 20 years? Isn't it boring?' But every week you are exposed to new things. It's exciting!" Nguyen says.

Part of this excitement comes from the encouragement given by management at the institute to ask big questions.

One of the biggest questions Nguyen has tackled draws on results from the Dubbo Osteoporosis Epidemiology Study. Nguyen estimates a dozen PhD theses have been produced from the data accrued in the 25-year study.

However, he is quick to stress that he and his group are interested in more than just scientific data. "We get money from taxpayers, so we have to do something for them. We have to make a difference to the person on the street," says Nguyen.

To achieve this goal of translational research, his research group developed a predictive model of bone fracture that incorporated five risk factors: age, sex, bone density, the number of falls a person had recently, and any history of fracture.

But rather than just publish the model in an academic journal, they also implemented it as an online calculator hosted on the Garvan's website (see fractureriskcalculator.com).

Professor Nguyen is also interested in personalised medicine, a goal he shares with the Garvan.

He argues that most people who experience bone fracture have a normal bone density, but may have a very high risk due to other factors, such as low muscle mass, a dangerous environment or carrying high-risk genes. The research group is now focused on incorporating genetic factors into these predictive models by taking advantage of the ever-shrinking cost of genome sequencing.

"Back in the 1990s when we started a genome-wide study, each patient cost more than $1,000 for only 500 markers," he says.

"Now I can do 500,000 markers for less than $1,000. And that's amazing. The application of bioinformatics and biostatistics to translate this huge amount of information into individualised diagnosis, prevention and treatment is the future."
– *Philip English*

The Garvan Institute celebrated its 50th anniversary (1963-2013) with a commemorative publication titled "Pathway to Excellence: 50 Years of the Garvan Institute" in which Tuan V. Nguyen was featured. (2013)

Chapter Eight

Crafting Prediction

The Garvan Institute was a platform where I, the first Vietnamese scientist to reach a leadership position, had the privilege of leaving my mark. One of my most cherished contributions to Garvan's global renown was the development of the Garvan Fracture Risk Calculator (FRC). But the story behind this tool, a silent guardian against fractures, is a lesser-known chapter waiting to be unraveled.

Osteoporosis, dubbed a silent thief of bone strength, had long been my area of focus. It is a two-pronged attack—bone mineral density (BMD), which diminishes with age, and bone microstructure, which deteriorates, leaving bones brittle and prone to fracture. These fractures, often from seemingly minor falls or even a sneeze, could occur anywhere, but the spine, hip, wrist, and ribs were the most vulnerable battlegrounds.

An estimated twenty-five percent of women and ten percent of men over fifty have osteoporosis. These statistics highlight a substantial public health challenge, with many cases likely undiagnosed. While the exact number cannot be calculated solely on the prevalence rate, osteoporosis affects a staggering number of people worldwide. Estimates suggest roughly 200 million women may have osteoporosis. Each year, an estimated 178 million new fractures occur globally. These fractures can be incredibly debilitating, causing significant pain, disability, and even death.

For many, osteoporosis flew under the radar, a common condition dismissed as an annoyance of aging. Yet, this seemingly innocuous disease lurked as a silent threat. We discovered that surviving a fracture from osteoporosis wasn't just a one-time event; it significantly increased the risk of future fractures. This domino effect led to limited mobility, a decline in quality of life, and even a greater risk of complications like stroke and depression. The mortality rate associated with osteoporosis fractures was particularly alarming. The shocking truth is that twenty to twenty-five percent of hip fracture patients wouldn't survive the first year. This number even surpassed the mortality rate of breast cancer. Spinal fractures, too, were linked to a shortened lifespan. These groundbreaking findings became cornerstones in the medical literature, and my own seminal publications based on the Dubbo data significantly contributed to this recognition of the true dangers of osteoporosis.

Diagnosing osteoporosis relies on BMD measurements and the derived value called "T-score." This score compares an individual's current BMD to what it "should" be at their peak (around twenty to thirty years old). A T-score of -2.5 or lower indicates osteoporosis, a threshold that my research group also helped establish. For these patients, treatment was the next step, proving successful in managing and preventing osteoporosis in those over fifty.

However, the T-score threshold of -2.5 for the diagnosis of osteoporosis wasn't universally embraced. One renowned researcher, Professor Richard Wasnich (then at the Hawaii Osteoporosis Center, Hawaii, USA), penned a critical piece in a leading journal. His words sparked a firestorm in my mind. He argued that the T-score alone wasn't enough and that it didn't account for individual risk factors. His words, challenging but compelling, set me on a new course:

"What are the issues surrounding the use of T-scores, as recommended by the WHO panel? On the one side, they seemingly offer simplicity, which is sorely needed. However, they are not readily translated into interventional guidelines. The opposing viewpoint is that T-scores are a major step backwards into the realm of 'fracture thresholds.'

Fundamental to this debate is the fact that bone density is a risk factor, and not a diagnostic test. So making a 'diagnosis' of osteoporosis based on the presence of a single risk factor, at a single point in time, is already a tenuous concept.

Although bone density is potentially a very useful risk factor, it is not the only risk factor to be considered when making diagnostic and therapeutic decisions. For example, what about the patient who has a 'normal' T-score, but who has also had a non-violent fracture? These patients do exist. Would she be denied treatment because she has a 'normal' T-score? What about other risk factors, both those currently known and those yet to be discovered? Can they be incorporated into the T-score model, or will we require entirely new 'guidelines' every time a new risk factor is discovered?

... what we need is an estimate of absolute fracture rate, and that information can be derived directly from the bone density value. It is also apparent from this figure that when the desired outcome is absolute fracture incidence rate, it makes absolutely no difference which skeletal site is employed, so long as the nature of the BMD/fracture relationship has been established."

Professor Wasnich's critique struck a chord with me. It mirrored the disquiet I harbored for some time—the T-score, while a valuable tool, painted a limited picture of fracture risk. It couldn't capture the intricate profile of individual risk woven from factors beyond just BMD. This realization ignited a fire within me, a determination to forge a more comprehensive approach to fracture risk assessment.

Our Dubbo data revealed an interesting correlation between bone density and fracture risk. It wasn't a simple on/off switch. People with different BMDs (e.g., T-scores) were scattered across a spectrum. Here's the key takeaway: even people with "good" bone density (higher T-scores) could still experience fractures, although it was less likely compared to those with "lower" bone density (lower T-scores). This means that there isn't a single perfect line that separates high and low fracture risk for everyone.

The World Health Organization (WHO) had to choose a specific T-score for diagnosing osteoporosis. They considered several factors, such as how many people would be diagnosed with osteoporosis at this T-score, whether this T-score seems to be linked to a higher risk of fractures in real-world situations, and whether the chosen T-score feels like a reasonable cut-off point for defining osteoporosis based on expert experience. They ultimately chose a T-score of -2.5 so that the prevalence of osteoporosis is equivalent to the lifetime risk of fracture among Caucasian women, which was estimated to be thirty percent. For this population group, having a T-score of -2.5 or lower puts an individual at a similar risk of fracture as the average woman experiences in her lifetime.

However, my analysis of the Dubbo data revealed a significantly higher life-time fracture risk than previously estimated (forty-four percent—not thirty percent—for women and twenty-five percent for men), further solidifying our resolve to personalize fracture risk assessment.

Together with my PhD student, Dr. Nguyên Đình Nguyễn, I embarked on a new research direction. Our quest? To identify additional factors beyond BMD that might contribute to fracture risk. We delved into the realm of clinical factors: age, gender, past fractures, and a history of falls.

Nguyen's brilliant analysis yielded a fascinating truth—a strong correlation between the number of previous fractures and falls in the past year and the likelihood of future fractures. These findings, published in two important papers in *Osteoporosis International* (2007 and 2008), challenged the sole reliance on BMD. In the opening lines of the 2007 paper, we boldly wrote:

"The ultimate aim of developing a prognostic model is to provide clinicians and each individual with their risk estimate to guide clinical decisions. At present, individuals with low bone mineral density (i.e., T-scores being less than -2.5) or with a history of prior low trauma fracture are recommended for therapeutic intervention. This recommendation is logical and appropriate, since these individuals—as shown in this study and previous studies—have higher risk of fracture, and treatment can reduce their risk of fracture. However, because fracture is a multifactorial event, there is more than one way that an individual can attain the risk conferred by either low BMD or a prior fracture. Indeed, virtually all women aged 70 years with BMD T-scores less than -1.5 and all 80-year-old men with BMD T-scores less than -1.0 can be considered 'high risk'. On the other hand, no 60-year-old men or women without a prior fracture and a fall are considered high risk, even when their BMD

T-scores were below -2.5. This demonstrates the informativeness of a multi-variable prognostic model, and the limitation of a risk stratification-based approach for risk assessment for an individual.

...

Each individual is important and unique. Individualization of risk—or the prediction of risk for an individual given a risk profile—is a fundamental aspect of the present models. The present models considered all continuous risk factors (e.g., BMD, body weight and age) in their original units of measurement. This consideration is different from previous models, which categorized continuous risk factors into distinct groups based on some thresholds. While the categorization is appealing for its simplicity, it implicitly assumes a discontinuous relationship, which is unlikely to be true for well-known risk factors, such as BMD and body weight. Such a categorization is also known to reduce statistical power. Furthermore, the risk estimates based on categorization of continuous risk factors can only be applied to a group of individuals, not to an individual. Prognosis is about imparting information of fracture risk to an individual and each individual is a unique case, because there exists no 'average individual' in the population. The more risk factors are considered, the greater likelihood of uniqueness of an individual's profile being defined. Therefore, by modeling risk factors in their continuous scale the present models can be uniquely tailored to an individual."

The "individualized assessment" approach we proposed felt like a revelation. Instead of relying solely on the T-score's binary verdict—"normal" or "osteoporosis"—we envisioned a more nuanced picture. We'd weave together BMD with demographic and clinical details such as age, gender, past fractures, and fall history, creating a unique "risk profile" for each individual. This personalized map would allow clinicians to predict fracture risk with greater precision, enabling them to tailor treatment plans accordingly.

Developing this method was a significant leap forward. It transcended the limitations of the T-score, embracing the complexities of fracture risk and empowering doctors to provide more effective care. The concept of "individualization" wasn't entirely new; I observed colleagues in cancer research using similar principles. Their "nomograms" for predicting cancer risk seemed strikingly effective, and I yearned to understand why.

While seasoned clinicians could make informed predictions, their assessments were often subjective and lacked consistency. Scientifically speaking, they weren't reproducible. Reproducibility—the ability to get the same results repeatedly—is the bedrock of science. Relying solely on subjective evaluations wouldn't suffice.

Statistical prediction models, on the other hand, consistently trumped subjective assessments. They could objectively integrate multiple risk factors and provide consistent, reproducible predictions. This realization became the spark that ignited the development of the Garvan Fracture Risk Calculator model.

After publishing the groundwork in two scientific papers, we were met with an overwhelming wave of support from colleagues around the world. They conducted studies to validate the FRC's accuracy, and the results were consistently positive. The FRC began gaining traction as a valuable tool for assessing fracture risk.

Some colleagues fondly called it the "Nguyen Model," named after the lead authors, Dr. Nguyên Đình Nguyễn and me. However, the Garvan Institute favored a more formal name—the *Garvan Fracture Risk Calculator*.

Publishing the papers was a crucial first step, but the real challenge lay in translating the FRC model into everyday practice. First, we developed a user-friendly website that allowed anyone to access and calculate their fracture risk. Next, we embarked on a mission to gain acceptance from medical associations across Australia and internationally.

Today, numerous medical associations in Australia, New Zealand, Europe, and the United States have endorsed the FRC model alongside the WHO model for fracture risk assessment. This widespread acceptance was a remarkable achievement.

One prominent professor even penned an editorial in a leading journal, hailing the arrival of fracture risk prediction models as a "revolution" and a "major advance" in osteoporosis research.

As Vietnamese-born scientists, it filled us with immense pride to have played a significant role in this "revolution," contributing to the global fight against osteoporosis and fractures.

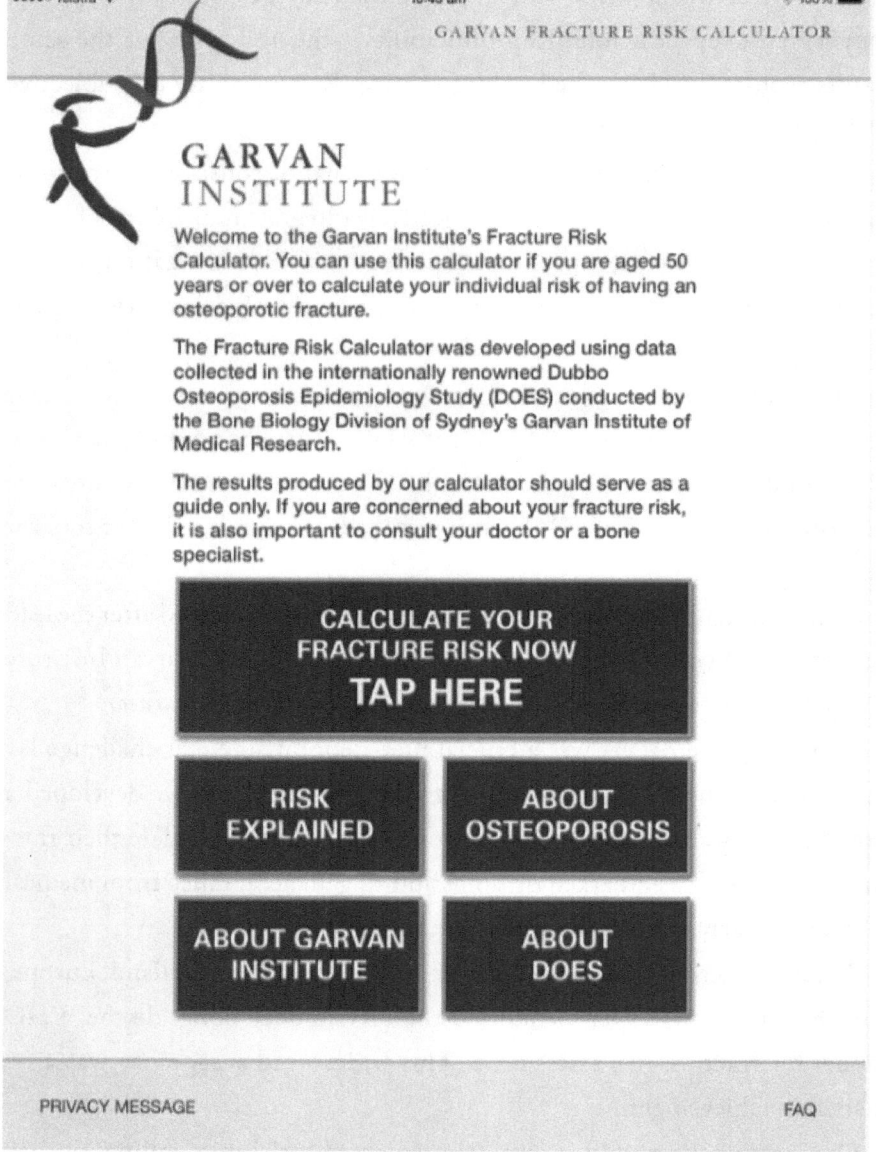

The Garvan Fracture Risk Calculator is available at fractureriskcalculator.com.

Over the past fifteen years, the Garvan Fracture Risk Calculator has become a recognized name throughout the medical world. A search on PubMed, the global medical literature database, yields thousands of studies that have utilized or simulated our model. Even medical guidelines, like Qmax, incorporate our approach.

The journey has led to numerous opportunities, including invitations to write reviews, editorials, book chapters, and lectures at medical conferences worldwide. It has also garnered recognition through awards for this groundbreaking research. Dr. Nguyễn Đình Nguyên, the lead author, completed his Ph.D. and received the prestigious UNSW/Garvan Best Thesis award, with his name proudly imprinted in the Garvan Institute's halls. This achievement further cemented the institute's reputation in the field of bone research.

The Garvan Fracture Risk Calculator's journey, from a spark of an idea to a globally impactful tool, demonstrates the power of scientific collaboration and the pursuit of personalized medicine. It has been a tremendous privilege to be part of this story and contribute to improving the lives of millions affected by osteoporosis.

Genes: A New Frontier in Fracture Risk Assessment

The Garvan Fracture Risk Calculator, a tool with immense potential, had entered the real world. Yet, a nagging doubt lingered in my mind. The calculator, while helpful, wasn't perfect. Individuals deemed "high risk" sometimes defied the odds and remained fracture-free, while others categorized as "low risk" ended up suffering fractures. This discrepancy gnawed at me. How could we refine our predictive abilities?

For twenty-five years, the whispers of genes had been a constant presence in my research on osteoporosis. My lab, along with collaborators around the globe, has unearthed over thirty genes linked to bone mineral density, a key factor in fracture risk. It was a significant milestone, a demonstration of the collective effort of researchers worldwide. However, there was a twist—the effect of these individual genes was subtle. Each variant only slightly nudged the odds of fracture, typically by five to fifteen percent. Such a minute influence rendered them impractical for pinpointing high-risk individuals in the general population.

So, the question loomed: how could doctors leverage the power of genes for fracture risk prediction? The answer lay in harnessing the collective effect of these genetic variants. I envisioned a "genetic signature"—a score unique to each individual, calculated by summing the impact of all these trait-associated genes, weighted by their influence. This score would essentially represent an individual's overall genetic susceptibility to fractures.

With this vision in mind, Thảo Hồ Lê, my brilliant PhD student, and I embarked on creating such a score. We christened it the "Osteogenomic Profile," a reflection of the interplay of genes and bone health. This profile, independent of age and other clinical factors, offered a new way to predict fracture risk. Publishing our findings in the prestigious *Journal of Bone and Mineral Research* (September 20, 2016) felt like the culmination of years of dedicated research. The work earned Thảo Hồ Lê a well-deserved Young Investigator Award from the American Society for Bone and Mineral Research.

But the true satisfaction came in the form of a wave of global media attention. On the October 14, 2016, the Garvan Institute of Medical Research put out a press release titled, "Outwitting the 'silent thief': how clues in our genes could help prevent osteoporotic fracture," capturing the essence of our work.

As Dr. Meredith Ross captured in her piece, our discovery hit like the creak of a forgotten door swinging wide, unlocking, for the first time globally, how a person's genetic blueprint could refine forecasts of those devastating osteoporosis fractures. This milestone pulsed from the resilient core of the Dubbo Osteoporosis Epidemiology Study, a twenty-seven-year saga tracking the rhythms of health in a unassuming New South Wales community, standing as the deepest dive yet into bone vulnerability across genders.

At the forefront, steering from the Garvan Institute and the University of Technology Sydney, I laid it out straightforwardly: blend those telltale genetic signals with the tried-and-true markers—age, gender, bone density scans, falls, and prior fractures—and the forecast clears like dawn breaking fog. "This crushes the old skepticism that DNA's hand in patient care is too light to lift," I noted. We had long charted gene mutations tied to brittle bones and snaps, yet each tugged with a feather's weight, barely audible in the clinical din. Our breakthrough? Bundling sixty-two such delicate DNA tweaks—SNPs, those one-letter flips in life's code—into a single, potent "genetic risk score" drawn from more than 1,400 people in Dubbo.

Spanning ten years of vigilant watch, we measured it head-to-head with our Garvan Fracture Risk Calculator, the benchmark we've polished for doctors the world over. The payoff? A twelve percent boost in sharpness, pushing spot-on high- or low-risk reads beyond eighty percent, transforming guesswork from a blurred sketch into a crisp aerial blueprint.

It was a moment of immense gratification, not just for the recognition, but for the potential impact. This new tool, the osteogenomic profile, offered a new way to predict and potentially prevent these devastating fractures before they occur. The fight against osteoporosis had just taken a significant step forward, and I, along with my team, stood at the forefront of this exciting new chapter.

The Bones Tell All: Unveiling Skeletal Age

Our research group had become a "Grim Reaper" of sorts, the first to unveil the undeniable link between fractures and a shortened lifespan. Our initial publication in *The Lancet,* back in the late 1990s, sent a shockwave through the medical community, demonstrating that a fracture wasn't just a broken bone, but a potential harbinger of mortality. The paper garnered over 2,000 citations, highlighting its great impact. We followed this up with two additional studies in the *Journal of the American Medical Association*, further solidifying the association, and accruing another 2,500 citations.

But how do you translate such complex medical jargon into something the public could grasp? Probability, the language of risk assessment in healthcare, often felt like a foreign tongue to lay audiences. *"You have a 5% risk of death"* could easily morph into *"my survival probability is 95%,"* diminishing the urgency of the matter.

This disconnect fueled my search for a more impactful and understandable approach. Inspiration, surprisingly, bloomed from a personal story from my great grandmother.

L-R: Professor Tuấn Nguyễn and Professor John Eisman, with University of Technology Sydney researcher Thảo Phương Hồ Lê. (Photo credit: Garvan)

In her eighties during the 1970s, my great grandmother defied expectations. Remarkably agile and mentally sharp, her independence was legendary. Disagreements with family? She'd simply hop in her small boat and paddle off to visit another child or grandchild. Upset with my grandfather? A canoe trip to our doorstep became her peaceful protest, returning only after appeasement from my mother. At home, she maintained a bustling pace, gathering firewood, coconut leaves, and essential household items. Her hair was only partially gray; her skin was wrinkled, but her gait was steady. Despite her chronological age, she possessed the vitality of a woman decades younger.

My great grandmother's story underscored an interesting truth—chronological age wasn't the sole measure of our well-being. An individual could be eighty-two, like her, yet have "younger" biological organs. Conversely, someone in their eighties, like US President Joe Biden, might exhibit the wear and tear of an "older' heart, brain, and bones.

Science had a way of expressing this disparity—the difference between chronological age and biological age. The former was simply the number of years lived, the latter a complex construct woven from DNA analysis, organ assessment, and intricate calculations. Chronological age was the obvious measure, while biological age resided in the intricate script of our DNA.

By the time we reach sixty-five, life has etched its story onto our bodies. Out of every hundred individuals past that milestone, eighty would grapple with at least one chronic condition—cardiovascular disease, pneumonia, diabetes, cancer, a constellation of ailments that conspired to shorten lifespans.

This decline stemmed from our cells' slow descent into aging, or more poetically, "senescence." The building blocks of these cells were DNA molecules, and aging itself could be understood as DNA senescence.

Cells within our bodies undergo a replication and editing process called "methylation." Think of it like a lock on a gene door; methylation could either open it or slam it shut, altering how the gene is expressed. This process gave birth to a new scientific field—epigenetics.

One of the factors influencing biological age was telomeres, repetitive DNA sequences found at the chromosome's tips. Imagine them as the plastic caps on shoelaces. The frayed caps of an old shoelace spoke of wear and tear, similar to how shorter telomeres signaled aging in our cells.

In simpler terms, telomere length held the key to longevity. Older individuals typically had shorter telomeres compared to their younger counterparts. As these caps frayed, our lifespans diminished. Epidemiological studies have shown that for each standard deviation decrease in telomere length, our lifespan shrinks by about a year. So, if you're sixty years old and your telomeres are shorter than someone your age, your body might actually be functioning more like a sixty-one-year-old.

Patients who had sustained fractures exhibited shorter telomeres than the general population. This could explain the increased mortality risk observed in patients with fractures. Perhaps telomeres were also a signal that bones themselves were "aging" when fractures occurred.

This revelation led me to develop an innovative metric known as "Skeletal Age." It was essentially the age of the skeleton as reflected by osteoporosis or fractures, a reflection of its biological health. Skeletal Age can be determined by the number of life years lost following a fracture or by risk factors (like low bone mineral density) that increase mortality risk.

Building on this concept, I teamed up with Dr. Trần Sơn Thạch to analyze data from over 200,000 fracture patients in Denmark. This vast dataset allowed us to estimate the number of life years lost following a fracture. For instance, patients with hip fractures could expect a reduction in life expectancy ranging from three to seven years, depending on their age, gender, and associated medical conditions.

The concept of Skeletal Age could be easily grasped through illustration. Imagine a sixty-year-old female patient with a hip fracture. Her Skeletal Age would be estimated at sixty-seven, indicating that her bone health was equivalent to that of a sixty-seven-year-old. Similarly, a seventy-year-old male patient with a spinal fracture might have a Skeletal Age of around seventy-three.

An elevated Skeletal Age compared to chronological age held two crucial implications:

• *Reduced life expectancy:* A higher Skeletal Age signified a diminished lifespan due to osteoporosis and fractures.

• *Increased fracture risk:* Individuals with a higher Skeletal Age, even within the same chronological age group, were at a greater risk of future fractures compared to those with lower Skeletal Ages.

Our research on Skeletal Age was published in the prestigious scientific journal *eLife*, creating a ripple effect across the globe. The University of Technology Sydney (UTS) issued a press release, and I was invited for numerous interviews on local, national, and international television and radio programs, including SBS. Major media outlets worldwide, including those in the United Kingdom, France, and the United States, covered this innovative concept.

I am deeply optimistic that the concept of Skeletal Age will empower the public to gain a deeper understanding of bone health and the impact of fractures on mortality. Armed with this knowledge, individuals can make informed lifestyle choices and consult with their healthcare providers to explore strategies for reducing their Skeletal Age and, consequently, improving their overall health and longevity.

The journey from a simple observation—the link between fractures and mortality—to the development of Skeletal Age has demonstrated the power of scientific exploration. I hope that this concept will not only empower individuals but also inspire further research into the intricate connection between bone health, aging, and overall well-being. After all, strong bones are the foundation for a strong life, and understanding their story—their Skeletal Age—can pave the way for a healthier future for all.

On May 15, 2023, the University of Technology Sydney issued a press release titled, "How old is your skeleton?" highlighting the groundbreaking concept of Skeletal Age. This announcement, celebrating the work of our research team, captured the attention of global media outlets. The media coverage catapulted our team and our research on Skeletal Age into the international arena of osteoporosis research. This recognition not only validated our dedication to this field but also underscored the potential impact of Skeletal Age on improving bone health diagnosis and treatment strategies worldwide.

The Evolution Continues

Over a decade has passed since the FRC first stepped onto the world stage. It has been a humbling journey, watching it transform from a novel idea into a tool that has been widely adopted by the medical community worldwide. However, as with all things scientific, progress demands a restless spirit and a willingness to push beyond the existing paradigm.

Several factors compelled me to advocate for innovation in fracture risk prediction. Years of research, both by our team and colleagues, have unveiled the undeniable link between fracture risk and genetics. We identified several genes associated with susceptibility, yet incorporating this genetic information into the equation remained elusive. Furthermore, psychological studies shed light on potential shortcomings in how we currently communicate risk information.

These insights fueled several commentaries I penned, urging the field to embrace a new wave of innovation. But words alone weren't enough. I felt compelled to take concrete steps to identify and address the shortcomings in the current model:

The Timeframe: Models like Garvan FRC and FRAX offer ten-year predictions, a timeframe that might feel distant and irrelevant for older populations. For someone in their seventies or eighties, a ten-year risk might hold little practical value. I proposed a shift to a 5-year assessment approach, one that is more immediate and relatable to the public.

Treatment Context: For those diagnosed with osteoporosis, antiresorptive or bone-building medications can significantly reduce fracture risk by up to fifty percent. However, this treatment benefit wasn't factored into current tools—a crucial oversight in my mind.

The Refracture Risk: Our research had painted a clear picture—individuals who had already survived a fracture faced a significantly higher risk of experiencing another one. Yet, current models remained silent on this critical issue.

Mortality and the Missing Link: Fractures, particularly hip fractures, are associated with a heightened risk of mortality. This information, too, was absent from current tools, a significant omission in my view.

The Unmeasured Risk: For someone who hadn't yet had their bone mineral density (BMD) measured, there was no way to estimate their osteoporosis risk using existing models. This left a crucial gap unaddressed.

BMD Reassessment: For those whose BMD had been measured and didn't meet the criteria for osteoporosis, a crucial question remained unanswered: when should they be reassessed to monitor changes in bone health? Current models offered no guidance.

Prevention Beyond Prediction: While providing risk information is essential, empowering individuals with knowledge on fracture prevention is equally important. Equipping them with actionable steps to reduce their risk, rather than solely relying on treatment, is an area where current tools fall short.

These shortcomings underscore the urgent need for a more comprehensive, personalized, and patient-centric approach to fracture risk assessment. I remain committed to collaborating with my colleagues, pushing the boundaries of the existing models, and developing innovative tools that address these limitations. The ultimate goal? To provide a more holistic understanding of fracture risk, leading to improved patient outcomes and potentially a reduction in healthcare costs. It's an ongoing journey, one I'm determined to see through to the end.

BONEcheck™: Empowering the Fight Against Osteoporosis

The limitations of existing models, coupled with the revolutionary concept of Skeletal Age, fueled my vision for a complete overhaul of the Garvan Fracture Risk Calculator. Digital Health's potential for disease prevention was profoundly meaningful to me, and I shared this transformative vision with my team. Our revamped model aimed to achieve several key goals:

- Five-Year Fracture Risk: Providing precise predictions for the next five years.
- Treatment Efficacy: Integrating treatment effectiveness data to empower patients.
- Refracture Risk Assessment: Offering a two-year refracture risk assessment.
- Mortality and Skeletal Age: Incorporating data on mortality risk and Skeletal Age.
- Osteoporosis Risk Prediction: Estimating osteoporosis risk for individuals without BMD measurements.
- BMD Reassessment Intervals: Predicting the optimal timeframe for BMD reassessment.
- Comprehensive Prevention Guidance: Equipping users with actionable steps to reduce fracture risk.

Accessibility was paramount. The new model had to be entirely free, ensuring inclusivity for all.

A meticulously crafted work plan followed, with me at the helm as project designer and coordinator. While my Australian research students tackled the scientific and technical aspects, programmers from Hà Tĩnh University and network specialists in Việt Nam joined forces to implement the model. After six months of dedicated effort, our groundbreaking tool was born.

No longer affiliated with the Garvan Institute, the new creation needed a name. During a lab meeting, "BONEcheck" emerged, resonating with everyone present. The name was promptly trademarked with the New South Wales Intellectual Property Office to secure legal protection.

May 2023 saw the triumphant launch of BONEcheck^{TM} online (bonecheck. org) and on dedicated mobile apps. The University of Technology Sydney issued a press release, and BONEcheck^{TM} quickly attracted global media attention. Within six months, over 15,000 users from a staggering 165 countries had utilized BONEcheck^{TM}, with France leading the pack, followed by Australia, Việt Nam, New Zealand, and the US. Western Europe was also well-represented.

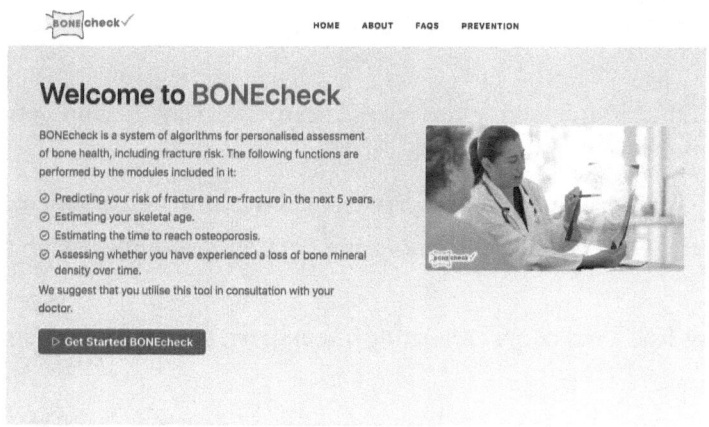

BONEcheck^{TM} is freely available through the website bonecheck. org

Letters of encouragement and support flooded in from colleagues, commending BONEcheck^{TM}'s innovative features. Professional associations eagerly requested presentations, expressing keen interest in adopting the tool. Scientific collaborations blossomed, and BONEcheck™ was translated into Thai, Malay, and Vietnamese. Currently, Chinese, Korean, Japanese, Pakistani, and Indian versions are underway.

BONEcheck™'s success reflects the power of collaboration, innovation, and a global commitment to bone health. The widespread adoption and positive impact of this groundbreaking tool fill me with immense honor. The fight against osteoporosis continues, and I remain persistent in my dedication to empowering individuals to take proactive steps toward lifelong bone health and well-being.

A Eureka Moment in the Fight Against Hip Fractures

The walls of my lab/office had sometimes become a second home. Countless hours hunched over data sets, the whirring of machinery a constant hum. As an investigator in the Dubbo Osteoporosis Epidemiology Study, I have published hundreds of papers, each a piece of the puzzle in the battle against a debilitating enemy—hip fractures. Yet, one study stands out, not just for its impact, but for the unexpected journey it took me on.

Published in the prestigious *Journal of Bone and Mineral Research* on August 28, 2023, the paper delved into the realm of hip fracture prevention. These fractures, a harsh reality for 1.6 million individuals globally each year, steal mobility, inflate healthcare costs, and leave a trail of shattered lives in their wake. Worse still, for many seniors, a hip fracture can be a death sentence.

The conventional wisdom, the very foundation upon which we built our research, was clear—individuals with osteoporosis, characterized by weakened bones, were at the highest risk of hip fractures. Treatment for this group, with medications that increase bone density, seemed the most logical course of action. Our research confirmed this, demonstrating a fifty percent reduction in fracture risk with treatment. Even treating those who already suffered a fracture offered a glimmer of hope, potentially lowering their mortality.

But a nagging question burrowed into my mind. Was this targeted approach enough? My calculations revealed a sobering truth. Osteoporosis, while a major risk factor, only affects around twenty percent of women over fifty. Treating them, while crucial, could only realistically prevent roughly twenty-five percent of all fractures in the general population. My gaze shifted to the larger group – those diagnosed with osteopenia, a precursor to osteoporosis. Astonishingly, sixty to seventy percent of all fractures occurred in this group. Surely, there had to be a better way.

This quest for a more comprehensive solution led me to Dr. Trần Sơn Thạch, a brilliant collaborator. Together, we delved into the rich data trove of the Dubbo Study. We discovered a fascinating trend. Between 1990 and 2000, there was an average increase of three percent in bone mineral density across the population. Yet, during this same period, the incidence of hip fractures plummeted by a staggering forty-five percent. This defied the expected correlation—such a decrease typically corresponded to a ten percent rise in bone density.

This seemingly contradictory outcome had a name: *the prevention paradox.* Imagine this—wearing a seatbelt might seem insignificant to an individual with a low chance of being in an accident. Yet, seatbelts save countless lives on a societal level. This paper argued that the same principle applied to hip fractures. Even a modest increase in bone density at a population level, achieved through public health measures, could lead to a significant decrease in hip fractures.

This concept wasn't entirely new. Decades earlier, the renowned epidemiologist Geoffrey Rose had laid the groundwork, demonstrating how minor interventions targeting widespread risk factors could drastically affect disease outcomes. Drawing inspiration from this legacy, our paper advocated for population-wide strategies like smoking cessation, adequate calcium and vitamin D intake, and regular exercise. These seemingly simple steps, when embraced by a community, could have a profound impact.

The impact of our research was electrifying. Media outlets like *The Sydney Morning Herald* (September 7, 2023) took notice, spreading the word far and wide. Radio and television interviews became a regular occurrence, allowing me to share this message of hope with a global audience.

But the true reward went beyond the accolades. The realization that a seemingly small shift in perspective could lead to a significant decrease in suffering was a moment of pure scientific triumph. It was a reminder that the fight against debilitating diseases is not just about individual interventions, but about empowering communities to create a healthier future, one lifestyle change at a time.

Gazing back on over three decades of dedicated research in osteoporosis, a profound sense of gratitude washes over me. The journey has been a captivating blend of intellectual curiosity, a relentless pursuit of scientific rigor, and a deep commitment to advancing our understanding of osteoporosis and its global impact.

A core principle guiding my research has been the concept of personalized fracture risk assessment. I've long advocated for a more individualized approach to osteoporosis management, recognizing that each patient is unique, with their own risk factors, genetic predispositions, and lifestyle choices. This emphasis has opened new avenues of research and contributed to a more nuanced understanding of osteoporosis risk stratification.

My research has been fueled by a fascination with the intricate interplay between genetic factors and the development of osteoporosis. My contributions have helped to unravel the genetic underpinnings of osteoporosis, paving the way for potential genetic testing and targeted therapies in the future.

The recognition and appreciation from colleagues humble me. Being the first Vietnamese researcher in this domain, leaving an indelible mark for future generations, is a source of immense pride. My legacy, I hope, will inspire future scientists to build upon my work and further push the boundaries of osteoporosis research.

The future of osteoporosis research is bright. New technologies, such as genomics, epigenetics, and artificial intelligence, hold immense potential to unlock new insights into the mechanisms of osteoporosis, leading to more effective prevention strategies and personalized treatments. The next generation of researchers will undoubtedly build upon the foundations laid by those who came before them. This will pave the way for a future where osteoporosis is no longer a debilitating condition, but a manageable one, empowering individuals to live healthy, active lives well into their golden years.

Chapter Nine

Earning Doctorates

The path to knowledge is rarely a straight one. For me, it was a winding journey that culminated in not one, but two doctorate degrees. The decision to pursue a double doctorate wasn't born out of a singular ambition, but rather a series of intellectual detours and a thirst for understanding osteoporosis from multiple angles. Here, I reflect on my academic experiences, from mastering the art of scientific writing to presenting complex research at conferences. It's a story of continuous learning, intellectual curiosity, and the challenges of forging a path as a scholar while facing down prejudice.

Investigating Bone Fractures: A PhD Journey

Australia had been my home for eleven years by 1993. I'd buried myself in the dusty files and bone scans of the Dubbo Osteoporosis Epidemiology Study for over two years, meticulously collecting and analyzing data. Then, one day, a spark ignited a fire in my gut. Another doctor was pursuing a PhD based on the very data I'd helped gather and analyze. A competitive fire flickered to life within me. I held a Master's degree and had completed a year of PhD studies at the University of Sydney, with a deep well of research experience. Yet, here I was, watching from the sidelines.

That was when the idea for my own PhD thesis took root. I envisioned a project that dug deeper, exploring the "whys" behind fractures, using real patient cases and the latest research. My plan? To leverage the existing Dubbo data and create a more comprehensive fracture risk assessment model for Australians. Armed with a five-page proposal outlining this ambitious vision, I marched into the office of my esteemed mentor, Professor John Eisman.

Professor Eisman's eyes lit up with the same competitive fire I felt burning inside me. He saw the potential in my idea, but also the need to explore the often-overlooked issue of osteoporosis in men. However, his expertise lay outside the realm of epidemiology. That was when he introduced me to Professor Richard Heller, the epidemiology heavyweight who would become my co-supervisor. Professor Eisman, ever the strategist, then suggested involving Dr. Philip Sambrook, a renowned rheumatologist, to round out my supervisory team. Dr. Sambrook was just as enthusiastic as the others, and just like that, I found myself under the tutelage of three academic giants, each bringing their unique expertise to my ambitious project.

Securing my place in the program was refreshingly straightforward. My qualifications, research experience, and proposal spoke volumes. The university craved novelty—fresh ideas, methods, interpretations—and mine ticked all the boxes. Enrolling at the University of New South Wales' Faculty of Medicine was a straightforward process: I submitted my credentials, research proposal, and supervisor's recommendation letter. Interviews? Apparently, having such esteemed professors championing my work bypassed that formality.

While technically a PhD student, my daily grind remained essentially unchanged as research was still my lifeblood. The crucial difference now was a laser focus on a concrete goal: completing a PhD thesis. My routine expanded to include mandatory attendance at seminars, rounds, and invited lectures. Weekly meetings with my supervisors ensured that the data flowed freely, keeping me on track. Every three months, the department hosted research showcases where intellectual exchanges crackled with energy and fostered a constant learning curve for everyone involved. This tradition of collaboration was profoundly meaningful to me, and I later implemented it in my own lab, fostering a similar spirit of teamwork.

Unlike the typical, young PhD student, I was a seasoned researcher... some might even say a *"slow buffalo drinking muddy water,"* as my friends would tease. However, experience was my secret weapon —a bedrock of knowledge that gave my research focus and purpose. While I had three esteemed supervisors guiding me, I craved (and fiercely protected) a sense of independent ownership. I devoured research papers, participated in case discussions with a newfound hunger, designed my own research protocols, meticulously analyzed data, and drafted the first versions of my papers, all driven by a thirst for autonomy. The final call on journals, however, rested with my supervisors, a necessary partnership in this academic dance. But from concept to (almost) completion, I carved my own path, demonstrating that a PhD journey could be as unique as the researcher undertaking it.

By 1997, a baker's dozen of first-authored scientific papers, proudly bearing my name, graced the pages of prestigious journals. One even managed to crack the coveted *British Medical Journal*, a personal Everest I scaled. Invitations to speak at conferences flowed in like a research grant windfall. Professor Eisman saw the momentum building and declared, with a mischievous glint in his eye, "Enough preening and pontificating! Time to write that thesis!"

Unlike the more streamlined Scandinavian models, where a handful of published papers could qualify as a PhD, the Australian system demanded a more holistic approach. My thesis needed to be a hefty tome, a monograph weaving a cohesive narrative from the disparate threads of my research. Chapter by painstaking chapter, the thesis came together. Each iteration was a brutal ballet of writing, revising, and receiving feedback from my formidable supervisor team.

Nearly six months later, a behemoth of a document, clocking in at a substantial 400 pages, materialized on my desk. It felt like a scientific Frankenstein's monster, a jumble of ideas stitched together with frantic late-night editing. Thankfully, a diet of ruthless red pens from my supervisors helped me whittle the beast down to a more manageable 350 pages. I christened my magnum opus: "Contributions of Genetic and Environmental Factors to the Determination of Fracture Risk."

The title captured the essence of my research, but Professor Eisman, ever the wordsmith, had a final, crucial note. With a chuckle, he pointed out that despite the "Doctor of Philosophy" title, a PhD thesis wasn't about philosophical musings. Back to the drawing board I went! Three more months of revisions ensued, each one a step closer to transforming my Frankenstein's monster into a polished, scientific dissertation. It was a lesson I wouldn't soon forget—the devil, or in this case, the essence of a good thesis, is truly in the details.

The initial spark for the genetic twist in my thesis title came from a stroke of unexpected luck. My proposal had been laser-focused on clinical factors influencing osteoporosis, but a chance encounter with a twin bone density study ignited a new flame of curiosity. Bone density, the Achilles' heel of strong bones, was measured through DXA scans, and the numbers varied wildly from person to person. Why? That million-dollar question hung in the air.

Enter genetics, a fascinating and unexplored avenue. Twin studies, a technique pioneered by the legendary Francis Galton centuries ago, offered a way to untangle this genetic influence. Identical (MZ) twins, like two peas in a pod, shared 100% of their genes, while fraternal (DZ) twins shared only half. If bone density were heavily influenced by genetics, identical twins should exhibit a stronger similarity in bone density compared to fraternal twins. To quantify this "similarity," I turned to a statistical measure called the correlation coefficient, a brainchild of Karl Pearson.

Inspired by this model, I spearheaded a study involving over 200 pairs of MZ and DZ twins. While leading a research project was a rare feat for a PhD student, in this case, it fell to me. The results were a resounding echo of Galton's prediction. The correlation coefficient for bone density in identical twins was a staggering 0.80, nearly double that of fraternal twins. Further analyses revealed a fascinating fact: genetics could contribute to a whopping eighty percent of bone density variation. This research fueled a series of scientific papers and laid the crucial groundwork for the discovery of the VDR gene, a story for another chapter.

Delving into genetics came at a personal financial cost. The Garvan Institute wouldn't sponsor this new frontier, so I dug deep into my own pockets, investing $5,000 to study genetics at the University of Colorado (Denver). It was a gamble, but one I felt compelled to take.

This genetic odyssey found its way into the final thesis, ready to face the scrutiny of a three-headed monster—university-appointed thesis reviewers. One of them even hailed from an international institution, all chosen from the cream of the crop in the top fifty universities in the world. Apparently, UNSW subscribed to a philosophy of "birds of a feather flock together," seeking association with the academic elite.

Six agonizing months later, the reviews arrived. Despite boasting thirteen published papers in top journals, the response was a daunting twenty-page document! Praise, critique, and revision requests swirled before my eyes like a scientific snowstorm. Yet, a glimmer of hope remained—all three reviewers deemed the thesis worthy of a PhD.

Deciphering the feedback wasn't an insurmountable Everest. My supervisors and I tackled the response within a month, and four weeks later, a revised thesis and a nearly one-hundred-page response landed on my supervisor's desk. He devoured it with a focus I hadn't seen before, not changing a single word. Was it indifference or quiet confidence? The answer, it turned out, was the latter. He trusted my revisions, perhaps bolstered by the input of the second supervisor.

Finally, in 1997, the verdict arrived: UNSW deemed the thesis worthy of a PhD. This worthiness wasn't a consolation prize; it was the gold standard at this institution. Then came the news that would forever etch itself in my memory—my thesis was chosen as the *UNSW Best Thesis of the Year*! Ecstatic, I basked in the recognition. The Garvan Institute, in a rare show of pride, engraved my name alongside other outstanding doctors in their main hall. Today, it stands as a recognition of the accomplishments of two Vietnamese doctors: myself and my student, Dr. Nguyên Đình Nguyễn.

On May 22, 1998, I donned the Doctor of Philosophy gown, officially graduating from the UNSW School of Medicine. This milestone has etched my name in history as the first Vietnamese-born individual to receive this degree from the institution. The PhD journey, though challenging, was a transformative experience. It propelled me deep into the intricacies of bone density research, allowing me to make significant contributions to the field.

I proudly wore the Doctor of Philosophy gown, marking my graduation from the UNSW Medicine. (May 22nd, 1998)

Beyond the PhD: Embracing the DSc Journey

By 2015, osteoporosis research had become an integral part of my professional identity. With over 250 papers published in leading journals, my contributions to the field were well-documented. My work has been cited more than 20,000 times by other researchers, placing me in the top 1% of medical researchers worldwide. Osteoporosis research was no longer just a part of my work; it had become a defining aspect of my career, one that I embraced with pride.

The Dubbo Osteoporosis Epidemiology Study, my initial foray into the field, felt like a long-lost friend. I yearned to share its story and its groundbreaking findings with the public. Two chapters of a book aimed at a general audience were already drafted, a passion project simmering on the back burner.

Then fate intervened, not in a dramatic way, but through a casual conversation with a respected senior colleague. We were discussing the ongoing battle against osteoporosis when he casually tossed out a suggestion that sent my plans careening in a different direction. "Why not write a Doctor of Science (DSc) thesis?" he asked, his words sparking a new fire in my imagination.

Intrigued, I delved deeper into the DSc degree. Unlike a PhD, which focuses on original research, a DSc celebrates a researcher's lifetime contributions to a field. It was a chance not only to tell the story of the Dubbo study, but also to connect it to the larger context of osteoporosis research —a context I helped create. The unfinished book could wait, but a Doctor of Science thesis was a challenge I couldn't resist.

The Doctor of Science degree, I discovered, was the Everest of academia in the prestigious British and Australian educational systems. Reserved for seasoned veterans, typically accomplished professors a decade past their PhDs, it shimmered with an allure I hadn't anticipated. Honorary DSc degrees existed for distinguished contributions, but mine, if I dared to pursue it, would be the hard-won kind. The University of New South Wales, my academic home, outlined the criteria for this prestigious honor. It wasn't for the faint of heart. A comprehensive set of requirements awaited, each a stepping stone on the path to this ultimate recognition:

1. The Council may grant the degree of Doctor of Science on the recommendation of the Academic Board for an original contribution or contributions of distinguished merit to some branch of science.

2. A candidate for the degree of Doctor of Science shall be either: (a) a graduate of the University of New South Wales of at least ten years standing; or (b) a graduate of another approved university of at least ten years standing who has been a full-time member of the academic staff of the University of New South Wales and has been engaged in advanced study and research in the University for a period of not less than four years.

3. The degree shall be awarded on the published work of the candidate.

4. A candidate for the degree shall forward to the Dean of Graduate Research an application together with: (a) Four copies (wherever possible) of the work referred to in paragraph 3; (b) A declaration indicating those sections of the work, if any, which have been submitted previously for a degree or other award in any university.

5. In submitting published work, every candidate shall submit a short discourse describing the research activities embodied in the submission. The discourse shall clearly outline the extent of originality and the candidate's contribution to any collaborative work.

6. The Dean of Graduate Research shall forward the discourse and list of published work to the Presiding Member of the relevant faculty, or if not appropriate, to the Committee on Research for determination of the membership of an ad hoc committee which shall conduct the examination.

7. Following the adoption of a report from the ad hoc committee that the work referred to in paragraph 3 above is prima facie worthy of examination, the work shall be submitted to three examiners appointed by the Committee on Research on the recommendation of the ad hoc committee.

8. At the conclusion of the examination, each member shall submit a report on the published work and shall recommend whether or not the degree be awarded. The ad-hoc committee shall, after considering the examiners' reports, recom-

mend to the Committee on Research whether or not the candidate should be awarded the degree.

9. The Committee on Research shall, after consideration of the ad-hoc committee's recommendation and the examiners' reports, recommend to the Academic Board whether or not the candidate be awarded the degree.

10. A candidate shall pay such fees as may be determined from time to time by the Council.

The application process for a DSc felt like a scientific gauntlet, mirroring the process of securing prestigious fellowships. The applicant presents his CV, a meticulously honed document showcasing his research journey, alongside ten of his most impactful research papers. The Higher Degree Committee, a group of academic titans, would scrutinize these with an eagle eye, measuring the applicant's contributions against a rigorous yardstick. Published research and groundbreaking achievements were the holy grail, the currency of academia. There were no classes, no rote memorization—just a deep dive into a chosen topic, a thesis that would become one's crowning achievement.

Initially, the process overwhelmed me. It was a labyrinth of rules and regulations. But a colleague at the Garvan, a kind soul who recognized the years I'd poured into research, nudged me forward. He saw the potential, and his words echoed a truth I couldn't ignore. This honor wouldn't just be mine; it would be a reflection on the Garvan Institute as well.

The topic was an easy choice—osteoporosis, the field I'd called home for over two decades. The real challenge? Narrowing it down. Would it be genetics, where I'd made significant contributions, or fracture risk assessment, the area where I was most recognized? Seeking advice from a network of international colleagues, the answer was unanimous: fracture risk assessment, particularly in the realm of personalized prediction.

With a topic locked in, I didn't waste a moment. On March 30, 2015, I formally declared my candidacy. A concise letter brimming with intent, along with a meticulously prepared application, landed on the desk of the Dean of the Graduate School. Then, the waiting game began. Days bled into weeks, then months, each one a slow tick of the anticipation clock. Finally, on November 11, the Higher Degree Committee convened and reviewed my application. A surge of elation coursed through me: I had been accepted into the DSc program. The official letter, dated December 18, 2015, arrived with the weight of a royal decree, spelling out the news in black and white: the journey to Doctor of Science had officially begun.

I am writing to you regarding your application for admission to the Doctor of Science at UNSW. The faculty Higher Degree Committee (HDC) met on Wednesday, 11 November, to consider your application. The Committee decided to seek further advice, which would then be considered by the Faculty Executive of the HDC before a decision was made. I am pleased to advise that they have approved your admission to the Doctor of Science program, and this will now proceed to examination.

Could you please submit three copies of the published work and three copies of the discourse to Dominic Mooney in the Graduate Research School as per the Conditions for Award of Higher Doctorates Policy. The requirements for both documents are outlined in section 4.3.4 of the Policy.

The Faculty of Medicine Higher Degree Committee will nominate two external examiners who will be provided with a copy of the publications and the discourse once these are submitted. The examiner's recommendations will be considered by the Faculty HDC and the University Higher Degree Research Committee (UHDRC) before a final decision by the Academic Board. You will then be advised of the outcome.

If you have any questions, please do not hesitate to contact Dominic Mooney at the contact details provided below.

Yours Sincerely,
Professor Laura Poole-Warren
Pro Vice-Chancellor (Research Training)
& Dean of Graduate Research

With the official green light, the thrill of acceptance morphed into the familiar hum of research. The DSc thesis, the final hurdle before this academic Everest was conquered, loomed large. Thankfully, years of dedicated research had gifted me a treasure trove of material.

I chose the broad title "Contributions to Osteoporosis Research," as it aptly encompassed the diverse aspects of my work. The thesis would unfold like a three-act play. The first act, an engaging introduction, would highlight the key moments of my research journey. Act two, a detailed examination of the research methodology, would emphasize the quality and rigor of my work. The final act, showcasing the global influence of my research, would illustrate its significant impact on the international stage.

The opening line, the first sentence that would set the tone for this magnum opus, practically wrote itself. It flowed effortlessly, a distillation of years of dedication and breakthroughs, ready to be incorporated into the narrative of my thesis:

"I arrived in Australia thirty-five years ago as a refugee from Vietnam. After working for a few years as a kitchen hand and research assistant, I entered the field of osteoporosis through a fortunate incident. This wasn't just the start of a thesis; it was the start of my story."

The application dossier, a substantial record of my twenty-five-year career, was finally out of my hands. Enclosed within the manila folder were a detailed curriculum vitae, a fifty-page summary documenting my extensive journey in osteoporosis research, and a comprehensive list of my published papers—each representing the countless hours spent analyzing data. With a sigh of relief, I mailed the application, trusting it would find its way through the university's administrative maze.

The waiting game, a familiar dance by now, began anew. Days blurred into weeks, each one a slow tick on the anticipation clock. Work continued, of course. Research never truly sleeps. But a sliver of my attention remained fixated on that manila envelope, its fate now in the hands of the Higher Degree Committee.

Nearly a year passed slowly, with each milestone—a conference presentation or a published paper—serving as a bittersweet reminder of the DSc still pending. Then, one crisp October morning, the anticipation finally snapped. An email, emblazoned with the official university seal, arrived in my mailbox. My heart hammered a frantic rhythm against my ribs as I opened it. Inside, nestled amongst official letterhead, was the document I'd yearned for: a letter dated October 26, 2016, from the Dean of the Graduate School.

Dear Professor Nguyen,

I am pleased to advise you that the Academic Board at its meeting on the 4th of October 2016 determined that you be admitted to the degree of Doctor of Science. Please accept my warm congratulations on the recognition of your substantial and distinguished contribution.

The UNSW Graduation Office will contact you shortly about arrangements for your graduation, which I hope to be able to attend.

Best Regards,

Professor Laura Poole-Warren

Pro-Vice Chancellor (Research Training)

& Dean of Graduate Research

Graduate Research School

Euphoria! The news of my DSc acceptance wasn't quiet satisfaction; it was a full-blown eruption of joy. The culmination of years of research, late nights, and countless breakthroughs finally had a tangible reward. But the official ceremony, the moment I'd don the doctoral gown and hood once more, wasn't until July 17, 2017. For those curious enough to see it, visit https://www.youtube.com/watch?v=X0F6ekEiqhc and forward to one hour and eleven minutes. This is a moment I'll cherish forever.

Standing there, bathed in the warm glow of the spotlight, a lump formed in my throat as presiding professor Terry Campbell, who was also from my St. Vincent's campus, read a citation that chronicled not just my publications, but the impact my research had on the fight against osteoporosis. It was a beautiful mix of pride and emotion, a validation of the long and sometimes arduous journey I'd taken.

Proudly wearing my Doctor of Science gown from UNSW Medicine, July 17, 2017—flanked by my niece Kim Thoa and her soon-to-be husband Trúc Phạm.

This second doctorate wasn't just a badge of honor or a line on a CV; it was a chance to solidify my footprint in the field I'd dedicated my life to. The years of research, the late nights spent chasing answers, the countless dead ends that led to breakthroughs, all culminated in this moment. It was demanding, yes, but the rewards were immeasurable. This accomplishment wasn't a finish line, but a wellspring of renewed passion, fueling me to push even further in my ongoing research endeavors.

As fate would have it, graduation week coincided with Refugee Week in Australia. *The Guardian*, perhaps sensing the significance of this confluence, reached out for an interview. An hour of conversation and filming followed, culminating in an article titled "'I Just needed a chance': from refugee to the heights of Australian medical research," published on June 19, 2017. I couldn't wait to read it, but the reporter kept the details close to his chest. What words would he use to capture my story, the journey from a young Vietnamese refugee to a Doctor of Science?

The article, when it finally arrived, began with a line that sent shivers down my spine:

"After fleeing Vietnam by boat in 1981, a dishwashing job at St Vincent's hospital was Tuan Nguyen's lucky break. Tuan Nguyen's lucky break came in the form of a Mrs. Ramsay, who cast an eye over his CV and offered him a job washing dishes in St Vincent's hospital kitchen in Sydney. That was 1982 and Nguyen was a refugee, having fled communist persecution in his native Vietnam, and only days in the country.

Thirty-six years later, Nguyen is still at St Vincent's, only now he is Professor Nguyen, and on Saturday was awarded a doctorate of science from the University of New South Wales for a quarter of a century researching osteoporosis and bone fractures at the Garvan Institute."

In celebration of academic achievement and dedication, the Garvan Institute of Medical Research proudly announced the awarding of a DSc degree to me on June 16, 2017:

The Garvan Institute of Medical Research congratulates Professor Tuan Nguyen, who has received a Doctorate of Science (DSc) from the University of New South Wales.

'I just needed a chance': from refugee to the heights of Australian medical research

After fleeing Vietnam by boat in 1981, a dishwashing job at St Vincent's hospital was Tuan Nguyen's lucky break

📷 Nguyen is still at St Vincent's, only now he is Prof Nguyen and has been awarded a doctorate of science from UNSW for a quarter of a century of research at the Garvan Institute. Photograph: Jonny Weeks/The Guardian

The Guardian's article of Tuan Nguyen for Refugee Week in Australia. (June 19, 2017)

The two professors mentioned in the newsletter, Ted Kraegen and Don Chisholm, were also my seniors at the Garvan Institute. Professor Kraegen, a quiet giant in the field of diabetes research, had a profound impact with his groundbreaking work. Yet, the man himself was the picture of humility, a gentle smile that embodied the spirit of a true Aussie. Professor Chisholm, another pillar of the Garvan, was there from the very beginning. Often hailed as a gentleman and a scholar by his colleagues, I couldn't agree more. He was a constant source of support for his juniors, his encouragement devoid of any harshness. Years later, I had the privilege of inviting Professor Chisholm to Vietnam to share his expertise with local doctors. His warmth and knowledge were appreciated by everyone he met. These experiences solidified the belief that great minds needn't be loud; sometimes, the most profound impact is made with a gentle hand and a kind heart.

During my PhD and DSc candidature, I learned numerous invaluable lessons that weren't found in textbooks. Beyond the research, I gained valuable insights into understanding the complexities of academia, forming professional relationships, and communicating my research effectively. These experiences shaped my development as a scholar and equipped me with skills essential for a satisfying academic career.

Know Your Place

My first, harsh lesson in academic culture remains vivid. A worn copy of *Nature* held a paper riddled with flawed methodology. Fueled by youthful naiveté, I drafted a scathing rebuttal—a letter to the editor that dissected the research with surgical precision. Proud of my exposé, I marched to my mentor's office, eager to expose the flaws.

Professor Eisman barely glanced at the letter before ushering me in. Concern etched lines on his brow as he scanned the page. The lecture that followed wasn't harsh, but it dismantled my righteous fury. In his calm, professorial way, Professor Eisman explained that criticizing a senior scientist, especially a giant in the field, was a minefield. "Wrong" wasn't the word to use, even if the research was demonstrably flawed. There was a language reserved for senior figures, a lexicon I wasn't privy to as a young researcher. It was an unwritten rule, a secret code learned at the knee of a mentor. He patiently explained the hierarchy: science is divided into "doers" like me, the foot soldiers of research, and the "talkers" and "thinkers" above. My place, for now, was decidedly at the bottom of the ladder.

That day, the weight of academia settled on my shoulders. My relatively youthful enthusiasm was tempered and replaced by a cautious understanding of the unspoken rules that governed scientific discourse. It was not quite a harsh lesson, but one that propelled me forward, determined to climb the ladder, not just with research, but with the language that would eventually allow me to speak my truth.

The scientific hierarchy wasn't just an abstract concept; I was about to experience it firsthand. The early 1990s found me, a wide-eyed newcomer to the world of osteoporosis research, presenting my findings on calcium and bone fractures at a national conference in Sydney. Little did I know, I was about to be schooled in the harsh realities of academic power dynamics.

My presentation concluded, and a hush fell over the room. Then, a towering figure rose—Professor Christopher Nordin, a legend in the field of calcium metabolism research. Though well into his sixties or seventies, his voice boomed with the authority of a seasoned warrior. "My dear," he addressed me, a subtle edge of condescension in his tone, "your findings, while interesting, are hardly groundbreaking. The link between low calcium and weakened bones is well-established."

A ripple of unease spread through the audience. This wasn't the reception I'd envisioned. Professor Nordin's statement sparked a heated debate, with dissenting voices challenging his long-held belief. Lost in the maelstrom, I stood frozen on the podium, a hapless newcomer caught in the crossfire. The moderators, sensing my distress, mercifully intervened, steering the discussion towards the next presenter.

Later, I came to understand the full weight of Professor Nordin's words. He was a man who embodied the Vietnamese saying, *"Nhất nghệ tinh, nhất thân vinh"*—master one art, and be honored. For him, calcium was the holy grail of bone health, a belief he championed throughout his long career.

Years later, when a study challenged this notion, Professor Nordin was met with a deluge of rebuttals. He penned scathing editorials, wielded statistics like a weapon, and even took to the media to defend his position. Ironically, during one such rebuttal, he sought my assistance, acknowledging the value of a fresh perspective. A strange camaraderie blossomed. We disagreed at times, but his fondness for me was evident in his endearing term, "My dear young man."

Professor Nordin was a man of strong principles. He disliked the growing influence of pharmaceutical companies on conferences, once famously shaming a colleague for presenting research that was blatantly sponsored by a drug company. He was a champion of academic integrity, and his fiery pronouncements left a lasting impression on the scientific community. His view on the relationship between the pharmaceutical industry and medical research prompted me to question the potential biases that could taint research, the delicate balance between progress and profit. As a young researcher, I vowed to maintain a healthy skepticism, to ensure my findings were driven by data, not dollars.

His dedication to his work was legendary. Even after retirement, the hospital attempted to "kick him out," but his passion for research remained unstoppable. He continued his work at another institute well into his nineties, demonstrating his indefatigable spirit.

Professor Nordin's presence at conferences was a constant reminder of the commitment required for scientific progress. He wasn't a mere spectator; he actively engaged in debates and his sharp mind exercised statistics with the dexterity of a seasoned swordsman. Imagine a man over ninety, fingers flying across the keyboard, analyzing data on the spot to refute a presentation. That was Professor Nordin, a force of nature who defied the limitations of age.

My encounters with Professor Nordin were not just scientific lessons; they were a crash course in the complex world of scientific hierarchy and the passionate battles that fuel discovery. He may have been a man of the past, clinging to his statistical software of choice, Minitab. Still, his solid dedication and fiery spirit continue to inspire me, a reminder that the pursuit of knowledge transcends age and circumstance.

The inevitability of his absence hung heavy in the air, an unspoken truth we all acknowledged. The ANZBMS, in a fitting tribute, established an award in his and his wife's name. The future conferences would be a quieter affair without him, but he wouldn't truly be gone. His spirit would live on in the Christopher & Maggie Nordin Young Investigator Award, an honor for which I was humbled to chair from 2020 to 2024. It was a privilege to shepherd new researchers into the fold, a continuation of the mentorship he so readily offered throughout his career.

At an osteoporosis conference in Adelaide, Professor Nordin, his wife Margaret, and I engaged in discussions about our research.

Learning How to Write

The path from a wide-eyed PhD student to a confident scientific author wasn't a straight shot. It was a journey filled with discovery, fueled by a thirst for knowledge and a desire to communicate my research effectively. Looking back, I can pinpoint several key lessons that transformed my approach to scientific writing. May these lessons benefit aspiring researchers on their own journeys.

My initiation into the world of scientific writing was a baptism by fire with Professor John Eisman as the high priest. We were aiming for the holy grail—a publication in the prestigious *New England Journal of Medicine*. The pressure was a constant hum in the lab, electrifying the air. Professor Eisman, a seasoned warrior in the publishing trenches, pointed me towards past issues of the journal. "Absorb them," he commanded. "Learn from the masters before you attempt to join their ranks." Back then, the library was my battlefield—long afternoons spent surrounded by mountains of photocopied papers, their black and white ink the war paint of countless successful campaigns.

Lesson One: Knowledge is power. In the realm of scientific writing, the power comes from studying the victors.

Eight weeks of writing, diagramming, and editing felt like an eternity. Armed with my meticulously crafted thirty-page behemoth, I approached Professor Eisman with the misplaced confidence of a fresh recruit. His response? A sigh that echoed in the lab and a toss—thankfully not in the bin, but onto his desk. My heart pounded a frantic tattoo against my ribs. Was my English that bad?

He chuckled, dispelling the tension with a single breath. What followed was a masterclass that would forever change my approach to writing. "Science isn't Shakespeare, my dear," he said, his voice laced with a gentle amusement. "It's about clarity, precision, and maybe a touch of the visual." He spent the next hour wielding his red pen like a surgeon's scalpel, meticulously dissecting my flowery prose and transforming it into a lean, mean, data-driven machine.

Lesson Two: Scientific writing is a language of its own. Ditch the poetry, embrace the facts.

Clarity was just one facet of the battlefield. Professor Eisman drilled me on the importance of the message. "Why is this research important?" he'd ask, a question that could leave me stumped for days. "Imagine you're explaining this to a taxi driver on your way home," he'd say, a mischievous twinkle in his eye. "Can they grasp the significance of your findings?" Until now, I still vividly remember those words.

Lesson Three: Distill complexity into clarity. Your research might be groundbreaking, but if no one understands its impact, it's like a tree falling in an empty forest.

Data were the foot soldiers in this war, but presentation was the general. Professor Eisman wouldn't tolerate a single sloppy graph or blurry image. He'd quote something equivalent to a Vietnamese proverb: "People are beautiful because of silk." It drove home the point—data, no matter how elegant, needs an elegant presentation. Choosing the right colors, fonts, and spacing... it all mattered.

Lesson Four: Data visualization is an art form, transforming raw numbers into a captivating story that can convince even the most skeptical minds.

The revisions were a grueling gauntlet. My mentor put me through the wringer at least five times, each edit a strategic maneuver honing my skills. But the most rigorous revisions, and the final say, came from the senior professor, the paper's corresponding author. He was the general leading the charge, his reputation and experience securing us a place at the table. Authorship order, I learned, wasn't just a courtesy; it reflected a hierarchy of contribution and responsibility.

Lesson Five: Authorship is a currency, a tangible recognition of your role in the scientific enterprise.

Finally, the paper, polished to a diamond-like sheen, was snail-mailed to its destination. Six agonizing months later, the verdict arrived: eight pages of reviewer comments, a mix of praise and critique. The top journal, the *New England Journal of Medicine*, wasn't a fit this time. Rejection stung, but Professor Eisman offered a stoic lesson: rejection is a rite of passage, a scar that marks your growth as a scientist.

Lesson Six: The path to publication is paved with rejection letters. Each one is a battle lost, but a lesson learned, a stepping stone on the path to victory.

We rewrote, submitted to a different journal, and this time, the response was more positive. Three months of revisions followed, a diplomatic dance of responding to reviewers' concerns, addressing opposing viewpoints, and backing everything with data, not defensiveness.

Lesson Seven: Responding to reviewers is a science—respectful, evidence-based, and focused on improvement. It's about building bridges of understanding, not burning them with arrogance.

Learning How to Speak

Scientific English, a language as foreign as my native Vietnamese, felt like a tangled jungle path compared to the sterile clarity of research papers. But conferences, those bustling hives of international researchers, presented an even steeper learning curve.

The American Society for Bone and Mineral Research conference in Minneapolis (1992) was a scientific wonderland teeming with thousands of eager minds. My first international presentation loomed—a flimsy research paper clutched in my sweaty hand, a meager shield against the coming storm.

Being selected for an oral presentation was a victory, after spending countless sleepless nights hunched over microscopes and data. Yet, my mentor, Professor John Eisman, wasn't one for pats on the back. This was a battlefield, and my presentation was the weapon.

The days leading up to the conference were marked by meticulous preparation, a flurry of careful planning, and organization. Slides, printed on clunky transparencies—a far cry from the digital future—were endlessly scrutinized. Font size, color palette, and every detail held the potential to trip me up. Despite a decade in Australia, my pronunciation remained suspect in Professor Eisman's critical ears. Memorization became my mantra, every sentence a meticulously rehearsed line in a scientific play.

Even the transpacific flight wasn't a respite. Professor Eisman, a phantom haunting the business class, materialized beside my cramped economy seat mid-flight. Flight attendants, perpetually pushing carts of in-flight meals, became a comical obstacle course as I fumbled through my presentation under his watchful (and slightly terrifying) gaze.

The hotel room transformed into a makeshift stage. Professor Eisman became a stern director, dissecting my every move in front of the mirror. Timing was paramount; every second was meticulously measured. Three grueling rehearsals later, his approval, a rare commodity, was finally bestowed.

Presentation day arrived, and with it, a fresh wave of panic. I sought refuge in the front row, desperately trying to project calm. Professor Eisman, a phantom once more, materialized just moments before my name echoed through the hall. His touch on my shoulder, a jolt of nervous energy, was his only reassurance. "Make us proud," he whispered, his voice a low rumble.

Taking the stage, the harsh glare of the spotlight felt like a physical weight. Yet, the opening lines, drilled into my memory, flowed effortlessly. Slide after meticulously crafted slide flickered by, my voice a steady current guiding the audience through my research. The final sentence, a triumphant declaration, resounded in the vast hall.

The real test, however, arrived with the Q&A. The cavernous room, once manageable, morphed into a sea of disembodied faces. The first few questions, pre-prepared and practiced, were navigated with ease. Then, a voice from the abyss: "What about weight? How does it impact fracture risk?"

My carefully constructed world tilted on its axis. Weight? It must have been body sway—the very topic of my presentation. Relief washed over me as I launched into a well-rehearsed explanation of sway and its connection to fractures. The questioner seemed satisfied, and with that, I sank back into my chair, a wave of accomplishment drenching me.

But John's expression told a different story. His face, a thundercloud, unleashed a single, scathing sentence: "You didn't answer the question." The world spun. My justification died in my throat. He elaborated, his voice low and cold. *Weight, not sway*, was the question.

Shame burned in my cheeks as I mumbled apologies. "Don't worry," he sighed, a hint of sympathy flickering in his eyes. "His English was terrible, the question poorly phrased. Congratulations." I knew better. The lousy English was mine, my misunderstanding a gaping hole in my preparation.

Minneapolis wasn't just the stage for my scientific debut; it was a "baptism by fire." It hammered home the unforgiving nature of scientific discourse, the importance of razor-sharp focus, and the art of thinking on your feet. More importantly, it underscored the paramount need for crystal-clear communication, not just within my presentations but in every interaction within the scientific arena. Minneapolis was the crucible that shaped me into a more confident and adaptable researcher, forever prepared to face the unforgiving spotlight of scientific inquiry.

Reflecting on my academic journey, which culminated in two doctoral degrees, I am filled with a sense of humility and gratitude. The path was fraught with challenges and required perseverance, but it was also gratifying. My pursuit of advanced degrees was driven by a deep-seated curiosity and a desire to make meaningful contributions to the field of osteoporosis. The support and guidance of my mentors were invaluable; without them, my achievements would not have been possible. The collaborative spirit of the scientific community also played a crucial role in shaping my work. These accomplishments are not just personal milestones but reflections of collective efforts and shared passion for advancing medical knowledge. As I move forward, I am committed to continuing this work with the same dedication and a renewed appreciation for the learning and growth each step of this journey has brought me.

Chapter Ten

Striving for Recognition

The public sees medical research as a realm of steady progress, with pronouncements of breakthroughs echoing across news channels. But the reality is a constant, gnawing anxiety. It isn't the long hours hunched over microscopes, the frustration of failed experiments, or the sacrifices of weekends spent wrestling with data analysis. It is the ever-present shadow of funding.

Grant proposals became my personal Moby Dick, a monstrous white whale I relentlessly chased. Weeks bled into months as I meticulously crafted documents, outlining the research with the precision of a surgeon, detailing the methodology with the clarity of a preacher, and emphasizing the potential impact with the fervor of an evangelist. Each rejection felt like a punch to the gut, stealing a breath from my scientific fire. The sting wasn't just professional; it was deeply personal. Every 'no' chipped away at the foundation I'd built, whispering doubts about the value of my work and the validity of my ideas.

The irony was that good research was the key to securing funding, yet funding was essential for doing good research. It was a cruel Catch-22. Without grants, cutting-edge equipment remained out of reach, limiting the scope of my investigations. Smaller studies, conducted with shoestring budgets, struggled to generate the kind of groundbreaking results that grabbed the attention of prestigious journals, the very publications that supposedly validated the research in the eyes of funding agencies.

This pressure cooker of competition fostered a culture of secrecy. We, the researchers, guarded our ideas like jealous dragons, fearing that a shared thought might be stolen and published before our own work saw the light of day. Collaboration, the cornerstone of scientific progress, became a hesitant dance, fraught with the risk of betrayal. A constant undercurrent of tension replaced the camaraderie I'd envisioned in this ivory tower of discovery.

There were triumphs, of course. The elation of a published paper, the thrill of a breakthrough finding, the quiet satisfaction of mentoring a bright young mind—these were the moments that fueled my passion and kept me going. But the specter of funding never truly receded. It was a constant undercurrent, a low hum of worry that colored every accomplishment, every milestone. It was the price of admission in this high-stakes game, the invisible tax on the pursuit of knowledge. The battle for funding wasn't just about securing resources—it was about the very soul of scientific discovery.

The lifeblood of Australian science flowed from a single, powerful wellspring: the National Health and Medical Research Council (NHMRC). Understanding this grand institution meant taking a peek beneath the surface of the whole Antipodean scientific landscape. It wasn't your fancy American NIH, oh no. This is a "poorer" brother/sister, with a budget that is a fraction of its US counterparts, yet it wields it with the sharp focus of a laser. Their mission? To find the brightest minds Down Under, the hidden gems buried in our universities and research labs. They weren't handing out participation trophies here. This was about cultivating an elite force, the best of the best, the future leaders of Australian science.

And the ultimate prize in this high-stakes game? The NHMRC fellowship. Now, that was something special. It wasn't just a grant, mind you. It was the holy grail, the shining star that only a select few could ever reach. Professors, those seasoned veterans who'd been climbing the academic mountain for years, would lock horns in this prestigious competition. The odds of winning? Well, let's just say it was enough to make you chew your nails right down to the nubs. We're talking about a ten percent success rate. Ten percent! That meant for every ten brilliant minds who poured their heart and soul into their applications, only one would reach the summit and claim the fellowship as their own. It was a brutal test, but the rewards were sweeter than any victory could ever be.

A decade had spun by since I'd walked through the doors of the Garvan Institute, a fresh-faced researcher with a head full of dreams and a heart brimming with ambition. By 2005, those dreams had sharpened into a laser focus, and that ambition had morphed into a burning desire—to establish myself as an independent scientist in my own right. The tenure track was a comfortable path, with a steady paycheck as a welcome constant. However, a different kind of constant aggravated me—a yearning for the freedom to chart my own course in the vast ocean of scientific inquiry.

The answer, it seemed, lay in the coveted NHMRC Research Fellowship. Back in the early 2000s, a hierarchy existed within these fellowships. Research Fellow, Senior Research Fellow, and Principal Research Fellow were each a title on a rung higher up on the ladder. First-time applicants, no matter their achievements, couldn't dream of the top rungs. Those positions were reserved for seasoned researchers seeking promotion. For those who secured a fellowship, the privilege, or perhaps the honor, was undeniable. The coveted title, "NHMRC Fellow," became a prefix, a mark of distinction worn proudly before one's name. It was the golden ticket, the passport to a world where I wouldn't be beholden to the priorities of others, where my research could blossom untamed. Sure, there was the undeniable personal triumph—– the validation and recognition by my peers. But this fellowship held a significance that transcended the individual. Securing it wouldn't just alleviate the institute's burden of funding my salary for the next five years (a truth I wouldn't deny was a welcome relief!), it would be a victory writ large.

I envisioned it as a battering ram against the invisible walls that hemmed in so many scientists from backgrounds like mine. The statistics revealed a harsh reality—the lack of diversity was a gap that needed to be closed. The NHMRC fellowship, in my hands, could be the crowbar. It could be the symbol of shattering that glass ceiling, of proving that brilliance wasn't the sole domain of a privileged few. It could be a beacon for the next generation, showing that science wasn't a monolithic entity, but a vibrant enterprise woven from threads of experience as diverse as the world itself.

The NHMRC fellowship became more than an award; it became a cause, a crusade for my future. And as I embarked on the process of crafting my proposal, a quiet strength bloomed within me. This wasn't just about my own future; it was about ensuring that the future of science mirrored the richness of the world it strove to understand. The fight was on, and I, armed with a decade of experience and the support of a hidden community, was ready.

The grant journey itself was an odyssey—a year-long saga of applications, peer reviews, and a nerve-wracking interview.

The Application

The NHMRC application template itself was a rigid affair, a world away from free-form writing. "All written material must be at least 11 point font." No exceptions. Stray from this format, and your application would be promptly returned, relegated to next year's cycle. No room for error, no distinction of applicant stature. Those colleagues' feedback sessions were a lifeline in this unforgiving system.

It was a strange mix of art and science. You had to choose the perfect words, each one a brushstroke, painting a picture of your research, its impact, and its future potential. Metrics, publications, grants secured... every bullet point reflected my dedication to the field. No wasted space, but all the key terms shimmering bright. Then there was the science part, the numbers and logic that built the foundation. I loved the structure, the challenge of making it all sing.

For me, the application wasn't entirely foreign territory. During summer breaks at my provincial home, Kiên Giang Hospital (Vietnam), I meticulously pieced it together, my experience a guiding light. Three colleagues, true lifesavers, reviewed my application, offering frank but invaluable feedback. Gaps were identified, areas needing emphasis highlighted, presentation styles critiqued, and even the occasional typo unearthed. Without their keen eyes, a complete application would have remained a distant dream.

But there was a snag, a cultural hurdle. Growing up, modesty was deeply ingrained. Using "I" felt like bragging, like taking credit for something that was often a team effort. Most of my research was a collaborative dance, each study a creation with multiple minds.

So, the first draft went out, and my mentor—a seasoned warrior in the grant trenches—took one look and said, "Not quite there yet." He leaned back and explained. This fellowship wasn't for a team, it was for me. A recognition of what I could achieve. He smiled, a twinkle in his eye, and said, "Go on, be bold. Tell them what you can do."

It was a turning point. The "I" became a powerful tool—a way to showcase my journey and my vision. It wasn't about bragging; it was about owning my potential. And with that shift, the application started to take shape, not just a scientific proposal, but a glimpse into the scientist I was becoming.

The Review

Once the applications flooded in, they were whisked away by the committee and distributed to a quartet of external reviewers, sometimes even reaching colleagues overseas. Anonymity was paramount in this dance—who held the fate of your research in their hands remained a mystery. But you, the applicant, were granted a small element of control. You could nominate reviewers you felt were well-suited, and even exclude some, with a justification for each move on the chessboard. Collaborators, mentors—anyone whom you had tangoed with professionally or personally—were automatically disqualified. Potential biases were constant specters in this scientific waltz.

But the committee, ever vigilant, rarely swayed on these exclusions. There were even whispers of a surprising move—they might assign your application to the very reviewers you'd tried to banish! This dance kept you on your toes.

Based on these independent evaluations, the first cut was made. A hefty chunk, a good seventy to eighty percent of hopefuls, would see their dreams fall by the wayside. Only a select few, that coveted twenty to thirty percent, would remain.

These were the chosen ones who'd get to showcase their moves on the interview stage... the final, most nerve-wracking step in the dance.

The Interview

This interview... oh, the interview! It was the ultimate filter, separating the merely good from the truly exceptional. Remember, everyone here had already cleared the basic hurdles. But with a limited budget, the NHMRC had to make a final, agonizing choice. The interview, then, became a way to whittle down the numbers, a kind of scientific musical chairs where only a lucky few would remain standing when the music stopped. The pressure was immense, the stakes impossibly high. It was here, under the harsh glare of expert scrutiny, that your research would be dissected, your passion evaluated, and your future as an independent scientist decided.

Imagine a room filled with eminent scientists, their faces a mix of curiosity and skepticism. For the next hour, they would dissect my research, testing the depth of my knowledge, the soundness of my methodology, and the viability of my plans. It was an intellectual duel, a test not just of scientific prowess, but also of mental fortitude. Here, the ability to anticipate their questions, to counter their arguments, and to think on my feet was paramount.

Five years prior, a time etched in my memory not for grand achievements, but for a stinging rejection. I believed my application had been strong. My publication record gleamed, exceeding expectations for someone at my stage. But confidence, it seemed, wasn't enough. The interview should have been a victory lap, a chance to showcase the research I'd poured my heart into. Instead, it felt like fumbling in the dark. My intellectual leadership, the very quality that sets strong researchers apart, remained frustratingly out of reach. The questions, sharp and probing, exposed a gap I hadn't realized existed. Rejection. The word hung heavy in the air, a lead weight settling in my gut.

It wasn't just a missed job opportunity. This was a blow to the ego, a chink in the armor I'd so carefully built. The other contenders—department heads, research group leaders, even institute directors—radiated a seasoned air I desperately craved. Compared to their professional gravitas, I felt woefully underprepared, a wide-eyed newcomer at a high-stakes poker game.

The sting of rejection was sharp, but it wasn't enough to break me. After all, I'd grown up with a saying that had become a personal mantra: "If one glue fails, use another." Dejected but not defeated, I picked myself up, dusted myself off, and began to meticulously plan my next move. Five years, I decided, would be my investment in redemption. Five years of honing my research, sharpening my leadership skills, and preparing for another shot at the NHMRC fellowship. This time, I wouldn't just be ready—I'd be undeniable.

This time, after almost six agonizing months of waiting, the email arrived: an interview invitation and a plane ticket. The NHMRC, ever-generous, shouldered the travel expenses for far-flung candidates. This year, my university wasn't alone in the fellowship race. Six of us, four from my own Garvan Institute, had been chosen. News of this windfall triggered a flurry of activity within the university. Their reputation was at stake, and they threw everything they had at us 'home-grown' candidates.

A communication expert lectured us on the art of interview responses, body language, and demeanor—the unspoken cues that could make or break an interview. An NHMRC fellow, a warhorse of the interview circuit, shared his experiences, offering battle-tested advice on how to answer those dreaded questions. Finally, the pièce de résistance—mock interviews. These weren't mere rehearsals; they were full-fledged interrogations, complete with a barrage of potential questions. Some, the more meticulous among us, even went so far as to compile lists of anticipated questions and meticulously craft responses!

Weeks bled into one another and the interview day loomed large. I woke at 4 am, clutching notes in sweaty palms. The city was still asleep as I drove to the airport, the questions swirling like a storm in my head. The early flight, the cheapest on offer, whisked me to Melbourne. The morning rush at the airport was a chaotic symphony of hurried footsteps and booming announcements. In the taxi to the hotel (a four-star affair, courtesy of the NHMRC), I attempted conversation with the driver, anything to distract myself from the impending battle. 'Good luck, professor,' he rumbled, a touch of empathy in his voice. 'May you succeed.' I thanked him, a silent thought echoing in my mind: who wouldn't crave success? But success and failure, I knew, were the flip sides of the same coin.

Forty-five minutes early, I arrived at the hotel. The NHMRC receptionist ushered me into a comfortable waiting room, a haven of internet access, coffee, and breakfast treats. Newspapers and a flickering television in the background were ignored by the intensely-focused gathering. Some, young and wide-eyed, attempted cheerful smiles despite the telltale tremor in their hands. Others, their hair dusted with silver, exuded the quiet confidence of seasoned warriors. I struck up a conversation with a colleague, whose age mirrored mine, from South Australia. He regaled me with tales from his interview experiences, one particularly memorable involving a fiery exchange between a distinguished professor and a young panelist. Age discrimination, it seemed, was a landmine some were braver (or foolhardier) to tread upon. Yet, the professor, despite the outburst, had secured the fellowship. I was reassured by the interview committee's emphasis on merit rather than manners.

This glimpse into the interview battlefield both intrigued and terrified me. Here, in this opulent waiting room, the air crackled with a mix of ambition, anxiety, and a healthy dose of professional pride. Each candidate, an accomplished scientist in their own right, had clawed their way through a grueling application process. Now, we were the chosen few, finalists vying for a coveted slot amongst Australia's scientific elite. The interview, the final hurdle, loomed large. It was a chance to showcase not only the meticulously documented research achievements listed in our applications, but also the passion, vision, and very essence of who we were as scientists. Little did I know, the real battle was about to begin, a battle not just of intellect but of nerve, strategy, and the ability to think on my feet under the withering gaze of the NHMRC interview panel.

Professor GL's booming laugh echoed down the hallway, momentarily snapping me out of my reverie. Interview time. He introduced himself, his handshake firm and warm, then ushered me towards the meeting room. His small talk—the weather, the upcoming elections—offered a welcome respite from the churning anxieties in my gut.

The room itself was a picture of calculated comfort. Soft lighting cast a warm glow, and a discreet heater fought the Melbourne chill. A variety of beverages sat on the table, a silent invitation to calmness. The seating arrangement, however, held a distinct formality. I sat at a separate table, facing the chairperson and two other committee members. The spokesperson, a stern figure, sat at the opposite corner with a recording device and a laptop. Every word exchanged, I realized, would be documented, a safeguard against future disputes.

After introductions, the spokesperson laid out the ground rules with military precision: a thirty-minute interview plus a possible five-minute grace period; the right to object to questions, not to argue; concise answers, avoiding lengthy justifications; and finally, a five-minute window for my own questions. Across the table, yellow, red, and green highlighter markings bled through thick packets of my profile—evidence of their meticulous preparation.

The interview began with a familiar question, a seemingly innocuous one: "Why the NHMRC fellowship?" Two minutes, they said. A lifetime, it felt like. It was a classic icebreaker, a test of articulation and focus. My response, carefully honed through countless mock interviews, had to showcase how perfectly my goals aligned with the fellowship's objectives—a concise, coherent narrative, crafted to convince them that I was the ideal candidate.

The chairperson, an old professor, leaned forward with a hint of a smile, occasionally jotting notes, his eyes flitting between me and his watch. The questions came in rapid succession, fired from all corners of the table. Highlight three significant contributions to my field—in two minutes! Explain my publication record, its impact, and plans for scientific productivity. Were my editorial board positions more about prestige than actual contribution? How would I balance research with a professorship? Funding strategies? Training plans? The gauntlet had been thrown, a barrage designed to assess not just my research acumen but also my resourcefulness, my vision, and my commitment to Australian science.

One question, in particular, caught me off guard: "Why help Vietnam? Shouldn't the fellowship funds go towards Australian research?" The implication was clear—was I spreading myself too thin? But I was prepared. My response, shaped by years of working in international scientific collaborations, emphasized the interconnectedness of Australian science. Australian science, I argued, couldn't exist in a vacuum. Fostering partnerships with developing countries like Vietnam wasn't only altruistic but also strategically beneficial. A rising tide lifts all boats, after all. By nurturing young Vietnamese scientists, we were creating future collaborators and potential partners for groundbreaking research projects. Ultimately, a strong regional scientific network benefitted everyone—Australia included. Just as I readied a counter-offensive, the chairperson stepped in with a gentle reminder: "Professor Nguyen, remember, you can answer or object to questions, not engage in debate." And just like that, they moved on.

The clock ticked relentlessly, each second a beat of my escalating anxiety. But with each question, I felt myself gaining momentum, my answers flowing more confidently. The initial nervousness gave way to a sense of purpose, a determination to showcase the scientist I truly was. Here, in this brightly lit room, I wasn't just presenting my research achievements; I was painting a portrait of my scientific vision, my passion for discovery, and my commitment to propelling Australian research to even greater heights.

Finally, the allotted time elapsed. It was time for my five minutes of questions... a chance to showcase my genuine interest in the fellowship. I inquired about specific research initiatives the NHMRC was funding, the committee's vision for the future of Australian science, and anything that demonstrated my understanding of the bigger picture. Leaving the room, I felt drained but strangely exhilarated. The interview, a nerve-wracking ordeal, was over. Had it been enough? Only time would tell. But one thing was certain—I had given it my all, facing the NHMRC interview panel with a heart full of passion and a mind brimming with a scientist's determination.

The overall atmosphere, I noted with surprise, was far from the cutthroat environment I'd anticipated. The committee members were nothing like the intimidating interview drill sergeants I imagined; they exuded an air of courtesy and friendliness. Perhaps it was simply a matter of personalities. Or perhaps, an awareness of the power dynamic at play, leading them to adopt a different demeanor. Whatever the reason, even potentially sensitive questions were delivered with a careful touch, softened by gentle phrasing and non-threatening body language. In contrast to previous interviews where criticism was blunt and direct, they seemed to prefer letting the candidate do the self-evaluation here.

"You publish a lot," a question from years ago echoed in my mind, "but are you truly the lead investigator or just a participant?" This time, there were no such inquiries about the authorship of my publications. Instead, they focused on quality, prompting me to assess my own work from their perspective.

Australian medical research, a fiercely competitive landscape, was even more so for foreign-born scientists like myself. Coming from outside, in my case Vietnam, meant constantly striving to outshine native-born counterparts by a factor of "one to two heads," as the saying went. It was a harsh reality I'd come to accept; this wasn't my homeland, after all. Their higher expectations, I suppose, were understandable.

Nine long months crawled by before the news arrived. In mid-2007, it was good news. Not just for me, but for the Garvan Institute—two of my colleagues had also been awarded fellowships! A cause for celebration, indeed. And as the festivities unfolded, a wave of pride washed over me. The first Vietnamese-born scientist to receive this prestigious fellowship—a title I would wear with immense honor.

The Cycle Continues

The NHMRC fellowship, prestigious as it was, wasn't a permanent golden ticket. Regulations dictated a five-year term, with a fortunate six-year extension in my case. Then, the inevitable reapplication. The same interview gauntlet, the same nerve-wracking wait. This time, however, the outcome was a bitter pill to swallow. Failure. Just 0.2 points shy of the coveted Principal Research Fellowship. A seemingly minuscule margin, yet a chasm nonetheless. Science, with its relentless pursuit of objectivity, offered no room for sentimentality. Success and failure—two sides of the same coin, and both have to be accepted.

Despite the fellowship setback, NHMRC's DOES research project funding provided a lifeline, enough to keep the lab running, to pay salaries, and nurture the next generation of researchers. Postdoctoral fellows and research assistants continued their work, and several talented students joined the fold. Those years saw our research on osteoporosis genetics culminate in significant publications, adding luster to our scientific reputation.

Meanwhile, the landscape at NHMRC was shifting. Australia's economic climate tightened, and NHMRC's budget dwindled like a shrinking tide. The fight for funding grew more fierce. The once ten to fifteen success rate plummeted to a meager nine percent. Rejection, more often than not, wasn't a mark of inferior research; it simply reflected NHMRC's dwindling resources. A reorganization followed, ushering in a new fellowship program with five tiers for various stages in a scientist's career. The highest tier, Leadership 3, was a direct descendant of the esteemed "Australia Fellowship"—the pinnacle of recognition, both prestigious and financially rewarding.

Five years later, I felt I had amassed enough "materials"—a solid body of research and a proven track record—to make another run at an NHMRC fellowship. Professorial rank now placed me firmly in the "highest tier" applicant pool. Anxiety gnawed at me. How would the new system translate to my candidacy? In 2018, with a deep breath, I submitted my application for the Australia Fellowship. Ten agonizing months later, the verdict arrived: failure. This time, the bar had been set just 0.1 point higher, and I fell short. A collective sigh of disappointment echoed through the Garvan Institute. Yet, for me, the sting was softened by years of experience in dealing with the unpredictable nature of scientific funding. Success and failure, intertwined companions, demanded a certain equanimity. I had tasted both, learned from both, and would continue to push forward, fueled by a passion for scientific discovery.

The sting of that second rejection lingered, but it wouldn't deter me. The Gavan Institute, recognizing my potential and the closeness of the previous attempt, assigned a mentor to guide me in revising my application. But the support network extended far beyond that. Friends and colleagues became invaluable allies, each with their own expertise to contribute: calculating impact indexes, crafting strategic narratives, and presenting data in a compelling visual format. Their collective efforts were a crucial piece of the puzzle, highlighting the true spirit of scientific collaboration.

And the result, when it arrived on that crisp November 30th in 2020, was pure exhilaration. A letter from NHMRC, bearing the weight of the Minister of Health's authority, announced my selection for the coveted Australia Fellowship. The accompanying budget was substantial enough to secure my own salary, fund scholarships for five postgraduate students, and hire talented postdoctoral researchers. The news rippled outwards, a wave of celebration washing over the University of New South Wales. Five leadership fellowships, culminating in two at the highest tier, marked a banner year for the university, and the Garvan Institute joined in the jubilation with press releases heralding the achievement.

Personally, it was a moment of profound satisfaction. A lifeline tossed to a drowning man, a culmination of years filled with triumphs and tribulations. This, finally, was the pinnacle, the highest and most prestigious fellowship bestowed upon me. An more profound sense of significance was felt within, as I was the first Vietnamese-born scientist to receive this honor. This, I decided, would be my final NHMRC foray. It was time to pass the torch, to offer the next generation of researchers the opportunity to chase their own scientific dreams. Fortuitously, during this period, another lifebuoy arrived: a substantial research grant from Amgen, a pharmaceutical powerhouse, to investigate the complexities of osteoporosis in the elderly.

The prestigious Australia Fellowship was more than a financial boon; it was a validation of my dedication, a recognition of the path I had forged. It marked a turning point, a transition from a scientist constantly vying for support to one who could now mentor and empower the next wave of scientific minds. The years of traversing the labyrinthine world of research funding and the elation of victories interspersed with the sting of rejections honed my resilience and shaped my leadership style. Now, with a secure research base and a team of talented young researchers under my wing, I could focus on fostering their scientific curiosity, guiding them through the treacherous terrain of grant applications, and nurturing their own research visions.

My journey wasn't over, but it had entered a new chapter, one filled with fresh challenges and the responsibility of guiding others towards their own scientific summits and even greater scientific discoveries.

A Brush with Bias

The shadow of prejudice loomed large in those early years. Each grant rejection triggered a chorus of murmurs from my colleagues, whispers tinged with the lingering scars of the "White Australia Policy." As a Vietnamese refugee arriving in the early 1980s, I'd landed in a country cautiously embracing diversity. Whispers of acceptance hung heavy in the air, a contrast to the turmoil we'd left behind. Thankfully, the overwhelming feeling was one of welcome from a nation extending a helping hand. But even within this warmth, pockets of prejudice festered, particularly in remote areas. Unwritten "No Asians" policies on pub doors and discriminatory clubs served as a reminder that true integration was a constant battle.

"Discrimination in academia?" became a question that echoed in my ears, a constant refrain from concerned friends, and a nagging voice within myself. Their eyes, searching mine, mirrored my inner struggle. My answer was always an honest "no," at least not in the blatant, exclusionary sense. Yet, a nagging feeling of unfairness persisted, a subtle undercurrent that occasionally surfaced.

One such instance, forever imprinted in my memory, was a rejection of my NHMRC fellowship. The initial review comments were encouraging, filled with compliments on the quality of my research. Then, the tone shifted abruptly. "Invited to give keynote lectures at international conferences," the assessor wrote, "but almost half of these were in Asia (e.g., Osaka, Nagoya, Seoul, Bangkok)." The implication was clear: a blatant devaluation of Asian scientific discourse. It was a gut punch, a moment that ripped away the illusion of a level playing field. The path to progress, I realized then, wasn't always paved with equality.

My mentor, a Jewish refugee from Poland, saw the red flags I'd initially tried to ignore. Reading the comment, he erupted in righteous anger. "Prejudice?" he boomed, his voice thick with indignation. "Prejudice against Asian academia, hidden in plain sight!" He strongly urged me to challenge it by writing a protest letter to the NHMRC.

The truth was, I was conflicted. Part of me, the scientist seeking recognition, wanted to fight. But another part, the weary immigrant still adjusting to a new world, shrank from confrontation. Would a public challenge paint me as a troublemaker, jeopardizing future funding opportunities? Would it be seen as sour grapes, a petty reaction to rejection? The internal battle raged.

In the end, I chose silence. It wasn't a surrender, but a strategic retreat. I channeled my frustration into further refining my research, into securing even more prestigious speaking engagements—not just in Asia, but across the globe. I built an undeniable record, one that transcended geographic bias. Years later, when I finally secured that NHMRC fellowship, the validation was all the sweeter, a victory not just for my work, but against the subtle prejudice I'd faced.

Looking back, my scientific journey has been a relatively rough ride. Systematic discrimination based solely on my Asian heritage? I wouldn't say so. Yet, the subtle sting of bias remained. A recent survey by the University of Melbourne painted a concerning picture: a mere sixteen percent of faculty and professors in Australia's top universities were Asian. This number dwindled further for leadership positions, where Asian representation remained a dismal three percent.

Those numbers echoed my own observations—a glass ceiling for Asian scientists, hindering their ascent to the top echelons of academia. This disparity was even more evident in research funding. While Asian applicants comprised twenty percent of early-career fellowships, they made up a mere 3.5% of the highest funding tier.

Despite these challenges, my path took a positive turn. Leadership roles beckoned, culminating in the honor of becoming a Fellow of the Australian Academy of Health and Medical Sciences. Interestingly, my academic career in the US and Australia felt relatively equal, with a surprising twist. American colleagues sometimes seemed more welcoming than my Australian counterparts. Perhaps the smaller size of the Australian scientific community fostered a more competitive, insular environment.

Ironically, it was back home in Vietnam where I encountered a more blatant form of discrimination. Returning overseas Vietnamese like myself often faced a wall of suspicion, bureaucratic roadblocks, and a lack of support that never appeared in the US or Australia. One experience that stood out was when a grant application for my Vietnamese research team was brutally rejected by the FIRST program. Four international reviewers had been glowing, but a single Vietnamese reviewer, writing in broken English, deemed me a "foreigner," unnecessary for Vietnamese research (genomics, no less!). Our team's contributions were apparently deemed insignificant. This incident highlighted the plight of returning Vietnamese: valued abroad, ostracized at home.

The NHMRC fellowship was more than just a grant—it was a battle cry. Securing it was a grueling ascent, reflecting relentless determination and strategic planning in the face of constant rejections. Each application, review, and interview was a nerve-wracking test, highlighting the brutal competition and sometimes cultural biases embedded in the system. Yet, reaching the summit wasn't just personal validation; it was a symbol of breaking barriers within academia. This hard-won award became an encouragement for others to fight for equity and recognition. Now, as I mentor the next generation, I share not just knowledge, but the resilience forged in this crucible. Together, we can transform this competitive landscape, fostering a community where diverse voices fuel innovation and the pursuit of knowledge becomes an inclusive climb for all.

Looking forward, Australia is evolving towards a more inclusive society, with a growing awareness of racial inequities. I hold onto the belief that one day, regardless of race or ethnicity, everyone will find a welcoming and respectful environment in this nation. And for the scientific community, the fight against the "glass ceiling" continues. My story is just a chapter in this ongoing struggle, a demonstration of the resilience and determination of Vietnamese scientists in the face of unseen hurdles. The path may be challenging, but the goal of a truly equitable scientific landscape is a prize worth fighting for.

Chapter Eleven

Climbing the Academic Ladder

They say a professorship at a prestigious university is a pinnacle of achievement, a crown bestowed upon the most esteemed scholars. But the truth, at least for me, was far less glamorous. Back then (2000s), I found contentment in the quiet hum of my research, deriving my greatest satisfaction from the contributions I made to the field of medicine. The title "Professor" wasn't a trophy I chased, but in its whimsical way, chose me. This is the story of how I found myself, unexpectedly, on the winding road towards a professorship in Australia—a journey far more nuanced than the public might imagine. Here, I'll pull back the curtain and reveal the grit, the dedication, and the unexpected turns that truly defined this remarkable chapter in my life.

As you might recall from the previous chapter, I landed a fellowship from the NHMRC in 2007. That felt like a sturdy rung ascended on the precarious ladder of academia. The NHMRC grant meant I wasn't solely reliant on the Garvan Institute for funding, which was a huge weight off my shoulders. Here at the University of New South Wales (now called UNSW Sydney), that ladder stretched before me, a daunting five rungs high. Lecturer, Senior Lecturer, Associate Professor, Full Professor—and then, the distant peak, a title that shimmered with possibility: Distinguished Professor.

Full Professor. It was a title I hadn't necessarily sought, but as life took its unexpected turn, it became a new horizon beckoning me forward. My mentor, Professor John Eisman, was a constant source of encouragement. "With the NHMRC under your belt," he boomed, his laugh echoing through his office, "you're a shoo-in for promotion."

Five years had flown by since I became an Associate Professor. Gazing up at the established "big guys" in the institute, a seed of doubt sprouted in my mind. Am I even qualified? The question echoed persistently like a nagging hum. Full Professor felt like a distant peak, reserved for those who had scaled the academic ladder with seemingly effortless grace.

But John, bless him, saw a different picture. Perhaps he glimpsed a flicker of his own youthful ambition mirrored in my eyes. "Let's get you a meeting with Peter Smith, the Dean," he declared, his practiced fingers already dialing the number. A moment later, John put down the phone, a satisfied grin spreading across his face. "Meeting with Professor Smith, Dean of UNSW Medicine, next Tuesday. Consider it handled." Relief washed over me, mingled with a jolt of nervous anticipation. The climb to Full Professor had just taken its first, unexpected step.

The following week, clutching a hefty preliminary application, I found myself before the imposing oak doors of Dean Peter Smith's office. A friendly-eyed assistant to the dean, a guardian of his time, sat diligently outside the office.

Within the dean's office, I was surprised. It was modest, adorned with framed certificates and awards. The initial questions, however, threw me off guard. "When did you arrive in Australia?" he asked, followed by, "Why did you leave Vietnam?" A series of personal inquiries continued, leaving me bewildered. Where were the expected questions about my research, the impact of my work, and the very things the application showcased? Before I could voice my confusion, our allotted time abruptly ended. Peter rose, a hint of a smile lingering on his lips, as he escorted me out. I left baffled, the weight of the unanswered research questions heavy in my mind.

"Ah, almost forgot!" he called out as I reached for the handle. "You can apply. Good luck!" Then, with a cryptic detail that sent a jolt of nervous energy through me, he added, "Just make sure you submit it under the academic system, not the conjoint one." Relief washed over me—a glimmer of hope after the unexpected detour into my personal history.

"Sounds like an 80% chance," John quipped later, a twinkle in his eye.

The application process itself was a labyrinthine challenge. Alone, I wouldn't have stood a chance. Thankfully, the institute assigned a resourceful librarian, a woman with an eagle eye for detail, to navigate its twists and turns. The final document was a formidable 200+ pages chronicling my academic journey. Ten of my most impactful publications were included, each accompanied by a detailed breakdown of my contribution and its influence on the field. Grant proposals, research awards, invitations to prestigious conferences—the list went on. The librarian, with a dedication that mirrored my own, even unearthed evidence of my efforts to communicate science to the broader public such as appearances on Australian television programs and articles I'd written for mainstream newspapers. A piece I wrote for the *Sydney Morning Herald* about my experiences as a refugee found its way in, adding a human dimension to my profile and showcasing my ability to connect with a wider audience.

Eight copies were required. Eight reviewers scrutinized my work. The university would select four, while the remaining four were my choices. John, ever the strategist, suggested I choose Vietnamese-born professors or those I was familiar with. Unfortunately, Vietnamese professors were still a rarity in Australian academia at that time. Undeterred, he devised a new plan, selecting four luminaries from esteemed institutions in the US—the Mayo Clinic, Johns Hopkins, Stanford, and UCSD, as I later discovered. The university's chosen reviewers remained shrouded in anonymity, adding another layer of intrigue to the process.

The application process was a marathon test of endurance that demanded mountains of paperwork and a surprising number of personal inquiries. The next chapter would reveal the outcome of this academic odyssey, a culmination of years of research, dedication, and the invisible threads of support that had woven their way into the fabric of my career. Would I be deemed worthy of the coveted title of Full Professor? Only time would tell.

Then came the hard news. Six agonizing months later, the university email arrived with the interview date: October 16, 2008. My heart sank. That date was already fixed on my calendar, a day I'd committed months ago to deliver a series of lectures in Hà Nội. Panic clawed its way up my throat. This interview, the culmination of years of research and dedication, a potential turning point in my career, and I'd be absent? How could I explain this glaring gap in my meticulously prepared application to the academic board?

Professor Smith emerged as an unexpected lifeline. Explaining my predicament, my voice laced with desperation, I pleaded for a reschedule. The pre-arranged lecture in Vietnam, the plane tickets, the booked hotel room, the registered participants—all dominoes poised to tumble if the interview date remained fixed. But the dean was unyielding at first. The interview panel, meticulously chosen from across the academic landscape, couldn't be rearranged on a whim. Dejection threatened to engulf me. This opportunity, so painstakingly earned, seemed to be slipping through my grasp.

Finally, after much back-and-forth negotiation, a begrudging concession emerged: a phone interview. Less than ideal, to say the least. The image of the esteemed board members, gathered around a table, scrutinizing my every response through the impersonal barrier of a telephone line, filled me with dread. The fear of being perceived as flippant or unconcerned gnawed at my gut. But options were scarce. With a deep breath and a newfound resolve, I embraced the challenge.

The Garvan Institute rallied around me in those crucial days leading up to the interview. They orchestrated a mock interview, complete with a panel mirroring the real one—a chairperson, a spokesperson, and even professors playing the role of critical reviewers. Questions were anticipated, answers honed to a fine point, and body language meticulously coached. They addressed every detail, from the content of my responses to the art of delivering them in a way that appealed to the board. Most importantly, they urged me to suppress my natural tendency to argue, a well-meaning piece of advice that was profoundly meaningful. By the end of the rehearsal, a newfound confidence flickered within me, replacing the gnawing fear with a steely determination.

On October 14, 2008, Dr. Nguyễn Đình Nguyên, one of my doctoral students at the time, and I embarked on our trip to Hà Nội. The looming phone interview, scheduled for 10:00 AM Sydney time (a punishing 6:00 AM in Vietnam), cast a long shadow. Sleep eluded me that night. By 4:00 AM, restlessness had taken hold, propelling me out of bed. I meticulously reviewed the criteria for promotion, revisiting past lessons learned, and meticulously crafted answers to potential interview questions, transforming my hotel room into a makeshift war room for this academic battle.

The phone rang at precisely 6:00 AM, a jarring intrusion into the pre-dawn quiet. Professor Smith's voice, the Dean of UNSW Medicine, crackled through the receiver from miles away. His opening gambit—a query about Hà Nội's weather—struck me as oddly irrelevant, especially considering the nervous sweat beading on my brow. Thankfully, after a few more innocuous inquiries, he announced the official beginning of the interview.

First came a recitation of the interview rules: my right to object to questions, the limits of the questioner's inquiries (no personal or invasive territory), and the recording of all questions and answers. I was well acquainted with the standard protocol, having served as an interviewer myself. He then formally introduced the panel: eight professors, a diverse group drawn from the various disciplines of medicine (cardiology, endocrinology, neurology, epidemiology, and genetics), science, and even two from the University of Sydney. Eight strangers, I presumed, would ensure a fair and objective assessment. My mentor, while present in the room, could only observe; his voice was silenced during the interview itself. This unexpected twist, a phone interview on foreign soil, had transformed a traditional academic hurdle into a unique and somewhat surreal experience.

The eight professors on the other end of the line launched into their inquiries, a rapid-fire barrage that demanded focused responses within tight time constraints. Unlike the mock interview, their approach was stoic, devoid of commentary, their attention solely on my answers. Some questions stand out in my memory:

- "Why the pursuit of Full Professor? How do you measure yourself against the university's criteria?" This, the sole query from Professor Smith, carried a weight of expectation. Five minutes, they instructed, to condense years of research and dedication into a compelling narrative.

- "Tell us about three of your most impactful research projects. Briefly, the story behind them and their significance." It was a chance to showcase the breadth of my research, the fruits of tireless exploration in the field.

- "Recognition at international conferences? What defines you in your field?" A chance to trumpet my contributions to the global scientific discourse.

- "Authorship breakdown: Lead papers versus collaborations with doctoral students?" This one probed the balance between independent research and nurturing the next generation of scientists.

- "Independence from your mentor, Professor John Eisman?" A question hinting at a potential conflict, one I addressed by highlighting the evolution of our relationship from mentorship to collaborative partnership.

- "A dip in publications between 1999 and 2001?" Explaining the reasons for this temporary slowdown, I emphasized the strategic shift in research focus that ultimately led to more impactful work.

Other inquiries delved into my philosophy on doctoral training, the success of my postdoctoral students (attributing a healthy share of the credit to their own exceptional talents), and the future direction of my research lab. They even touched on the broader landscape of science and health policy, my views on evidence-based medicine, and the ideal trajectory for future medicine.

The limitations of the phone format were evident. The vast distance between Hà Nội and Sydney, combined with the assumed spaciousness of the interview room, resulted in muffled voices. Though protocol granted me the right to request them to speak louder, the awkwardness of my "absence" and the perceived vacation setting of Hà Nội made me hesitate. So, I persevered, straining to catch every word, the phone pressed tight against my ear.

After nearly forty-five minutes, the questioning ceased, a wave of relief washing over me. Minutes later, John called, his voice brimming with congratulations. "You did well," he declared.

While I, too, felt good about my responses, I clung to the belief that a do-over would yield even better results. The interview itself, however, held no surprises. Thorough preparation, courtesy of the university's briefing, had equipped me with the necessary knowledge of the process. A key principle, repeatedly emphasized, was to project an air of equality, to avoid appearing subservient, but most importantly, to never come across as seeking pity. John assured me that I had embodied this principle flawlessly. A hint of arrogance might have crept into a few of my answers, so I thought, but John disagreed, dismissing it as nothing more than a reflection of my confidence in my achievements.

The phone interview, a dramatic departure from the norm, had tested my adaptability and composure. Now, I awaited the verdict, the culmination of a long and arduous journey. Would the coveted title of Full Professor be bestowed upon me, or would I have to face another round of hurdles in the pursuit of this academic pinnacle?

Despite my best efforts, a couple of questions caught me off guard. One inquired about the number of uncited papers. Flustered, I sputtered a response that even my watchful boss recognized as rambling. The true surprise, however, came with the final question—"If you were the Minister of Education..." This wasn't part of the standard interview repertoire, and the notion of holding such a lofty position had never crossed my mind. A refugee would become a minister? No, I think. Later, it dawned on me—that question was a leadership test in disguise. In their eyes, a professor wasn't just an academic, but a leader, someone prepared for any challenge. I stammered through an answer, unsure of its effectiveness.

Overall, the interview felt less adversarial compared to the NHMRC fellowship grilling. The atmosphere, although I couldn't see it, seemed cordial, and opportunities were offered for clarification and justification. Two interviewers, however, adopted a more pointed approach. They scrutinized my publication chart, demanded a quantifiable measure of my independence, and even went so far as to suggest my achievements might be solely the work of my students, or perhaps mere credit-grabbing on behalf of my boss. These, I viewed as opportunities—a chance to elaborate, to turn weaknesses into strengths, as my grandparents would have said.

With the interview behind me, I dove back into my teaching schedule, pushing the experience to the back of my mind. After completing my lectures in Hà Nội, I returned to Sydney and resumed my routine work, deliberately setting aside the anticipation of good or bad news.

One morning in November 2008, I was chatting with the friendly receptionist at the Garvan Institute. Suddenly, Professor John Shine, the institute's director, materialized. Placing a reassuring hand on my shoulder, he declared, "It's all done, just waiting for the official announcement."

Bewildered, I tried to decipher his cryptic message. Professor Shine, sensing my confusion, clarified. It was about the promotion. He had just received a call from Professor Peter Smith, confirming my ascension to the rank of Full Professor. This year, the Garvan Institute boasted two newly minted full professors, and I was one of them!

A formal letter arrived in early December 2008, dated November 28th. It bore the official insignia of the University of New South Wales and the signature of Vice-Chancellor Fred Hilmer. The weight of the words within would forever etch themselves in my memory:

"Dear Tuan

I am pleased to advise you that I have approved the recommendation of the Qualifications Committee that you be promoted to Professor with effect from 1 January 2009.

You were recommended for promotion by your Faculty Promotions Committee, which itself shows the high regard in which you are held by your peers, and I am happy to say that this was endorsed by the University Promotions Committee.

Promotion to Professor at UNSW is a significant achievement, given the standard of scholarly work and effort reflected in the criteria. Please accept my warmest congratulations. I look forward to hearing more of your outstanding achievements in the years ahead.

Yours sincerely
Fred G. Hilmer
Vice-Chancellor"

The weight of the words settled on me, heavier than the years of research condensed into its pages. It was the culmination of an odyssey that began far from the lab, a journey etched in the memory of a refugee escaping a war-torn homeland. A simple sentence, yet one that encapsulated a momentous transformation. I am a Professor now.

The university's media team, ever opportunistic, saw a story in my background. The first Vietnamese-Australian Full Professor at UNSW was, they enthused, a story ripe for the picking. But I declined. Part of it was the lingering unease of public fanfare, the harsh glare of television lights. Public appearances have always left me with a lingering discomfort. But more importantly, the refugee label never felt like the defining factor.

The promotion marked a pivotal point in my career. It wasn't just about the title or the recognition; it was about the doors it opened. The ability to attract brighter doctoral students, to secure larger research grants, and to collaborate with esteemed colleagues on a global scale—these were the opportunities that now awaited me. Professor. The word held a weight of responsibility, a call to not only excel in my own research but to inspire and guide the next generation of scientific minds. The journey to Full Professor had been arduous, filled with challenges and triumphs alike. But as I stood at this new threshold, I couldn't help but feel a surge of excitement for the uncharted territory that lay ahead.

Beyond Professorship: The Fellowship Honor

The word "Academy" whispered promises of prestige even in my cramped student dorm in Vietnam. News of Vietnamese scientists elected to the *Académie Française* was met with national fanfare, highlighting the pinnacle of scientific achievement. Back then, the idea of being part of such a prestigious institution felt like a distant dream, a shimmering mirage in the harsh desert of reality.

Fast forward to my years as a researcher in Australia. A seemingly ordinary visit to my mentor, Professor John Eisman, turned into a life-altering moment. We were dissecting the latest research paper when he pivoted abruptly, a mischievous glint in his eye. "The Academy of Health and Medical Sciences," he declared, pronouncing each word with reverence. "Why haven't you applied?"

The Australian Academy of Health and Medical Sciences (AAHMS) is the *crème de la crème* of Australian medical science. Membership felt like an impossible dream. My initial reaction was a scoff of disbelief. But Professor Eisman, ever the wise guide, countered with a simple yet profound truth: "No knock, no answer." His belief, coupled with the undeniable allure of the challenge, ignited a spark within me. He even offered to be my Sherpa on this daunting climb, his guidance a lifeline in the face of the complex application process.

Professor Eisman's words hung heavy in the air long after our meeting. The ensuing months were a masterclass in self-discovery intertwined with an exploration of the AAHMS's lofty ideals. I spent countless hours delving into their website, their pronouncements a beacon guiding me towards a deeper understanding of their mission. This wasn't just about the shiny badge of Fellowship; it was about aligning myself with a collective dedicated to revolutionizing healthcare in Australia.

The criteria for Fellowship, however, were a daunting Everest. Exceptional leadership in my field? Check, but could it be considered truly exceptional? Ongoing engagement with healthcare issues? Absolutely, but were these contributions impactful enough? Each bullet point felt like a summit I had to conquer, and self-doubt, that unwelcome companion, began to whisper its insidious doubts.

To silence those whispers, I embarked on a quest to understand the esteemed company I aspired to join. I meticulously researched past Fellows, each name an indicator of brilliance. Their groundbreaking research, impactful contributions, and dedication to advancing the field both nationally and internationally became my guiding stars. Each story ignited a spark of inspiration, but also a sobering realization: the path ahead wasn't paved solely with my own accomplishments, but with the recognition and endorsement of my peers.

The application process itself became another revelation. Unlike other accolades, Fellowship wasn't simply a matter of submitting a self-congratulatory resume. No, this honor demanded a different kind of validation—a nomination from within the AAHMS itself. This realization struck a chord deep within me. It was a humbling reminder that the Fellowship wasn't just about my own achievements, but about earning the respect and recognition of my colleagues, the very community I aspired to join. It was a hurdle, yes, but one that only magnified the significance of the Fellowship itself.

Buoyed by the unexpected momentum, I wasted no time scheduling another meeting with Professor Eisman. His office, once a source of nervous anticipation, now felt like a launching pad for the next phase of my journey. The news I delivered—my burgeoning desire to apply for the AAHMS Fellowship—was met with a warm smile and a hearty congratulations. Relief washed over me as Professor Eisman readily agreed to be my nominator. His support was a cornerstone upon which I could build my case.

But even as I basked in the afterglow of his acceptance, Professor Eisman threw down a new gauntlet. "There's another hurdle, my friend," he said, his tone turning serious. "The nomination needs to be accompanied by recommendations from four external reviewers, and at least two must hail from prestigious institutions overseas." I could easily come up with a list of four potential reviewers, and Professor Eisman agreed.

The application was a series of forms meticulously documenting my research odyssey. It wasn't just a laundry list of publications; it was about weaving a narrative of how my work impacted global health. Did my research translate into better patient outcomes? Did it pave the way for future breakthroughs? Each question demanded a compelling response, forcing me to revisit not just the "what" but also the "why" of my scientific journey.

Another document meticulously detailed my contributions beyond the lab—my leadership roles, mentorship of budding scientists, and efforts to bridge the gap between research and public understanding. Here, the focus shifted from the intricacies of my research to its ripple effects on the broader medical landscape.

Finally, a concise explanation of my twenty most impactful research papers, written for a lay audience. This, I discovered, was a humbling exercise in translation. Years of complex research had to be condensed into clear, concise language, accessible to anyone with a curious mind. In the process, it wasn't just the public I was educating; I was rediscovering the core motivations that first propelled me into the world of science.

With the completed dossier in hand, I sought the expert eye of Professor Ken Ho, an esteemed colleague at the Garvan Institute and a fellow of AAHMS. His feedback, delivered within two short days, was refreshingly succinct: "You don't need any window dressing. Go ahead with the current version." His words were a vote of confidence, a green light that propelled me forward.

Professor Eisman, ever the champion, used the finalized dossier to formally nominate me in October 2018. The application process, with its challenges and revelations, was complete. Now, the waiting game began, a period filled with nervous anticipation as my fate rested in the hands of the AAHMS selection committee.

With the application submitted, a nerve-wracking waiting game began. The weeks stretched into an agonizing test of my patience. Each day felt like an eternity, the silence deafening as I awaited the AAHMS selection committee's decision. My fate hung in their hands. Discouraging rumors about high first-round rejection rates swirled in my head, tempering my hope with a dose of realism.

However, life occasionally brings surprises. Then, on a freezing July 31, 2019, an envelope arrived, bearing the official seal of the AAHMS. My heart pounded as I tore it open. The crisp letter within was signed by none other than Professor Ian Frazer, my scientific hero and President of the Academy. The words that followed were nothing short of a dream come true:

"Dear Professor Nguyen,

In recognition of the important contribution you have made to health and medical research in Australia, I am delighted to inform you that the Academy's Council has ratified your election to Fellowship of the Australian Academy of Health and

Medical Sciences. May I be the first to congratulate you on behalf of the Council and Fellowship."

A pinnacle moment: Professor Ian Frazer, President of the Academy of Health and Medical Sciences, bestowing the prestigious fellowship upon me—honored, humbled, and ready to pay it forward in the pursuit of better health for all.

A wave of emotions washed over me—relief, pride, and a profound sense of gratitude. This wasn't just an honor bestowed upon me; it was a validation of my life's work, a recognition of the impact my research had on the world stage.

Confidentiality was paramount until the official announcement at the Academy's Annual General and Scientific Meeting in Perth. The anticipation simmered for weeks, the knowledge of my Fellowship a closely guarded secret. But October 10 finally arrived, ushering in a whirlwind of celebratory events.

The gala that evening was a culmination of years of dedication. As I received my Fellowship certificate from Professor Frazer, a sense of accomplishment swept over me. Signing the Fellowship Book, I joined a lineage of esteemed scientists, forever etching my name in the Academy's history.

News of my election spread quite quickly. The university was happy, and a wave of congratulatory messages flooded my inbox. Among them, a particularly heartwarming letter from Professor Nicholas Fisk, Deputy Vice-Chancellor of the University of New South Wales, extended his congratulations on my election to the Academy. His letter read:

"Professor Tuan Nguyen FAHMS
Garvan Institute of Medical Research
Dear Tuan,
RE: Election to the Fellowship of the Australian Academy of Health & Medical Sciences
Congratulations on being elected to the fellowship of the Australian Academy of Health & Medical Sciences for 2019. This is wonderful recognition of your research and scholastic achievements, as well as your high standing in the field.
I know that I speak for the Vice-Chancellor when I say that we are very proud of you having been recognised by your peers in this way.
Kind regards,
Professor Nicholas Fisk FAHMS
Deputy Vice-Chancellor (Research)"

Later, I learned that I was not only one of forty new Fellows, but also the first Vietnamese member ever elected to the Academy. The Vice-Chancellor and President of my University, Professor Ian Jacobs, was also a new Fellow.

The Academy's Fellowship wasn't just about prestige; it was about belonging to a community of brilliant minds, united by a common purpose—to push the boundaries of science and improve human health. It wasn't the end of my journey, but a thrilling new chapter, brimming with opportunities for collaboration, discovery, and the chance to inspire the next generation of medical pioneers. This was my chance to not only contribute to the advancement of science but also to leave a lasting legacy for years to come.

While election to the Academy of Health and Medical Sciences carried immense prestige, it wasn't accompanied by a hefty paycheck. In fact, membership came with annual dues. Fortunately, the university, recognizing the honor bestowed upon them through my election, graciously covered this cost.

A Fellowship Among Australia's Elites

In 2022, the University of Technology Sydney (UTS) bestowed upon me a singular honor: a nomination for the Royal Society of New South Wales (RSNSW). Founded in 1821, the RSNSW stands as the oldest learned society in Australia, mirroring the prestigious Royal Society of England. Originally christened the 'Philosophical Society of Australia," it served as a forum for esteemed figures to engage in intellectual discourse on lofty subjects. By 1866, Queen Victoria herself bestowed the royal seal of approval, and the Royal Society was born. Today, this venerable institution has proudly stood for three centuries.

Unlike learned societies in socialist countries, their Western counterparts, like those in Australia, the US, and the UK, play a vital role as scientific advocates. The term "advocacy" doesn't fully capture their essence. Imagine a chorus of accomplished voices, united in their dedication to championing scientific causes. These societies advise governments and the broader community on scientific matters, ensuring informed decision-making. To fulfill this critical advisory role, membership is reserved for accomplished scientists—an election to a learned society signifies both honor and recognition.

The RSNSW is a veritable who's who of Australian excellence, encompassing science, medicine, arts, and humanities. Attending the induction ceremony felt surreal, a chance to rub shoulders with the very figures I'd revered for years. Many displayed medals on their chests, showcasing their distinguished careers in government, the military, science, industry, and community service. The gathering skewed male and, shall we say, seasoned. While I wouldn't call myself old, the majority of Fellows were my seniors. It was a humbling experience, a potent reminder of the giants upon whose shoulders I stood.

UTS, recognizing my contributions to Australia, encouraged me to apply with their full backing. Why not? I thought, and they expertly navigated the nomination and evaluation process, a task that was less complex than the challenges faced with AAHMS. After nearly a year of scrutiny, the RSNSW proudly announced my election as a Fellow. The news graced the institute's newsletter in April 2022, and from that day forward, FRSN became a proud addition to my name. More importantly, I etched my name in history as the first Vietnamese-origin Fellow in the RSNSW's distinguished 300-year legacy.

The day of my election brought a wave of heartwarming congratulations. The UTS Vice-Chancellor, a Fellow himself and formerly of UNSW, sent a particularly kind note. It was truly a delightful gesture. But beyond the personal accolades, a sense of responsibility settled upon me. As a newly minted Fellow, contemplation naturally turned towards the future: what contributions could I make?

I decided that my voice would champion medical research and its challenges. I envisioned myself representing my colleagues, advocating for their plight in the face of federal government policies that often seemed shortsighted or underfunded. Research is the lifeblood of medical progress, and its continued advancement requires support. The RSNSW platform offered a powerful amplifier for these concerns.

Another cause close to my heart—the horrific invasion of Ukraine—would also find a voice through the RSNSW. Science thrives on international collaboration, and this barbaric act of aggression threatens the very fabric of scientific progress. Whenever possible, I would leverage the Society's influence to condemn the violence and advocate for peace.

This esteemed institution offered a powerful platform to speak for those who couldn't speak for themselves, and the opportunity humbled me. It wasn't just about scientific advocacy; it was about using my voice for the greater good.

The year 2022 marked a significant milestone—forty years since I set foot in Australia. While "homeland" might ring with sentimentality, for four decades, Australia has undoubtedly become my second home, a place I plan to remain for the rest of my life. Forty years may seem like a vast stretch of time, but looking back, it feels like a fleeting moment. A young man when I arrived, I now find myself on the cusp of autumn. The journey has been exhilarating, filled with challenges and triumphs alike.

On March 28, 2022, my boss, Professor Andrew Parfitt, Vice-Chancellor and President of the University of Technology Sydney, extended his congratulations on my election to the Society. His letter read:

"Dr Tuan van Nguyen AM
Professor Of Predictive Medicine
School of Biomedical Engineering
University of Technology Sydney
Dear Tuan,
RE: Appointment as Fellow of the Royal Society of New South Wales
Congratulations on being appointed a Fellow of the Royal Society of New South Wales, for your significant contributions to osteoporosis research nationally and internationally.

Receiving this honour is a fantastic achievement and a testament to your academic and professional excellence. Your research in fracture risk assessment is improving the lives of individuals around the world.

The success and impact of our university are in no small part due to the hard work of our staff to advance knowledge and learning and on behalf of the entire UTS community, I thank you for the role you play in this.

I wish you all the very best in your upcoming research, and I look forward to hearing about your future successes.

Yours sincerely,
Professor Andrew Parfitt FTSE, FIEAust
Vice-Chancellor and President"

Over four decades, Vietnamese immigrants have become an integral part of Australian society. From the halls of academia to the halls of government, refugees have carved an indelible mark on nearly every facet of life here. I like to believe my journey is a small contribution to that, a contribution that has brought a flicker of glory to my adopted home on the world stage. The beauty of belonging to two homelands lies in how achievements in one echo in the other. The name Nguyễn forever binds me to both Việt Nam, the land of my birth, and Australia, the land of my rebirth.

Forty years ago, I arrived as a "boat person," a term often freighted with negativity. Back then, the concept of accolades or honors was a distant dream. Yet, here I stand, four decades later, a "boat person" no more, but a proud member of the esteemed New South Wales learned society. It was a fleeting moment, etched in time, yet the culmination of a long and arduous journey—a reflection of resilience, dedication, and the relentless pursuit of knowledge.

This prestigious Fellowship wasn't just a personal triumph; it was a powerful symbol of the transformative power of opportunity. A beacon of hope for refugees and immigrants everywhere, it whispered a message: that against all odds, a new life and a new beginning was indeed possible. And within that new life, the chance to excel, to contribute, and to leave a lasting legacy.

As I look back on my journey to becoming a Full Professor and securing prestigious fellowships, I realize that academic success is rarely a straightforward path. It's a demanding journey filled with twists and turns. As a Vietnamese refugee, I learned early on that I had to work harder than most to level the playing field in my new home.

From the initial steps of securing funding and understanding institutional hierarchies to the final, nerve-wracking moments of an interview, each stage demanded resilience, dedication, and strategic thinking. The support from mentors and colleagues, coupled with my relentless pursuit of excellence, paved the way for my eventual recognition and honors. This journey not only solidified my place within the academic community but also underscored the importance of perseverance and the transformative power of mentorship.

Frankly, titles and accolades are mere footnotes; the real reward lies in the journey itself. It's about witnessing a mentee blossom, a spark of curiosity growing into a roaring fire of scientific exploration. It's about fostering a scientific culture, where ideas bounce off each other like excited children, igniting innovation. This is the essence of academia—a shared quest for knowledge, a legacy that extends far beyond individual achievements. As I continue my research on osteoporosis,

I'm not just building my own career; I'm laying the foundation for the next generation of scientists, lighting the path for them to explore the unknown.

Chapter Twelve

Transformative Years

The year 2024 marked a decade of my affiliation with the University of Technology Sydney (UTS). UTS, though a young university by Australian standards, boasts a rich history, morphing from the New South Wales Institute of Technology (NSWIT) in 1988. Despite its relatively young age, UTS has carved a niche for itself as a leading research university, both nationally and globally. In Australia, it ranks a respectable seventh, trailing only slightly behind the University of Queensland's sixth place (THE ranking 2026). Globally, the QS World University Rankings for 2025 place UTS at an impressive eighty-eighth position. Today, it thrives by shaping the future of over 40,000 students.

My association with UTS began in 2014 with a phone call. Professor Nguyễn Thế Hùng, , whom I affectionately call Hùng, reached out from his position as Dean of the Faculty of Engineering and Information Technology (FEIT). Hùng, a fellow Vietnamese and a highly respected figure in the Australian academic community, spoke in his characteristically soft and gentle manner. He proposed a novel idea: joining UTS as a part-time faculty.

At the time, I had been firmly established at the Garvan Institute, a full professor at the University of New South Wales, already a powerhouse in Australian and global academia. I was also a conjoint professor of the University of Notre

Dame Australia. Another university affiliation seemed unnecessary. I voiced this hesitation, requesting a week to mull it over.

Hùng persisted, presenting a compelling argument. Universities, he explained, offered a degree of stability compared to research institutes. The ever-present threat of funding cuts and layoffs that haunted research institutes wasn't a concern at universities. He hit a nerve. In the world of research, funding is the lifeblood; a brilliant idea withers without financial backing. His logic appealed to me, and I agreed to join UTS as a part-time faculty. The Garvan Institute, surprisingly, welcomed the arrangement. This collaboration allowed them to shed some of the financial burden (now borne by UTS) while retaining ownership of my research—a clever solution indeed!

February 2014 marked the beginning of my affiliation with UTS. Initially, the notion of a "Distinguished Professor"—the highest academic title in Australia—was floated by Hùng. However, after a few months, this path diverged. The university stipulated that such a prestigious title was reserved for full-time faculty with a minimum five-year contribution. I wasn't fazed. To me, titles were ephemeral or fleeting accolades compared to the lasting impact of one's achievements. Titles, like clothes, are subject to change like impermanent adornments.

The Chancellor's Medal of Exceptional Research

The years at the Garvan had been marked by intense research efforts and the gratifying recognition of external awards. Stepping into the bustling world of UTS, I discovered their own system of accolades, a glittering constellation recognizing all sorts of achievements. One evening, at an award ceremony alive with anticipation, I browsed the program. There were prizes for rising stars in research, established faculty who'd shaped the academic landscape, educational leaders, and even dedicated service staff—the unsung heroes of the university.

A kind colleague nudged me with a smile. "Why not go for the highest honor, the Chancellor's Medal of Exceptional Research?" Her words struck a chord, a quiet challenge that ignited the competitive fire that had always flickered within me.

Diving into the application criteria, I felt a surge of purpose. It demanded a sustained track record of excellence, impactful publications that had sparked dialogues in respected journals, demonstrable societal contributions that went beyond the ivory tower, and evidence of competitive funding that validated the significance of my research. Reviewing my work at UTS, a sense of satisfaction washed over me. It all fit. Each criterion aligned perfectly with the path I'd carved at this new institution.

With the enthusiastic support of the head of school and dean , I crafted my application in 2017. It was a meticulous process, demanding a clear narrative that showcased the impact of my research. The following months were a slow burn of anticipation. A rigorous selection process unfolded as external professors scrutinized my work and a UTS panel carefully evaluated the application. Six agonizing months later, the news arrived in a crisp email: I was shortlisted for the medal! The wait intensified, as only the award committee held the key to who would be bestowed the ultimate honor.

The ceremony night buzzed with a nervous energy. My boss, the deputy vice-chancellor for research, took the stage as the MC, her voice carrying weight as she announced each award and its nominees. My category, the most prestigious of the evening, was saved for last. Mingling with colleagues, the possibility of winning gradually faded from my mind, replaced by the joy of being shortlisted amongst such esteemed colleagues.

Suddenly, my name pierced the excited chatter. I had won the medal! Elation washed over me, a wave of vindication for the countless hours poured into my research. As I stepped onto the stage, a kaleidoscope of emotions swirled within me: gratitude, pride, and a renewed sense of purpose to share a few words with the captivated audience. Taking a deep breath, I focused on expressing my heartfelt thanks. I acknowledged the incredible support system at UTS, the brilliant minds who collaborated with me, and the dedication of my students. It was a victory not just for me, but for the collective effort that propelled this research forward.

"Friends and colleagues:

Wow, this is a real bone of contention! I'm incredibly honored to receive the Chancellor's Medal for Exceptional Research. It's humbling to be recognized for my work in personalized fracture risk assessment. Let's just say, this award feels like the culmination of years spent obsessing over all things bone-related. I may have driven my family a little crazy explaining bone density at every dinner table, but hey, at least they all know their risk factors now!

This medal is a testament to the amazing team I've had the privilege to work with, and of course, to all the tireless volunteers who participated in our research. Here's to building a stronger future, one healthy bone at a time!"

Looking out at the sea of proud faces, I couldn't help but reminisce. The journey to this stage had been long and arduous. There were moments of doubt and setbacks that threatened to derail my progress. But the passion for osteoporosis research, the desire to make a tangible difference in people's lives, had always guided me forward. This award, then, became more than just a recognition of past achievements. It was a powerful validation, a beacon that illuminated the path ahead.

I concluded my speech by saying, "In all seriousness, this is a tremendous honor. Thank you to the committee for recognizing the importance of this research. Here's to building stronger bones, and even stronger research in the future!'

Holding the Chancellor's Medal, a symbol of exceptional research, I knew this was a defining moment in my career. The weight of the medal wasn't just metal; it was the responsibility to continue pushing boundaries, to delve deeper into the complexities of osteoporosis, and ultimately, to translate research into real-world solutions that could improve the lives of millions. It was a responsibility I embraced with newfound fervor, the fire of curiosity and dedication burning brighter than ever before.

The end of 2021 brought another decision point. After a fruitful thirty years with the Garvan Institute, I opted to join UTS full-time. Parting with a place woven into the fabric of my professional and scientific life was an emotional step. But as the saying goes, "No one steps into the same river twice." Change is inevitable.

My joining UTS coincided with an exciting new opportunity for Hùng—, a deputy vice-chancellor position at Swinburne University. During his tenure, Hùngestablished the Centre for Health Technologies at UTS. With his departure, the director's position became vacant. The mantle fell upon me, and I set about revitalizing the center, ensuring its continued development to this day.

My journey with UTS has been one of collaboration, growth, and a bridge between two esteemed institutions. It's a sign of the interconnectedness of the academic world, where knowledge flows freely between institutions, fostering innovation and progress. And as I look towards the future, I eagerly anticipate the next chapter UTS and I will write together.

Distinguished Professorship

As 2021 drew to a close, a colleague at UTS, perhaps sensing a shift in my perspective, gently nudged me to reconsider the "Distinguished Professor" title. Time, the great healer, had softened the sting of the earlier rejection. Their encouragement, coupled with a renewed sense of belonging at UTS, sparked a renewed interest in the title. This time, the application process felt less like a hurdle and more like a chance to tell the story of my academic journey.

The application was a methodically crafted narrative itself. My curriculum vitae, a hefty tome, served as the foundation, chronicling my academic achievements. Documented leadership roles within the field and contributions to professional societies painted a picture of my active engagement with the broader scientific community. A meticulously crafted ten-page self-assessment went beyond merely enumerating publications. It delved into the impact of my work, the problems I tackled, and the advancements I helped pioneer. Ten select research papers, chosen with utmost care, were presented like prized jewels, each a reflection of years of dedicated research. Finally, letters of support arrived from esteemed colleagues outside UTS's walls, their words a chorus of endorsement for my work. The icing on the cake? A glowing recommendation from my department head—an indication of my achievements and the collaborative spirit that thrived within UTS.

The application embarked on a six-month odyssey, evaluated by four external experts, two even hailing from prestigious universities ranked within the top one hundred globally. The wait was filled with a mix of anticipation and nervous energy. Finally, the long-awaited news arrived: I had been appointed "Distinguished Professor!" But the significance of the achievement went far beyond the title itself. Not only did it mark a personal milestone, but it also made me the first Vietnamese-origin individual to hold this title at UTS. The weight of history settled upon me, a sense of responsibility to lead the way for others who might follow in my footsteps, to serve as a symbol of hope and determination, especially for young Vietnamese immigrants adjusting to the complexities of academia in a new land.

The vice-chancellor's letter, dated April 29, 2022, arrived with a flourish. Its contents were the formal confirmation of this significant achievement. But beyond the official pronouncements, it represented a culmination of the countless hours poured into research, the dedication to innovation that fueled my nights, and the pursuit of knowledge that had been the driving force of my life. It wasn't just about personal validation; it was a validation of the long and winding path that brought me to UTS, to Australia, and ultimately, to this remarkable moment. This prestigious title wasn't just an honor bestowed upon an individual; it was a symbol of the transformative power of opportunity, evidence of the resilience and determination of a young man who arrived in Australia on a boat, and against all odds, carved a niche for himself in the world of Australian science.

"Dear Tuan,

Appointment to Distinguished Professor

I am delighted to inform you that your nomination for appointment to the position of Distinguished Professor has been successful.

The panel was impressed by your internationally recognised research and reputation. In your role as Distinguished Professor, the panel would like to see you take on greater leadership responsibilities as would be expected of a distinguished professor.

As outlined in the Procedures for the Appointment of Distinguished Professor, a Distinguished Professor is recognised for their contribution towards achieving the UTS vision of becoming a world-leading university of technology. Distinguished Professors must also work to enhance the academic profile and reputation of UTS. Accordingly, recognition of your achievements through this promotion comes with an obligation to ensure that you continue to positively promote a culture of excellence and collegiality within UTS and contribute to building the reputation of UTS within and beyond the communities with which you engage.

I look forward to working with you and the other Distinguished Professors to build the academic leadership we need to achieve the vision for UTS as a public university of technology.

I would like to thank you for your contribution to the University and congratulate you on your successful appointment.

Professor Andrew Parfitt
Vice-Chancellor and President"

My UTS appointment, I later learned, wasn't merely an acquisition of talent, but a strategic investment. Teaching, though a cornerstone of academia, wasn't the primary focus. Instead, UTS envisioned me as a catalyst, someone who could attract the very fuel that propels academic progress: research funding. My established expertise and the citation count of my research publications wouldn't just bolster UTS's internal research prowess but also elevate their standing in the coveted global university rankings. It was a chess move, one where my established impact could draw not only recognition, but also the resources needed to push the boundaries of knowledge.

Looking back, I can confidently say I fulfilled that strategic vision. During my tenure at UTS, I spearheaded the acquisition of millions of dollars in research funding. These funds weren't mere numbers; they were the lifeblood of groundbreaking projects, the fuel for late nights spent poring over data, and the seed money for ambitious new ideas. My publications, meanwhile, soared to the top of the citation charts, making me one of the most-cited professors at UTS.

While the global university rankings are a complex dance of metrics that can feel somewhat arbitrary at times, I believe that UTS's impressive climb of ten positions to a commendable ninetieth place was partly propelled by the collective efforts of my dedicated colleagues and me. And for me, it was deeply gratifying to contribute to UTS's ascent, a place that had become an integral part of my academic journey. It was a symbiotic relationship; UTS provided the platform for my research to flourish, and in turn, my work helped elevate the university's standing on the global stage. It was a perfect example of how strategic investment can lead to remarkable achievements.

Chapter Thirteen

Nurturing the Next Generation

Science, for all its pursuit of objective truth, can be a surprisingly rigid world. During my doctoral years, the hierarchy was formidable, with senior researchers holding an almost mythical status. As my expertise grew, I found myself drawn to a different aspect of academia: guiding future generations. In nurturing bright, curious minds, I discovered a unique kind of satisfaction. However, the path to becoming a mentor was not simply about intellectual exchange; the undercurrent of prejudice and bureaucracy made this hierarchical world more complex.

Nurturing Minds: A Legacy Beyond Research

I always enjoy teaching and mentoring because I believe it is an excellent way for me to learn. Though I never received formal training in pedagogy, the desire to ignite curiosity in, and transmit knowledge to, young minds burned fiercely within me. From my early days in Việt Nam to now, nearly five decades have passed. Each year is filled with the energy of eager students. High school classrooms thrummed with youthful energy as I unveiled the intricacies of math and science. However, universities became my true calling, offering a stage for profound explorations into the mysteries of knowledge.

In the early 1980s, arriving in Australia with a strong urge to help young kids, having just stepped off the boat, so to speak, I found support at Bass Hill Primary School. The school generously provided a free classroom every weekend. For over ten years, I have conducted math and science tutorials for up to one hundred students at a time, including both refugees and local students. Despite grappling with limited English proficiency, our steadfast determination guided us through the complexities of these subjects in the Australian context. The truest measure of success, the wellspring of my deepest joy, resided in the triumphs of my students. High school students, once drowning in the complexities of math, blossomed into confident test-takers, equipped to tackle the highest levels. Witnessing such transformations and empowering them to forge their own destinies was a gift beyond measure.

The years at the university unfolded like a rich fabric woven from diverse threads. From a humble tutor to a professor, my path led me to guide doctoral dissertations, each one a unique voyage of discovery. Direct classroom instruction took a backseat, but mentorship blossomed, nurturing young researchers in their formative years. My laboratory teemed with a vibrant multicultural energy. Australian students mingled with research students from Sweden, China, Hong Kong, Taiwan, Iran, Thái Lan, and Việt Nam—a melting pot of brilliance. Each interaction became a learning experience, a chance to broaden my horizons through their unique perspectives. Even political tensions, like the simmering conflict between Việt Nam and China, became opportunities for understanding. I gathered my students, a microcosm of the global community, and fostered open dialogue, fostering empathy above all else.

With doctoral students, the joy transcended passing grades. To see them blossom into independent scientists, surpassing even myself in their expertise, was the ultimate reward. Their groundbreaking research, published in high-profile journals, their successful graduations, their postdoctoral positions at prestigious institutions—these milestones echoed an old Vietnamese metaphor I held dear: a "soul engineer." Indeed, I had sculpted minds, nurtured potential, and equipped them to build the future of science.

While I cherished students from all walks of life, four individuals stand out: Dr. Nguyễn Đình Nguyên, Dr. Steven Frost, Dr. Trần Hoàng Ngọc Bích, and Dr. Hồ Lê Phương Thảo. Their journeys, each unique yet intertwined with mine, are tributes to the boundless potential of the human spirit. From aspiring doctors to accomplished geneticists, they embodied the transformative power of education, not just for themselves, but for the scientific community at large.

The corridors of the Garvan Institute buzzed with the fervent energy of scientific inquiry. As a lone Vietnamese researcher, I often felt a pang of isolation. Then, fate intervened, sending Dr. Nguyễn Đình Nguyên waltzing into my lab. His initial interview seemed less than promising, a CV adorned with a few publications in "average journals." But a spark flickered in his eyes, an insatiable hunger for knowledge that mirrored my own. Overlooking the limitations on paper, my boss, Professor John Eisman, and I saw a potential that pulsed with promise.

Nguyên, a beacon of Vietnamese dedication, proved us a thousand times over. Fueled by his ardent thirst for learning and determination, our decade of collaboration yielded groundbreaking research. Working side-by-side, we etched our names into the annals of bone and mineral research, a spirit of collaboration that birthed groundbreaking works. The aptly named "Nguyễn's Model," a testament to our shared surname, became a cornerstone in the field. This scientific odyssey culminated in a delightful conference anecdote: a Canadian colleague mistaking us for father and son, a humorous reminder of the bonds forged in the pursuit of knowledge.

In the annals of our laboratory's history, Steven Frost's arrival stands as a serendipitous twist. It was a day like any other when Nguyên, one of my students, casually mentioned, "There's an Aussie fellow who's keen to join us. Says he's sharp as a tack. Fancy a chat with him?" In the midst of managing my numerous responsibilities, balancing multiple projects, delving into the complex fields of genetics and the epidemiology of fractures, I found myself nodding in assent. And so it was arranged.

Dr. Nguyễn Đình Nguyên earned a PhD in Medicine from UNSW.

My initial encounter with Steven unfolded in the usual manner, devoid of any premonition of the significant collaboration that lay ahead. He presented himself as a courteous yet assured individual fresh from completing his Master of Public Health. Though the realm of bone research was foreign to him, I impressed upon him the singular focus of our lab. And thus, it was decreed that his path forward would be paved with osteoporosis pursuits. Steven, in his capacity as a self-funded research student, officially became a member of our lab. The University of New South Wales, in its wisdom, sanctioned his enrollment as a part-time student, granting him a generous six-year window to weave his thesis.

In the nascent stages of his tenure, Steven's progress was measured, a slow but steady cadence. Yet, as the years unfurled, he etched his mark upon the annals of our research endeavors. Our collective curiosity had fixated upon the elusive realm of hip fracture prediction, transcending the conventional parameters of bone mineral density. Armed with the arcane weaponry of Bayesian inference, Steven undertook the formidable task of integrating disparate factors into a cohesive predictive model. Thus was born a tool of prognostication, a beacon guiding our understanding of hip fracture risks.

Drawing on his experience as a practicing nurse, Steven harbored a singular ambition: to redefine the temporal rhythms of bone mineral density remeasurement. In a landscape where convention dictated a standardized two-year interval, devoid of empirical grounding, he sought a more nuanced approach. Leveraging the rich data from the Dubbo Study, Steven meticulously crafted a model, distilled to its essence—gender, age, and prevailing bone mineral density—heralding an important shift in guidelines governing bone health assessments. Steven Frost's journey within our midst, a narrative imbued with tenacity and innovation.

Dr. Nguyên and Steven were not an "anomaly." The scientific universe conspired to send me another gem—Dr. Trần Hoàng Ngọc Bích. Bích exuded a vibrant energy, yet her scientific acumen called for refinement, while her fluency in English seemed to flutter with the breeze. But beneath the surface resided a fierce independence and the raw power of a burgeoning geneticist. Nguyên's clinical expertise and Bích's genetic prowess formed a perfect storm, propelling us into the burgeoning field of genetic profiling.

Budgetary constraints forced us to be resourceful—whole-genome analysis was a distant dream. But with a hefty dose of creativity, we used simulations, paving the way for the polygenic risk score (PRS) research that dominates today. Bích's defining moment arrived at the ASBMR conference, a scientific mecca. Our meticulous rehearsals paid off; her opening remarks were smooth and confident. But the Q&A took an unexpected turn. A Dutch colleague's question on study replication tripped her up, and the auditorium erupted in laughter. Flustered, Bích stood at the podium, a baptism by fire if ever there was one.

But fate, ever the jester, had another twist in store. The same Dutch professor, charmed by Bích's scientific prowess despite the language hiccup, offered her a postdoctoral fellowship in his European lab. An awkward presentation morphed into a career-defining opportunity! Today, Dr. Bích, adorned with prestigious awards, is a reflection of the dedication and intellectual prowess of a true diamond in the rough.

These serendipitous encounters with brilliant minds weren't mere blips on the scientific radar. They represent the cornerstone of my journey at the Garvan Institute. These students, with their dedication and thirst for knowledge, are the true legacy I leave behind.

My transition to the University of Technology Sydney (UTS) marked a new chapter, one I'll delve into later. There, I encountered Dr. Hồ Lê Phương Thảo, another serendipitous meeting. Freshly arrived from Việt Nam and seemingly adrift in search of a research topic, Phương Thảo joined my lab, proving to be a wise decision. Building upon Bích's work, she brought the "Osteogenomic Profile" to the research program. Phương Thảo's groundbreaking work, published in the esteemed journal eLife, laid the foundation for the concept of Skeletal Age.

Phương Thảo embodied the pinnacle of success within the lab. "Successful" in the sense that her research held profound meaning, yielded significant impact, and garnered numerous awards. Phương Thảo swept all five available awards during her studies, including the prestigious TJ Martin Award and the ASBMR Young Investigator Award.

Celebrating milestones at UTS: beaming with pride as my two exceptional students cross the stage—First Class Honours star Daniela Tesorioro on the left, and the brilliant Hồ Lê Phương Thảo on the right.

Each student made significant contributions, but these three represented distinct "eras" of the lab. Steven and Nguyên defined the era of building the Garvan Fracture Risk Calculator model. Bích contributed to the era of pioneering genetic research and the concept of "genetic profiling." And Phương Thảo, who took the baton of genetic research, developed the Osteogenomic Profile for osteoporosis and refined the fracture prediction model.

All eighteen students who graced my lab have secured national and international recognition. After meticulous counting, I discovered that my fifteen doctoral students alone have secured a staggering thirty-one national and international awards, not including conference accolades.

Passing The Torch in Việt Nam

While supervising students in Australia held its own rewards, guiding them in Việt Nam felt deeply personal. To me, mentoring PhD students in Việt Nam wasn't just a task; it was a chance to contribute directly to my homeland's scientific future.

I firmly believe Vietnamese students possess the potential for greatness. Given the right opportunities, they can excel. They need the chance to explore their ideas and the support of experienced mentors. Seeing PhD theses in Vietnam often fall short of what I'd expected in Australia was a wake-up call. Frankly, some PhD theses resembled undergraduate projects back home. This awakened a passion within me— to ignite a similar passion for scientific inquiry in Việt Nam's brightest minds. The thought of guiding these promising researchers, of watching them blossom into skilled investigators, fueled my every action. However, achieving this dream wasn't a simple journey; it was more like working through a labyrinth of bureaucratic obstacles.

My dream of mentoring Vietnamese research students faced a hurdle at Southern universities. They demanded formal teaching qualifications and fluent English as prerequisites for supervising local students, qualifications I lacked. This restriction unfortunately sidelined me from official advising roles at that time. However, unofficially, I'd already mentored over ten students on their research journeys, supporting them through the intricacies of designing studies, collecting and analyzing data, and mastering the complex process of writing and publishing scientific papers. While my name wasn't listed on their theses, it often appeared in the published works themselves, concrete evidence of the guidance I provided. Here was a treasure trove of experience, a reservoir of knowledge, seemingly rendered inert by bureaucratic barriers.

The North, however, offered a glimmer of hope. My colleagues there, with a refreshing absence of administrative knots, assured me that no regulations barred foreigners like me from supervising PhD students. And so began my metamorphosis, from a visiting professor at Tôn Đức Thắng University to another at Hà

Nội Medical University, followed by an honorary professorship at both Hà Nội University of Pharmacy and the University of Đà Nẵng. These titles, once elusive, became the key that unlocked the door of opportunity. Official supervision of Vietnamese research students was finally within grasp.

And grasp it I did. Seven doctoral students in Việt Nam have embarked on research journeys under my mentorship, each a shining example of the immense potential brimming within Việt Nam's young minds. Their dedication and hunger for knowledge mirrored my own youthful passion. The countless hours spent designing studies, analyzing data, meticulously dissecting findings, and crafting compelling arguments were sessions of shared discovery. We collaborated, with me offering guidance and them bringing their unique perspectives and insights to the table. Witnessing their research culminate in publications within esteemed international medical journals was a moment of immense pride. It wasn't just the publications themselves; it was a validation—a resounding confirmation—that Vietnamese research students, when equipped with proper training and support, could compete on equal footing with any student globally. They have become my extended academic family.

The Long-Distance Scholar

My first Vietnamese PhD student, Dr. Nguyễn Thị Thanh Hương, presented a unique challenge. Enrolled at the prestigious Karolinska Institute in Sweden, Hương needed a co-supervisor with expertise in osteoporosis. A funny email, addressed with a formal "Dear Sir" followed by friendly Vietnamese sentences, landed in my inbox. Hương, assuming my prolific research output meant advanced age, used the respectful term "cụ" (Sir). When we finally met in Hà Nội, her surprise at my middle age became a shared joke.

Hương's research path wasn't easy. The Karolinska Institute's requirement of four published papers before graduation loomed large. Yet, after five years of dedication, Hương successfully defended her thesis. It was immensely satisfying to have helped shape her research direction and witness her blossom into a visionary leader. Today, Dr. Hương spearheads medical research at the Đinh Tiên Hoàng

Medical Research Institute—an institution she fiercely advocated for—and I had the honor of being present at its inauguration.

From Professor to Supervisor

Fast forward to the early 2010s. A course in Sài Gòn brought me face-to-face with Associate Professor Nguyễn Thanh Bình from Hà Nội University of Pharmacy. His down-to-earth demeanor, even playful at times, made me mistake him for a PhD student. Little did I know, he'd become a valued colleague. Years later, after his promotion to Rector, Professor Bình surprised me by requesting my supervision for one of his students. The paperwork involved initially daunted me, but Professor Bình, with a hearty laugh, offered an Honorary Professorship as a solution. "The title comes with the task, teacher!" he declared, sealing our collaboration.

Dr. Hạnh Vân beaming at the center on her PhD graduation, with the esteemed Rector of Hà Nội University of Pharmacy, Prof. Nguyễn Thanh Bình, by her side (right).

Dr. Phạm Nữ Hạnh Vân, Professor Bình's student, became my first official PhD student at the Hà Nội University of Pharmacy. An instant connection formed as her quiet grace and thoughtful nature impressed me. Recognizing a gap in research on reasonable spending thresholds for osteoporosis treatment in Việt Nam, I presented it as a potential thesis topic. The initial hurdles were steep, but data from the Việt Nam Osteoporosis Study project proved invaluable. After nearly five years, Hạnh Vân not only defended her thesis with distinction but also became a prominent figure in Vietnamese osteoporosis pharmacoeconomics.

Resilience on the Road to Research

Mai Thị Hà represents the spirit of many Vietnamese students pursuing their dreams abroad. After graduating from Hà Nội Medical University, she embarked on a journey that led her to South Korea and eventually to Australia. It was through social media that our paths crossed. Despite financial constraints, I was determined to support her aspirations. Offering Hà a volunteer position, I witnessed her tears of gratitude, reflecting the struggles she faced as a Vietnamese immigrant in Australia. Her vulnerability solidified my commitment to her success.

Hà's dedication was remarkable. In just two years, she co-authored three scientific papers in prestigious journals, including a groundbreaking publication in the Journal of Clinical Endocrinology and Metabolism. This research challenged existing assumptions about osteoporosis and fracture prevention, showcasing Hà's immense potential. While pursuing research, Hà also earned a Bachelor of Nursing degree and secured permanent residency—a sign of her resilience and the power of mentorship.

From ICU Physician to Award-Winning Researcher

Dr. Hà Tấn Đức, an ICU physician from Cần Thơ, began our connection with a simple online inquiry about resuscitation scoring systems. Upon meeting at a conference, I was struck by his genuine kindness and humility, qualities that embodied the spirit of the Mê Kông Delta people. Đức's dedication to research led him to various courses I organized. When he felt ready, we discussed his proposed project: developing a mortality prediction model specifically for Vietnamese emergency patients.

The project was a collaborative effort. We evaluated existing models such as SAPS, REMS, and WPS for applicability in Vietnam, then designed a large-scale study involving 4,000 patients for model development and another 2,000 for validation. The promising results not only led to publications in international journals but also garnered the prestigious Alexandre Yersin Award. This research formed the bedrock of Đức's doctoral dissertation. Witnessing the challenges he faced during his defense exposed the complexities of the Vietnamese academic system, further solidifying my belief in advocating for streamlined and transparent research procedures.

The Unsung Hero

The first time I met Dr. Trần Minh Giang, he was just another face in the crowd at a training workshop organized by the University of Medicine and Pharmacy in Hồ Chí Minh City. Both of us hailed from the Mê Kông Delta, but that first encounter left no lasting impression. Perhaps it was the awkwardness of introductions, or maybe the sheer number of eager faces.

But Giang kept showing up. He enrolled in courses taught by Dr. Nguyễn Đình Nguyên, Dr. Trần Sơn Thạch, and me, demonstrating his dedication. It was then that I learned about his background as an intensivist at Gia Định People's Hospital, witnessing the daily struggles of ICU patients on ventilators. He saw firsthand the relentless scourge of infection and the frustration of antibiotic resistance.

He shared his idea: to research this very problem, to understand the enemy at a deeper level. My own research interests leaned towards the role of genes, and I saw an opportunity to elevate his project. We could weave genetic analysis into the study, adding a layer of scientific novelty worthy of a doctoral thesis.

The journey wasn't easy. Ethical clearances were hurdles to navigate, and funding was a constant challenge. While the Department of Science and Technology offered some support, it wasn't enough to cover the crucial genetic analysis. Just like countless other researchers before him, Giang dug deep, investing a significant sum—fifty thousand USD—of his own money to see the project through.

Finally, after tireless work, the study bore fruit. He published the findings in both Vietnamese and international journals. The results were striking: an alarmingly high prevalence of antibiotic resistance—nearly eighty percent for some common drugs. This groundbreaking research, published in *BMC Infectious Diseases*, has garnered almost one hundred citations—a true mark of its impact.

Seeing Giang's transformation from a curious clinician to a published researcher filled me with pride. It validated my approach to mentorship. But Giang's journey wasn't confined to the sterile walls of hospitals. He embodied the true spirit of Southern people: chivalrous, decisive, and in his pursuit of saving lives. This heroic spirit even manifested outside the hospital walls.

There was the time he attended a funeral, only to discover the mourners preparing to enshroud a seemingly deceased person. His medical instincts kicked in. He checked for a pulse, a faint but persistent flicker of life. In that moment, Dr. Giang refused to accept defeat. He insisted on rushing the "deceased" to the hospital, his tenacity saving a life on the very precipice of death. The story even made it to the local news.

An Osteoporosis Investigator in Kiên Giang

A trip back home to Kiên Giang province brought an unexpected but delightful encounter. There, I met Dr. Thái Viết Tặng, the Principal of Kiên Giang College of Medicine, a center primarily focused on training nurses and allied health professionals. Dr. Tặng, much like my esteemed student Dr. Hà Tấn Đức, possessed the warmth and genuineness that define our southern culture. His easygoing nature made our conversation flow effortlessly.

Little did I know, Tặng, then pursuing his PhD in mid 2012, was researching osteoporosis, a field in which I had gained international recognition. As fate would have it, his supervisor directed him towards me, granting me the opportunity to mentor him indirectly. Tặng's research compared the fracture prediction ability of the Garvan model, my brainchild, to the World Health Organization-backed FRAX model. I offered guidance on designing this study to meet the rigorous standards of a doctoral thesis.

Tặng had diligently collected data in Kiên Giang over several years. However, the sample size proved insufficient, necessitating ethical clearance to collect additional data in Cần Thơ. I vividly recall spending countless hours alongside him, meticulously guiding him through data analysis and interpretation. His dedication and passion for science were truly inspiring. Over the next five years, I witnessed him blossom into a skilled researcher.

The hard work paid off. The results were gratifying; the Garvan model outperformed FRAX, suggesting its potential application in Vietnamese patients. Tặng's research gained widespread recognition, with presentations at national meetings solidifying his reputation as a leading figure in osteoporosis research within the Mê Kông Delta region. In 2018, a stroke of serendipity brought me to Hà Nội on the very day Tặng defended his PhD thesis. I eagerly attended his defense in Hà Đông (just about twenty-five kilometers from Hà Nội), where I saw him navigate the rigorous yet respectful scrutiny of his colleagues and peer reviewers. The successful defense was met with jubilation. We, the delegation from Kiên Giang, celebrated Tặng's remarkable achievement at a traditional restaurant.

The Unassuming Vertebral Fracture Investigator

Dr. Nguyễn Thái Hoà, originally from Hậu Giang (a Mê Kông Delta province), joined the Vietnam Osteoporosis Study group upon my recommendation. I proposed a research project investigating vertebral fractures in middle-aged and elderly individuals. This meticulous undertaking involved X-ray analysis of over 4,000 people, followed by repeat X-rays two years later to identify new fractures. Additionally, the study aimed to pinpoint risk factors and develop a predictive model for high-risk individuals. Hoà embraced the project wholeheartedly, traveling from Cần Thơ to Sài Gòn every week to contribute to data collection and assist the research team.

His dedication went beyond research. Hoà actively participated in organizing research methodology courses and a continuous medical education (CME) program on osteoporosis in Cần Thơ. After three years of tireless effort, Hoà had gathered enough data for two scientific publications and embarked on his doctoral dissertation. Witnessing his intellectual growth during his defense was a source of immense pride. His initial presentation, though unrefined, revealed his potential. Over time, he honed his presentation skills, demonstrating remarkable progress and earning my utmost confidence. I do not doubt his future success and the valuable contributions he will make to the field of osteoporosis research.

A Contribution to Parkinson's Disease Research

Each student I've guided has embarked on a unique research journey, tackling important topics with dedication and a thirst for knowledge. Their work has not only enriched their own understanding but also made significant contributions to their respective fields. One such student is Dr. Lê Thị Thúy An, whose thesis on epigenetics and Parkinson's disease stands as evidence of the caliber of research being conducted in Việt Nam. Our collaboration began through a shared interest in the interplay between environmental factors and genetic predisposition in the development of Parkinson's disease. Thúy An's enthusiasm and dedication to the project were evident from the start, and her meticulous approach to data collection and analysis was truly inspiring.

The path to completing Thúy An's thesis was not without its challenges. The Covid-19 pandemic caused a significant disruption to our research schedule, delaying data collection and analysis. However, Thúy An's perseverance and resilience shone through, and she emerged from the experience a more accomplished researcher. In 2024, Thúy An successfully defended her thesis, marking the culmination of six years of hard work and dedication. Her thesis, which has since been published in a prestigious international journal, has made a significant contribution to our understanding of the complex mechanisms underlying Parkinson's disease.

Witnessing Thúy An's growth as a researcher has been a source of immense pride. From her initial steps in the field to her confident presentation of her findings, she has demonstrated remarkable progress. I am confident that the scientific knowledge and skills she has acquired during her doctoral studies will serve her well in her future endeavors.

A Bonfire for Student Mental Health

My experiences as a mentor extended beyond medical research. During a course I taught, I met Dr. Lê Minh Thuận, a student with a keen interest in pursuing researching depression among university students. I encouraged Thuan to explore this idea, and he enthusiastically enrolled in a doctoral program at the Vietnam Academy of Social Sciences in Hà Nội. While I initially worried about my lack of connections within the academy, the faculty surprisingly welcomed me as a mentor.

Together with Thuận and academy professors, we designed a comprehensive research project. The study involved surveying hundreds of students across various academic disciplines. Thuận's dedication to data collection was firm, and his perseverance paid off, enabling him to gather enough data to support his dissertation. Fortunately, he received invaluable support from the professors in Hà Nội who, like myself, believed in the significance of his research. Despite the challenges, Thuận's dissertation received high praise, and he completed his doctoral program. His dedication to this critical mental health issue among students left a lasting impression.

A Lasting Partnership

While many of my students have been formally enrolled PhD candidates, others have collaborated with me in an unofficial capacity. Dr. Trần Sơn Thạch stands out as a prominent example. Thạch, a physician who graduated from Hồ Chí Minh City University of Medicine and Pharmacy, later pursued a PhD in epidemiology at Prince of Songkla University in Thái Lan.

Our paths crossed during the mid-2010s when Thạch invited Dr. Nguyễn Đình Nguyên and me to deliver a short course at Hùng Vương Hospital in Sài Gòn. His calm demeanor, gentle nature, and meticulous approach to language left a positive impression. He then expressed his desire to join my lab at the Garvan Institute in Australia as an unpaid research fellow, driven by a passion to learn from a world-leading research institution.

Dr. Trần Sơn Thạch and I kicking back post-annual scientific meeting of the American Society for Bone and Mineral Research in Nashville, TN (USA) 2005.

Little did I know that this decision would solidify a long-lasting scientific partnership. After his fellowship at my lab, Thạch found himself drawn to the Australian environment and subsequently applied for permanent residency upon returning to Việt Nam. His impressive research experience readily secured his residency visa.

Once settled in Australia, Thạch flourished in medical research, publishing numerous groundbreaking papers in top-tier journals. He further expanded his knowledge by pursuing a Master's degree in Statistics at the University of Sydney, graduating with top honors.

For over a decade, Nguyên and I worked together on various significant research projects and educational programs in Việt Nam. Unfortunately, witnessing the constant struggle for research funding led our colleague, Dr. Nguyên, to pursue a different path. He established a private practice, a decision I fully supported. While Nguyên's departure from research created a temporary void, Thạch's presence filled it seamlessly. Over time, we developed a well-oiled collaboration, culminating in impactful research projects like BONEcheck™ and Bone Age, both bearing the indelible mark of Thạch's expertise.

Dr. Trần Sơn Thạch, Dr. Hà Tấn Đức, and I often joked about being a "scientific roadshow." For over a decade, we have run numerous educational programs across Việt Nam, delivering research methodology courses in Hà Nội, Hải Phòng, Huế, Đà Nẵng, Nha Trang, Sài Gòn, Đồng Tháp, Cần Thơ, and Kiên Giang. This program has empowered countless colleagues nationwide, and Thạch's contributions to its success remain invaluable.

Going Through the Maze of Doctoral Training in Vietnam

These seven students weren't merely my extended academic family in Việt Nam, they were the kindling that would ignite a fire of scientific inquiry. The skills they honed and the knowledge they assimilated would ripple outwards, inspiring countless future generations. They would become mentors themselves, passing on the torch of scientific exploration, fostering a spirit of critical thinking and problem-solving that would propel Vietnamese research to even greater heights.

I would like to think that my mentorship was about building a legacy—one of Vietnamese scientific excellence, nurtured by the dreams of a generation past and fueled by the boundless potential of a generation to come. It was about creating a self-sustaining ecosystem of research, where knowledge flowed freely, and breakthroughs became the norm, not the exception. And in the eyes of my students, their dedication and thirst for knowledge, I saw not just the culmination of my efforts, but the dawning of a brighter future for Vietnamese medical research.

However, the world of doctoral training in Việt Nam unfolded like a labyrinth compared to the well-trodden path I knew in Australia. Here, the transformation from eager student to polished researcher felt like a precarious tightrope walk, fraught with unforeseen twists and turns.

Australia's approach brings to mind a well-rehearsed dance. It is a process both gentle and rigorous. The dance begins with a student brimming with a research question, seeking a mentor—someone with expertise in their chosen field. Discussions flourished, and research proposals were crafted, outlining the context, objectives, and the anticipated journey ahead. This initial waltz culminates in securing funding—a competitive tango with the university or an external sponsor.

With funding secured, the student becomes fully immersed in the research lab or research group, conducting experiments and delving deep under the guidance of not just one, but often two supervisors. Weekly seminars are a cornerstone of this experience, fostering a community of scholars, sharing their progress, and receiving invaluable feedback from peers and professors alike.

But the university's watchful eye extends beyond the lab. Every six months, a committee reviews the progress of both student and supervisor. These meetings are surprisingly friendly; conversations designed to assess the student's needs and ensure they have the necessary support to excel. The supervisor's expertise and commitment are also evaluated, ensuring a healthy student-supervisor relationship.

Although not compulsory, publication is implicitly viewed as a crucial element of this journey. During their three or four years of research, students are encouraged (though not mandated) to publish their findings in international journals. Quality, not quantity, reigns supreme: a single paper in a prestigious journal could pave the way for a successful thesis. Supervisors, too, play a crucial role in guiding and supporting their students through the intricate process of publication.

Finally, after a period of publishing (typically two to three papers), the student receives the green light to write their thesis. This document isn't crafted in isolation; external professors are invited to review and provide feedback. Once incorporated, the committee, often composed of supervisors, delivers the final verdict—graduation or further revisions. Interestingly, Australia's doctoral program eschewed the formal thesis defense ceremony common in Europe. Instead, students present their research findings throughout their studies, honing their communication skills before a wider audience—a test of mettle.

Throughout this odyssey, the student shoulders no financial burden. From contacting external reviewers to administrative tasks, the university meticulously orchestrates the entire process. This, in essence, was the doctoral student's journey in Australia, a model mirrored in many advanced countries, albeit with slight variations.

The ideal vision of PhD training I'd carried from Australia crashed head-on with the reality I encountered in Việt Nam. Here, the doctoral journey wasn't a well-lit corridor leading to a brightly lit future, but a labyrinth with hidden corners and unexpected turns. Unlike the structured programs I knew, Vietnamese doctoral training felt like a curious blend of Soviet-style rigor and a sprinkle of French tradition—a system unlike anything I'd experienced before.

Forget supervisors offering pre-defined research projects – here, the onus of crafting a research question, a spark that would ignite their thesis fire, fell entirely on the students' shoulders. Sometimes, the esteemed professors assigned as supervisors weren't even specialists in the students' chosen fields. They were respected figures, yes, but their expertise might lie in a field that only vaguely overlapped with the students' research. While this system fostered a deep respect for hierarchy, it lacked the focused mentorship that I'd seen abroad. There, supervisors became partners in the research journey, guiding students with intensive focus and ensuring their research bloomed to its full potential. Here, guidance felt more like a distant lighthouse in a foggy sea, but not necessarily one illuminating the students' specific path.

Funding—the lifeblood of research—exposed another gaping difference. Unlike their full-time counterparts abroad, Vietnamese PhD students were more like research jugglers. Their days were occupied with hospital or university work, leaving precious little time for their research. This, in turn, became a part-time pursuit, financed not by generous grants but by personal savings or, more often, by family support. This financial burden created a physical separation, too. Limited lab time meant interaction with supervisors became a rare commodity. Forget the regular progress reports and collaborative brainstorming sessions I knew. Here, the system relied on nerve-wracking "defenses" at the departmental and university level.

The doctoral defenses, designed to be rigorous examinations, often felt like a gamble. While most committee members were undoubtedly well-intentioned, some seemed like misplaced puzzle pieces, lacking the specific expertise to truly assess the research at hand. This was particularly disheartening when these same individuals, with no history of publishing in prestigious international journals themselves, felt compelled to critique the work of students whose research had been published in the very same journals.

Imagine a student presenting groundbreaking research, published perhaps in *The Lancet* or the *New England Journal of Medicine*, only to face criticism from committee members who lacked experience at that level. What should have been a stimulating exchange of ideas often devolved into ordeals. Misplaced comments, even personal attacks, rained down, leaving students emotionally drained and questioning their own abilities.

The harassment wasn't confined to the committee room. Administrative staff, empowered by an uncaring system, could subject students to their own brand of humiliation. This constant pressure, a feeling Vietnamese students described as "holding your breath across the river," forced them to compromise their dignity simply to survive the process.

Adding insult to injury, the thesis defense itself became a logistical nightmare. The responsibility of wrangling committee members scattered across the country fell entirely on the student's shoulders. Travel, accommodation, and honorariums all became personal expenses. The university played a passive role, leaving students to navigate this bureaucratic maze alone. And the charade continued; summaries of theses had to be sent to fifty experts nationwide for comment. A performative act, with most recipients too busy to even glance at the research. Students, aware of this charade, resorted to elaborate ruses—forging comments and enlisting friends and family in a desperate attempt to fulfil these meaningless requirements.

Finally, after clearing this series of obstacles, the ordeal wasn't over. The Ministry of Education loomed, a specter of potential irregularities. In the medical field, this translated to producing records of hundreds, even thousands, of patients, a massive task that often culminated in a game of unspoken understanding. Students would "read" the records for inspectors, a charade highlighting the flaws of a broken system.

The starkness of this reality left me disheartened. Witnessing the struggles of Vietnamese Ph.D. students, I couldn't help but contrast it with the relative ease of doctoral training abroad. There, students weren't subject to the whims of unqualified committees or burdened with the financial and logistical nightmares of organizing their own defense. Their focus was on research—on pushing the boundaries of knowledge—not on bureaucratic hurdles.

This realization ignited a fire within me. The Vietnamese Ph.D. process, a relic of a bygone era, needed a complete overhaul. The model emphasizing departmental defenses and thesis summaries offered little value in a world driven by peer review. Change was imperative to liberate students from the shackles of administrative burdens and empower them to focus on scientific exploration. Only through reform could Vietnamese PhDs earn international recognition, their degrees respected passports to the world's leading universities. The goal wasn't simply producing more PhDs; it was about nurturing a generation of scientists and empowered researchers, not individuals scarred by lifelong spiritual wounds.

As I reflect on this chapter of my life, I am filled with a profound sense of gratitude for the opportunity to contribute to my homeland, for the privilege of working with such brilliant minds, and for the lasting friendships forged through shared intellectual pursuits. The legacy of this mentorship isn't just a collection of research papers or academic degrees; it's the enduring impact these individuals will have on the future of healthcare in Việt Nam. And that, for me, is the most fulfilling reward of all.

My approach to doctoral training draws a parallel to martial arts. After rigorous training, a martial artist hones their skills in another dojo before venturing out on their own. Similarly, upon completing their doctoral programs and publishing research, doctoral students embark on postdoctoral research in another lab before flourishing as independent scientists. Therefore, my greatest reward lies in witnessing my students blossom into independent researchers, quickly establishing their own brands within the scientific community. A student's success reflects the success of their teacher. I often tell my students that after four years, I yearn for the day they become the teachers who enlighten me about the specialized fields they delve into.

This vision extends beyond the confines of the lab. Mentorship isn't a singular act; it's a ripple effect that stretches outward. Many of my former students have established their own research groups, fostering the next generation of scientific minds. Witnessing this chain reaction of knowledge and discovery is a source of immense pride. It represents the peak of a philosophy that goes beyond simple instruction, fostering a love of research, a thirst for knowledge, and the determination to expand the limits of scientific exploration.

The students who have graced my lab haven't simply earned awards and accolades; they've become accomplished researchers, each with a unique fingerprint on the scientific landscape. Their stories are a combination of chance encounters, dedication, and the transformative power of mentorship. They are the legacy I carry forward, a legacy that extends far beyond the walls of a laboratory.

Throughout my career, I've been fortunate to have exceptional mentors who not only imparted scientific knowledge but also instilled in me the importance of fostering the next generation of researchers. Their guidance extended beyond the lab, shaping my approach to collaboration and communication. The lessons learned from these esteemed individuals continue to guide me as I mentor young researchers, providing them with the support, encouragement, and constructive criticism they need to flourish.

Mentorship is a two-way street. The enthusiasm and fresh perspectives of young researchers keep me invigorated and constantly learning. Witnessing their growth and accomplishments brings immense satisfaction. It's a privilege to play a role in shaping the future of scientific discovery.

Chapter Fourteen

Unmasking Science

My career in medical research has been multifaceted. I have donned many hats: a practising scientist in the trenches, the strategist leading a research lab in both Australia and Việt Nam, and even the captain establishing and steering an entire institute. Beyond the lab, I became a trusted voice, reviewing research papers for esteemed journals and appraising grant proposals for giants such as the NIH, the Wellcome Trust, and the NHMRC. I even had a hand in shaping the careers of future researchers on promotion committees. As an editor for various medical journals, I acted as a gatekeeper and curator of knowledge. This mixture of involvements, which I'll share in more detail here, offered a panoramic view of the scientific landscape, a window into the complexities, triumphs, and challenges that define the world of scientific research.

I witnessed the thrill of discovery—the relentless pursuit of knowledge that burned brightly in some researchers' eyes. But science, as beautiful as it can be, isn't always pristine. I observed biases and prejudices against scientists from developing countries. I saw egos inflate faster than a research balloon, prevalent narcissism, and the temptation to cut corners became sobering reminders. Sadly, I even encountered the devastating blow of outright fraud.

Biases and Prejudices

The dream of science, I used to think, was pure objectivity. A beacon of truth, shining regardless of where it came from. But that idealism started to crack when I became a lab head here Việt Nam. My colleagues, brilliant minds from Việt Nam and Thái Lan, faced hurdles I never imagined. The supposed safeguard of academic quality—the peer-review system—seemed to have a blind spot.

The gatekeepers of scientific merit—the prestigious journals—are fortresses built by Western academia, often in collaboration with giants like Springer Nature or Elsevier. Their editorial boards are populated with esteemed editors, most from wealthy nations with overflowing research coffers. Through their lens, research from developing countries can seem inherently flimsy. Limited funding means less cutting-edge equipment and smaller teams, which can be misconstrued as a lack of rigor. It's an unconscious bias, perhaps, but it can lead to sound research being dismissed before it even gets a fair hearing.

More than fifteen years ago (in mid-2010), my Vietnamese colleagues and I designed an "experiment" to investigate potential bias in scientific publishing. We meticulously wrote a manuscript on diabetes in Việt Nam, ensuring flawless English thanks to a native English endocrinology professor. With all authors listed as Vietnamese, we submitted it to a prestigious journal. Within a week, it was rejectedno review, no feedback, just a flat-out dismissal. Approximately four months later, we tried again with the same manuscript, but with one crucial change: we added the Australian professor as a co-author. This time, the paper breezed through peer review and got published. The science remained identical, but the perception had shifted dramatically. This experiment provided strong evidence supporting the hypothesis of unconscious bias against scientists from economically disadvantaged countries. It also served as a powerful illustration of the broader obstacles these researchers faced within the international scientific community.

Years had passed since that first sting of research bias, but the memory still simmered. Now, a new incident fanned those embers into a roaring fire, solidifying my resolve to fight for our research. My Vietnamese colleague, Dr.

Hồ-Phạm Thục Lan, and I poured our hearts into a manuscript. This was not just any manuscript, mind you; this was the culmination of countless nights spent hunched over data, dissecting research papers, and meticulously selecting participants. We'd recruited 105 Buddhist nuns who'd adhered to a strict vegan diet their entire lives. We then compared them to 105 omnivorous women from the general population, all meticulously matched for age, ethnicity, and clinical history. The sample size was robust, and the data were clean. We submitted the manuscript to a prestigious journal, brimming with anticipation. This research had the potential to contribute valuable insights to the ongoing debate about plant-based diets and bone health.

Weeks bled into a month, and then the email arrived. My heart hammered as I clicked it open. But as I scanned the reviewers' comments, a cold dread washed over me. The feedback wasn't about the methodology, the analysis, or our conclusion. It fixated on a seemingly insignificant detail—the sample size. The reviewer, in a tone dripping with skepticism, questioned how we managed to recruit precisely 105 participants per group. The reviewer's words reeked of suspicion, veiledly implying we'd fabricated something. Disappointment morphed into anger. Here we were, presenting meticulously collected data that could make a real difference, and they were hung up on a number?

We politely addressed the comment in our response. We detailed the painstaking recruitment process, explaining how the local community had been instrumental in connecting us with potential participants. We highlighted the rigorous matching criteria to ensure a statistically sound comparison. It was a frustrating detour, but we persevered, determined to see our research reach a wider audience.

This experience served as a reminder of the challenges researchers from developing countries face in the scientific publishing world. Sometimes, the biggest obstacles aren't flawed data or poor methodology, but rather preconceived notions and biases that can derail even the most well-designed studies. It was yet another battle in the ongoing war for recognition—a war I was determined to win.

Throughout my research career in Australia, I have never received comments regarding the quality of English in my papers, despite being aware that some of my manuscripts contained language errors. This was likely due to the presence of my mentors and native English-speaking Australian colleagues in these Australia-based papers. However, when I authored papers originating from Vietnam, with all authors having non-Anglicized names, my manuscripts were almost always criticized for poor English or labeled as "problematic," even though I was certain there were no issues with the language.

One instance stands out. We submitted a meticulously-crafted manuscript to a prestigious American journal. One reviewer lauded the writing, praising its clarity. The other, however, offered a single, damning comment: "Problematic English. Needs heavy editing." Not a single error highlighted, just a vague accusation hanging in the air.

The frustration was compounded by reviewers who, with misplaced confidence, tried to be my grammar guru. One expert deemed the sentence "*Individuals who experienced total paralysis were excluded from the study*" to be "*quite weird.*" Apparently, excluding folks who can't move wasn't the weird part; it was the way I wrote it! These experiences, though infuriating at times, became a sort of masterclass in the unconscious bias that can permeate even the hallowed halls of academia. It was a reminder that brilliance and meticulous research don't always shield you from misplaced critiques.

The thrill of a completed research paper—the culmination of months of meticulous data collection and analysis—used to be a familiar high. But that feeling had been tainted lately. The culprit? Reviewer bias, specifically the kind that felt suspiciously like veiled intimidation.

A prime example was our study on bone quality and type 2 diabetes in Việt Nam. We poured our hearts and expertise into the research, confident that it held valuable insights. Initially, the esteemed journal we submitted to seemed promising. Three reviewers praised our research design, methodology, and presentation. We were on cloud nine—until the editor's review arrived.

This heavyweight figure in the field, someone whose work I'd long admired, delivered a stinging critique. He claimed our statistical analysis—an area where I'd spent decades honing my expertise—was fundamentally flawed. Disappointment swiftly morphed into confusion. I meticulously scrutinized the feedback, and there it was, clear as day: the editor was simply wrong.

But what truly unsettled me was the concluding line. It wasn't phrased as constructive criticism, but as a thinly veiled threat. "... If this point is not addressed by the Authors, I am sorry to inform you that we cannot accept your manuscript..." Blackmail, couched in academic jargon.

This wasn't just about our paper anymore; it was about the integrity of the entire scientific process. Righteous anger fueled my response to the editorial board. I politely but firmly challenged the editor's competence in statistical matters. I demanded he be barred from future statistical reviews to prevent similar injustices. And I pushed further. "The editor's behavior is unacceptable," I wrote, my voice unwavering even on paper. "We demand a formal apology and request a different editor handle our manuscript."

It was a gamble, a stand against an established figure. But the thought of letting this blatant bias slide fueled my resolve. It took a few tense weeks, but eventually we received a response. The editor was reassigned, and our manuscript was reviewed by a statistician who found our analysis to be absolutely sound. Finally, the paper was published.

The victory felt bittersweet. While our research saw the light of day, the experience left a scar. It served as a reminder that even in the pursuit of knowledge, bias can fester. But it also ignited a fire within me. This wouldn't be the last time I stood up against the gatekeepers who, blinded by their own perceived authority, tried to silence good science.

Throughout my career, I've encountered a disheartening trend in scientific communication: unfair, dismissive, and even microaggressive behavior. It's a far cry from the collaborative environment science aspires to be. This kind of dismissive feedback isn't new, and it's finally getting the attention it deserves. Articles in prominent journals like *Nature* ("*Don't be a prig in peer review,*" January 9, 2020) and *Science* ("*Rude paper reviews are pervasive and sometimes harmful, study finds,*" December 12, 2019) highlight this very issue. Let's be clear, such disrespectful reviews are not only discouraging but potentially harmful.

It truly touched me when Richard Smith, former Editor-in-Chief of the *British Medical Journal,* addressed unconscious bias against research from low-income countries in a blog post. He cited studies showing that reviewers tend to rate abstracts lower when they believe they originate from such countries. These findings confirmed a suspicion I'd harbored for years—that bias can infiltrate even the seemingly objective world of scientific review. My own experiences mirrored these studies all too well.

Narcissism

My teenage self held a particular image of the scientist: a dispassionate truth-seeker, driven only by the pursuit of knowledge. But after a few years in the trenches of scientific research, that image began to crumble. I started to see scientists as multifaceted individuals, each with their own motivations and stories. It was a humbling realization that continues to shape my understanding of the scientific community.

Now, over three decades of interacting with scientists and doctors across the globe, I've encountered a vibrant spectrum of personalities. Some, at first, left me bewildered. There was a particular breed of scientists who reveled in self-promotion, boasting about their ever-growing publication count, the mountain of citations they'd accumulated, and the seemingly endless list of appointments they held at universities, professional societies, and even as editors of various journals. Their email signatures, sometimes stretching to half a page, served as testimony to their perceived importance.

This flamboyance was a striking contrast to my mentor's demeanor. He, a man of many accomplishments, never felt the need to brag. His email signature, a model of understated elegance, simply listed his name and affiliations. It was a constant reminder of a Vietnamese proverb I hold dear: *"Thùng rỗng kêu to"*—empty vessels make the most noise. My mentor embodied the wisdom of this proverb, letting his work speak for itself. He is not alone. History is filled with scientific titans whose groundbreaking work revolutionized our understanding of the world, yet many of these giants were known for their remarkable humility. Albert Einstein, the architect of relativity, famously downplayed his genius, attributing his success to "a holy curiosity about nature." Rosalyn Yalow, who pioneered the radioimmunoassay technique, deflected praise, emphasizing the collaborative nature of science. These towering figures serve as a constant reminder that true scientific progress is often fueled by a passion for discovery rather than personal aggrandizement.

Back then, I struggled to articulate the flamboyant self-promotion I witnessed in some scientists. Was such behavior even necessary? It wasn't until I stumbled upon Bruno Lemaitre's *"An Essay on Science and Narcissism"* that the term "narcissist" finally clicked.

My email conversations with the author were eye-opening. They shed new light on years of my observations. In his book, Lemaitre, a practicing scientist who has personally witnessed the dark side of academia, presents a powerful argument about the presence of narcissism within scientific circles. His experience serves as a striking illustration: Lemaitre's research directly led to the discovery of the Toll-like receptor, a monumental achievement that ultimately resulted in a Nobel Prize for his supervisor, Jules Hoffmann. This well-documented yet intricate incident fueled Lemaitre's investigation into how widespread and impactful narcissism is within the scientific community.

Lemaitre vividly describes two types of scientists: S-drive and N-drive. The S-drive scientists are characterized by their dedication to hard work, meticulous attention to detail, and genuine passion for generating solid, reproducible data. On the other hand, N-drive scientists, often referred to as the narcissistic type, possess a unique set of non-scientific skills: charisma, writing and public speaking, extensive networks, political connections, and board and editorial committee positions. Their focus wasn't necessarily the pursuit of knowledge or scientific progress, but rather the construction of a facade—a facade of success, power, and brilliance. These individuals, however, also exhibit a capacity for misconduct and unfair review practices, often leveraging their wealth and personal connections to their advantage.

While the exact number of narcissistic scientists remains unknown, my personal experience suggests they are present in significant numbers. Their presence is often readily apparent through university websites and email signatures, where their self-promotion shines brightly. However, their presence in science isn't entirely negative. They are driven by a desire for power and success and can effectively champion their research vision, thus benefiting their entire field. Additionally, their energized self-absorption often translates to a knack for public engagement, attracting more research funding than their less narcissistic counterparts.

While the presence of narcissism in science can have some positive effects, its potential for harm is significant and multifaceted. At its extreme, it can manifest as bullying, harassment, and data manipulation—all of which directly harm individual scientists and damage the integrity of the scientific process. This toxic environment can also discourage diversity and create an atmosphere of fear and distrust, ultimately tarnishing the public's perception of science.

However, even in its less extreme forms, narcissism can have subtle yet detrimental effects. The relentless focus on self-promotion and a need for admiration trumps collaboration. These narcissistic scientists often resort to bullying tactics to maintain control over research and downplay the contributions of others. This can manifest in various ways, from taking credit for another's work to sabotaging their research or deliberately excluding them from authorship on important findings. This bullying behavior not only harms the individual but also stifles scientific progress by creating a toxic environment that discourages open communication and information sharing.

A case in point: Australia's scientific community was shaken by the case of a highly decorated scientist whose groundbreaking work was ultimately revealed to be built on fabricated data. This individual, revered for his achievements and regarded as a leader in his field, had resorted to manipulating research findings to secure publication in prestigious journals. In 2023, an investigation into the allegations of his research misconduct painted a disturbing picture. The scientist was described as *"a bully who used his reputation, status, and power to intimidate"* colleagues and avoid scrutiny of his work. Ultimately, the investigation concluded that the scientist could not have possibly conducted all the experiments he claimed to have performed, exposing the fabricated nature of his research.

Narcissism is a well-established personality trait that has been linked to un-ethical behavior and decreased participation in communal activities across fields such as finance, banking, and politics. In science, I think narcissism might also be associated with various forms of misconduct, including biased peer review, exaggerated scientific claims, and outright fraud. The inherent trust placed in scientists to conduct research ethically creates a vulnerable environment where self-centered, unethical individuals can easily exploit the system. This vulnera-bility is further exacerbated by the lack of strong sanctions against fraud and the absence of robust controls within the evaluation process.

Unfortunately, universities and scientific institutions have often prioritized protecting their image and reputation over addressing instances of misconduct. This has led to a concerning trend of concealing such problems, further eroding the scientific community's connection to its core value: the pursuit of truth. When I assumed the role of Director at Tam Anh Research Institute, I imple-mented greater transparency across various processes, including research con-duct, peer review, and funding allocation. I believe that such measures are crucial steps toward mitigating the negative consequences of narcissism and restoring trust in the scientific enterprise.

Frauds

Scientists with narcissistic tendencies, fueled by a desire for recognition and a fragile sense of self-worth, may be more susceptible to manipulating data or fabricating results. Their inflated sense of ability can lead them to believe they can outsmart the system and get away with scientific fraud. Additionally, a narcissist's aversion to criticism might make them resistant to admitting mistakes or flaws in their research, further increasing the risk of deception. This tendency has led to several high-profile cases of scientific misconduct. The field of bone research is not immune to this, with numerous instances of fraud being discussed privately.

One particularly public case was that of Japanese professor Yoshihiro Sato. As an expert reviewer involved in this investigation, I can attest to the profound impact it had on the scientific community. The sheer scale of the fabricated data and the potential consequences for patient health underscored the importance of upholding ethical standards in research.

Professor Sato, a respected figure in the osteoporosis research community, succumbed to a dark temptation. Driven by the pressure to produce, he fabricated data in over 200 papers published in top journals. His results were too good to be true, boasting impossible patient recruitment speeds and "miraculous" outcomes that raised eyebrows amongst colleagues.

Initially, concerns were politely voiced through letters to editors, but Sato's respectful explanations and the prestige of his position kept the issue simmering beneath the surface. It wasn't until a team of New Zealand and UK scientists, Drs. Mark Bolland, Alison Avenell, and Greg Gamble meticulously analyzed Sato's published data that the truth began to unravel. Their analysis revealed serious inconsistencies in published data, suggesting the data were fabricated rather than the product of actual research. Despite the evidence, major journals hesitated to retract Sato's work, delaying exposure. They faced frustration as their attempts to publish their analysis were initially rejected by prominent journals such as *JAMA* and *JAMA Internal Medicine*.

In 2015, Bolland, Avenell, and Gamble submitted their manuscript to the *Journal of Bone and Mineral Research* (JBMR). As a member of the JBMR editorial board, I was tasked by the Editor-in-Chief with reviewing it. While I confirmed the authors' methodology was sound, I recommended against publication. My concern was the potentially devastating impact on Sato's career and the unpredictable consequences of such an exposé. Instead, I suggested retracting Sato's papers from JBMR, a decision I still believe was the most reasonable course of action.

Frustrated by the major journals' rejection, the authors turned to *Neurology*, where Sato had previously published. *Neurology* agreed to peer-review their manuscript, and in December 2016, after Sato had already retracted ten papers, *Neurology* published their analysis, marking a significant victory for their persistence. Bolland and Avenell were overjoyed, with Avenell even admitting to shedding tears of relief when the paper was accepted.

But the story took a tragic turn. Just a month after the publication, Professor Sato committed suicide. The news left Bolland and Avenell, still young researchers, devastated, never imagining their actions would lead to such a consequence. This case serves as a blunt reminder of the dangers of prioritizing publications over scientific integrity, highlighting the human cost of academic pressure and the ethical responsibility that comes with scientific research.

The Sato affair, a recent high-profile case of scientific misconduct in Australia, wasn't an anomaly. Blogs like *For Better Science* and *Retraction Watch* have documented thousands of similar issues, exposing a troubling trend of fraud and misconduct. These cases have led to numerous retractions, highlighting the devastating impact on the credibility of scientific research. Public frustration is evident; newspapers have begun questioning the very foundation of science with headlines like *"How Much Science is Fake?"* This widespread problem underscores the urgent need for stronger safeguards and a culture of openness within the scientific community.

Culture of Numbers

Early in my scientific career, I began to suspect a link between the relentless pursuit of recognition and a culture obsessed with numbers. Guest speakers were showered with praise based solely on citation counts and H-indexes, leaving me bewildered. One particularly prolific American professor stood out. He boasted a staggering record of 1,300 published papers and 40,000 citations! This translated to nearly a paper a week for thirty years, a level of output I couldn't even imagine, especially as I wrestled with publishing just a few high-quality papers each year. Despite his impressive metrics, I couldn't shake a sense of disappointment with the actual content of his work.

While reviewing COVID-19 research, I came across a paper by Professor Didier Raoult promoting hydroxychloroquine as a treatment. I critiqued the data analysis methods used in the study. A French colleague then surprised me by highlighting Professor Raoult's immense reputation in infectious diseases. He mentioned Raoult's prolific publication record: a staggering 2,053 papers between 1979 and 2018, averaging nearly one per week. This level of productivity was truly impressive, far exceeding what I could personally manage.

But how should a scientist's worth truly be measured? Surely, the most important factor is the impact of their work, both socially and scientifically. Consider Mrs. Tu Youyou, whose discovery of artemisinin revolutionized malaria treatment, saving millions of lives in Asia and Africa. Despite having published a few papers with fewer than a hundred citations, she deservedly received a Nobel Prize for her groundbreaking achievement.

While some scientists make groundbreaking, headline-grabbing discoveries, the vast majority, myself included, contribute in a different way. Our dedication yields progress in smaller, more incremental steps, often building upon the work of others. The impact of these contributions unfolds over time and may not be readily apparent in the short term. Evaluating these scientists and their vital role in scientific advancement, for promotion or grant funding, presents a unique challenge. As a result, the scientific community has devised a complex system of metrics to assess scientists' worth, attempting to capture the true value of their contributions.

Metric 1: The Quantity Game

The coveted title of "Professor" seemed solely dependent on one metric: publications. A scientist's calling card, it appeared, was a monstrous list of papers, stretching into the hundreds. To the untrained eye, this sheer volume spoke of dedication and a burning desire to push the frontiers of knowledge. But beneath this shiny surface lurked a dark side. The emphasis on quantity cast a long shadow, morphing into a relentless pressure to churn out publications at an alarming rate. The mantra became "publish, publish, publish," pushing the quality of the work, its originality, and its true contribution to the field, to the periphery. In this relentless pursuit of numbers, the very essence of scientific inquiry—the pursuit of knowledge—risked being lost.

This obsession with publication quantity has led to a disturbing trend of "salami tactics." Like a skilled butcher, researchers slice their findings into paper-thin slices, each one stretched across multiple publications, diluting their meaning in the process. Take a medical disorder, for example. It's often defined by a complex interplay of factors. Yet, under the pressure to publish, each factor is dissected and analyzed in relation to a series of disease outcomes, each analysis forming the basis of a PhD thesis or a separate scientific paper. This fragmentation, driven by the publication game, results in a sea of increasingly irrelevant information that drowns out truly groundbreaking research.

Remember the days when scientific journals were like grand libraries, housing diverse and fascinating research across disciplines? It seems like a distant memory now. The insatiable hunger for publications has spawned a new breed of journals: hyper-specialized publications focused on ever-narrower slivers of knowledge. Imagine a world with over 130,000 scientific journals, each year churning out more and more. It's a dizzying landscape where researchers are encouraged to become ultra-specialized, focusing on topics so esoteric that only a handful of insiders even understand them.

The logic is simple: the more niche your research, the easier it is to get published. So, you can become an expert in "the economic impact of osteoporosis on the Asian populations," and voilà, you have a journal to publish your findings. And within this tiny circle, everyone becomes reviewer and author, praising each other's work, ensuring a steady stream of publications for all. It's a strange world we've created, where knowledge is fragmented and siloed and where the pursuit of publication has eclipsed the joy of discovery. We've traded the grand libraries of diverse research for a labyrinth of hyper-specialized niches, each echoing with the same self-referential praise.

Remember the days when scientific papers were like solo journeys of discovery? One researcher, one lab, one quest for knowledge. Now, it's a team sport, with papers boasting ever-growing author lists. In 1957, a single scientist could publish a paper in the *Deutsche Ärzteblatt*. By 2008, the average number of authors per article had ballooned to 3.5.

This isn't just about the growing complexity of research, though. It's also about the pressure to publish and be seen as productive. Senior researchers, like professors and project leaders, wield their power, demanding inclusion on every paper from their team. The bigger the team, the more "honorary authorship" opportunities there are. Young scientists, desperate for career advancement, often feel pressured to include senior figures as co-authors. It's a way to boost their chances of publication, even if the senior researcher hasn't meaningfully contributed to the work. This "forced co-authorship," as Timo Rager called it, is particularly prevalent in medicine, where the average number of authors per article is already alarmingly high. Some journals have found that one in five papers has "phantom authors" who haven't actually contributed.

And it doesn't stop there. With each additional author, the paper gains more "friends" who cite it, regardless of its actual merit. It's a self-perpetuating cycle of self-citation in which quantity trumps quality. It's a far cry from the days of solitary scientific exploration. The pressure to publish has turned research into a numbers game, where authorship is a currency and collaboration can be a burden. We've lost sight of the individual scientist, the one driven by the pure joy of discovery.

Metric 2: The Impact Factor Game

But the playing field isn't level. Articles published in prestigious journals like *Nature* or *Science* hold considerably more weight than those appearing in lesser-known journals. To address this disparity, a new field emerged: *Scientometrics* or *Bibliometrics*. This discipline focuses on measuring and comparing scientific output, developing its own journals and increasingly intricate (though less transparent) methods. This is where metrics entered the scene.

A cornerstone of *Scientometrics* is citation analysis. The number of times a paper is cited reflects its reach and assumed quality. Highly cited papers are presumed to be well-read and influential. This logic allows citations to serve as a proxy for quality, enabling researchers to compare articles published in different journals. The resulting "objective" numbers are then used for rankings and comparisons, with some institutions prioritizing these metrics over actual research itself.

Back in the 1960s, Eugene Garfield, a bright mind with a knack for numbers, teamed up with Irving Sher to create a new metric: the Impact Factor (IF). It was meant to be a simple tool for librarians, a way to gauge which journals were worth subscribing to. They envisioned it as a quick snapshot of a journal's overall influence, calculated by averaging the number of citations its articles received over a two-year window.

But what started as a helpful tool morphed into something far more powerful—and ultimately problematic. Over the decades, the IF ballooned into a dominant force, becoming the ultimate measure of academic prestige and success. Universities used it to judge potential professors, funding agencies relied on it to allocate research grants, and researchers themselves became fixated on it.

The problem? As Goodhart's Law so aptly states, "When a measure becomes a target, it ceases to be a good measure." The IF, initially meant to be a rough indicator, became the be-all and end-all. This led to a perverse game of manipulation. Unscrupulous researchers found ways to artificially inflate their publications' citation counts, while journals adopted strategies to boost their own IFs. Self-citations became rampant, review articles (which tend to attract more citations) were prioritized, and publication timing was meticulously managed to maximize the citation window.

The IF, originally intended to reflect the influence of journals, ended up obscuring the true significance of individual research. High-quality work published in lower-impact journals could easily be overlooked, while mediocre articles in prestigious journals were often overvalued. The focus on journal-level metrics lost sight of the individual contributions, fragmenting valuable research and hindering collaboration.

The pressure to publish in high-impact journals became immense, driving scientists to prioritize quantity over quality. This led to a flood of marginally significant findings submitted to prestigious journals, diluting the scientific literature and impeding progress. The quest for the coveted "high-impact publication" even compromised research integrity, pushing some scientists towards questionable practices such as data dredging, p-hacking, and outright fabrication.

Perhaps the most concerning consequence was the exacerbation of inequities within the scientific community. Researchers from smaller institutions, developing countries, or less well-funded fields often struggle to publish in high-impact journals, marginalizing their contributions and hindering their career advancement. This created a skewed view of scientific progress, privileging certain areas of research over others and reducing the diversity of scientific inquiry.

The IF, a simple tool meant to be a helpful guide, became a symbol of the pressure and distortion that can arise when metrics are overused and misinterpreted. It serves as a reminder of the importance of critical thinking and a balanced approach to evaluating research, ensuring that the pursuit of knowledge remains focused on its true purpose: the advancement of understanding and the betterment of humanity.

Metric 3: The H-index Game

The obsession with metrics has become a pervasive force in academia, and the H-index is another example of its pitfalls. In 2005, the American physicist, Jorge Hirsch, introduced this new metric, promising a way to assess "the importance, significance, and broad impact of a scientist's cumulative research contributions." It combined the number of publications with the number of times those publications were cited, offering a seemingly objective scorecard.

The H-index quickly gained traction, becoming a benchmark for universities and funding agencies. Scientists became fixated on it, viewing it as a badge of honor and a measure of their standing within their field. While it offered a convenient comparison tool, the H-index became, for some, another metric to be maximized, potentially detracting from the true essence of scientific contribution.

I remember reading a report in *Médiapart*, a French newspaper, where a journalist described a researcher on Professor Didier Raoult's evaluation committee. The researcher was struck by Raoult's "obsession with his publications," evident in his immediate display of his H-index before the evaluation even began. This anecdote mirrored the growing "Culture of Numbers" I witnessed in academia, where algorithmic analysis of statistics became the perceived key to fair research evaluation.

The H-index, despite its popularity as a metric for assessing a researcher's productivity and citation impact, has several significant weaknesses that limit its effectiveness and fairness. It fails to consider the context of citations: highly cited papers might be groundbreaking or riddled with errors, but the H-index treats them equally. Additionally, it doesn't distinguish between single-authored and collaborative papers, obscuring individual contributions in large research teams. Furthermore, the H-index favors established researchers due to their longer publication history, potentially hindering the career advancement of early-career scientists. My H-index is naturally higher than my junior colleagues' due to my longer career as a researcher. However, this metric doesn't necessarily reflect the impact or quality of our individual contributions.

The H-index still emphasizes quantity over quality, potentially valuing numerous publications in lower-impact journals over fewer, but more influential, publications in high-impact journals. The H-index, relying on citation counts, can be vulnerable to manipulation. Practices such as self-citation can artificially inflate an H-index. Finally, the H-index is specific to each field, making it difficult to compare researchers across disciplines because citation practices and publication norms vary. Thus, relying solely on the H-index can lead to an incomplete and sometimes misleading picture of a researcher's influence and accomplishments.

I witnessed this firsthand during a faculty candidate search. A candidate presented impressive numbers: 800 publications, 35,000 citations, and an H-index of 101—all within nine years of his PhD. However, a closer look raised red flags. Nearly forty percent of the citations originated from the papers that he authored or co-authored, and further investigation revealed a network of researchers citing each other excessively, suggesting a potential "citation cartel." Despite these red flags, the selection committee ultimately chose to offer the candidate the professorship position.

The story of the professorship candidate is not an isolated incident. It highlights the systemic flaws in our current research evaluation system, where metrics like the citations and H-index have become the driving force, often overshadowing the quality and originality of the research itself. This pressure to publish and inflate metrics can lead to a culture of corner-cutting, unethical practices, and ultimately, a distorted view of scientific progress.

As we move forward, we need to find a more balanced approach to research evaluation. This requires a critical examination of existing metrics, a focus on qualitative assessments, and a recognition of the diverse ways in which scientific contributions can be made. Only then can we ensure that the pursuit of knowledge remains driven by the true spirit of inquiry, curiosity, and the desire to contribute to a better understanding of the world around us.

Fake Journals

Unfortunately, my suspicions about inflated metrics were further confirmed. Many highly-cited researchers, it turned out, had achieved their status through fabricated papers published in fake journals. This concerning trend, known as predatory publishing, involves the rise of sham academic journals solely motivated by profit. These journals prioritize revenue over quality and publish research with minimal to no regard for scientific validity or rigorous review processes.

The emergence of predatory publishing can be traced back to three key factors: the obsolescence of the traditional scientific publishing model, the development of the internet, and the potential for significant profit.

The traditional scientific publishing model, established in the 17th century and persisting until the early 21st century, has remained largely unchanged. Under this model, scientists submit manuscripts, which are then sent to experts for peer review. Based on the reviewers' recommendations, the editorial board decides whether to accept or reject the manuscript. Publishers in this system play a minimal role, with authors and their colleagues handling manuscript submission and editing, and the editorial board working essentially without compensation.

However, publishers own the brand and the printing press, allowing them to generate significant profits with minimal investment. Forget tech giants—science publishing might be the real king of profits. Some scientific publishers boast margins exceeding forty percent, putting them well ahead of companies like Apple and IBM. This high profitability stems from a unique combination of factors: a captive audience of researchers seeking to publish their work, limited competition for top journals, and recurring revenue from subscriptions and article processing charges. While a thirst for knowledge may drive the content itself, the business behind it thrives on a very different kind of currency.

This model, in which authors essentially pay to publish and lose copyright to their work, has been widely criticized. In response, the late 1990s saw the emergence of the Open Access model, where authors pay a publication fee to a legitimate publisher, retain copyright, and allow anyone in the world to access their work. This model, championed by groups like the Public Library of Science, has revolutionized scientific publishing.

The Open Access model, coupled with the development of the internet, has led to a permanent shift in the scientific publishing landscape. Traditional paper-based journals have largely given way to online platforms, with publishers requiring minimal investment due to the free labor of reviewers and the authors' responsibility for formatting. This shift has also led to the emergence of numerous online journals, such as *PLoS ONE* and *Scientific Reports*, which publish vast quantities of research papers and generate substantial revenue.

The lure of high profits in online publishing has spawned a troubling trend: "predatory" scientific journals. These deceptive publishers often masquerade as legitimate by using scientific-sounding titles and claiming to be Open Access. However, they prioritize profit over quality, churning out low-grade research with minimal to no peer review or editorial oversight. This has resulted in a concerning spread of misinformation and confusion within the scientific community.

In 2008, librarian Jeffrey Beall of the University of Colorado emerged as a champion against this trend. He compiled a renowned list of predatory journals (coining the term "predatory publishing" itself) that served as a crucial resource for researchers worldwide. Sadly, Beall faced relentless pressure from the university, which in turn faced the threat of lawsuits. This ultimately forced Beall to remove the list in 2017. While the closure of Beall's List was a significant setback, others have taken up the mantle, continuing his fight to expose predatory journals and ensure the integrity of scientific publishing.

The predatory publishing industry had been thriving. The sheer scale of this industry is quite alarming. Estimates suggest that there are currently over 11,000 fake journals publishing hundreds of thousands of papers annually. These journals often target early-career researchers and those from developing countries, further blurring the lines between legitimate and illegitimate research.

The most tragic aspect of the predatory publishing industry is the human cost it inflicts. Thousands of established scientists, often unaware of the deception, have published their work in these outlets, potentially jeopardizing their reputation and career advancement. Their research, conducted with rigor and genuine intent, becomes tainted by association with a fraudulent system.

The impact on early-career researchers and PhD students is particularly devastating. Eager to publish and establish themselves in their field, they are often targeted by predatory publishers that promise rapid publication and minimal review. Their hard-earned work, the culmination of years of study and research, gets published in journals with no credibility, potentially hindering their future opportunities and casting doubt on their academic integrity. The consequences can be particularly severe for students from developing countries, where access to legitimate publishing opportunities can be limited.

The damage extends beyond individual careers. Universities and funding agencies are also affected, because the proliferation of low-quality research papers published in predatory journals makes it difficult to assess the true value of research output. This can lead to wasted resources and funding being allocated to projects based on flawed or fabricated findings.

The presence of low-quality research published in predatory journals dilutes the pool of legitimate scientific information. This makes it difficult for researchers and the public to distinguish between credible findings and flawed or fabricated work. This can have serious consequences, potentially leading to misinformed decision-making and even harmful outcomes if flawed research is applied in real-world settings.

The Crisis of Reproducibility

There was a period in my research career that I now call the "VDR Fiasco,' or, perhaps more politely, the "VDR Incident" I mentioned earlier. For me, that little stumble turned into a massive lesson about the fickle nature of medical research, especially when it comes to a phenomenon's "reproducibility."

These days, reproducibility—or the lack thereof—has become a full-blown crisis in science. Think of it like a recipe. You follow the steps meticulously, gather the finest ingredients, and... the cake flops. Except in science, the "cake" can be a potential cure for cancer or a revolutionary new theory in psychology.

Here's the thing: reproducibility is what separates real science from pseudoscience or wishful thinking. It's the ability for other researchers, following the same methods, to get similar results. It's the cornerstone of building a reliable body of knowledge. And the scary part? Most research results just aren't cutting the mustard. They can't be reproduced.

This is a big deal. It throws a wrench into the whole scientific process. How can we trust findings that can't be replicated? How can we build on shaky ground? It's like trying to cook a new dish based on someone's vague recollection of their grandma's secret recipe. The results are bound to be inconsistent, frustrating, and ultimately a waste of time and resources.

My hard lesson in reproducibility stemmed from the VDR incident. After our major VDR paper was published in *Nature*, the scientific community went into a VDR frenzy. Research labs everywhere, including mine, were on a mission to find more genes linked to osteoporosis. The approach back then was pretty straightforward: based on biological reasoning, pick a gene, pick a single variation of that gene (an "allele"), and compare it between people with osteoporosis and healthy folks. We call it a "case-control" design. Find a difference in the allele frequency between the two groups and boom! You have found a candidate gene for osteoporosis. It was all about "Candidate Gene Association Studies" back then.

Now, here's the kicker: just because you find an association doesn't mean the gene variant causes the disease. It just means there's a signal, something worth digging deeper into. It also doesn't guarantee the specific allele you studied is the culprit. It could be linked to another variant you haven't even considered. Blinded by this enthusiasm, we, along with countless colleagues around the globe, reported over a hundred osteoporosis-linked genes. Seemed like a breakthrough, right?

Wrong. Reality soon hit us like a ton of bricks. Most of those associations, including—to my chagrin—our VDR gene finding, weren't reproducible. Some studies couldn't replicate our results, and others got conflicting data altogether. The lack of reproducibility wasn't just a problem in bone research, either. It was, I later discovered, a gremlin plaguing studies across the entire medical landscape. That's when I truly understood the fragility of medical research, the importance of rigorous methodology, and the need for independent confirmation before popping the champagne.

The VDR incident was a humbling experience, but ultimately, a valuable one. It taught me a crucial lesson: in science, especially medicine, flashy findings are just the beginning. It's the ability to consistently replicate them that separates the signal from the noise.

Most Published Research Findings Are False

Then came John Ioannidis. Florence. 2014. A beautiful city for a conference on pharmacogenetics, where I crossed paths with him—a soft-spoken professor from Stanford with a resume that could put a filing cabinet to shame: medicine, epidemiology, statistics, biomedical data science—the man wore more hats than a haberdashery.

One year later, in 2015, he dropped a bombshell on the medical world with a paper titled "*Why Most Published Research Findings Are False.*" Now, this paper was published in *PLoS Medicine*, a great open-access journal, but some considered it a notch below the big guns like the *New England Journal of Medicine*. The title itself was a shot across the bow, and the tone, well, let's just say it wasn't exactly establishment-friendly. It made me wonder if that's why such an important paper ended up in *PLoS Medicine*. Maybe the big journals choked on the audacity of it all.

Regardless, the impact was undeniable. It became the most-viewed paper *PLoS* had ever published. And here's the thing: Ioannidis wasn't just spouting off. He used cold, hard math—mathematical models—to back up his claims.

The core of his argument was elegantly simple. He compared a scientific paper to a medical diagnostic test, asking: "If a study shows something positive, how much more likely does it make the claim actually true?" It forced you to consider the bigger picture—the totality of the evidence—not just the flashy headline of a single study.

Ioannidis used an epidemiological concept called "positive predictive value" (PPV)—basically, the odds that a positive result actually reflects something real. Here's the kicker: his model showed that, under some common assumptions, the PPV could be less than fifty percent if only a handful of hypotheses in a field were true. In other words, in many medical areas, a coin toss might be just as good as a positive study result!

Bias, of course, was another gremlin in the system. Poor study designs and cherry-picked data can skew results. And the more research groups chasing the same hot topic, the worse it got. It was a phenomenon called "multiple hypothesis testing," and it basically meant that the more you dug, the more likely you were to unearth false positives.

John Ioannidis's paper was a bombshell, sure, but was it just academic theory? Sadly, real-world research painted a picture even bleaker than his predictions. Most published findings seemed destined to be either flat-out wrong or, at best, impossible to replicate.

Take for example the Reproducible Project in Cancer Biology (RPCB). These folks spent eight long years trying to replicate experiments from supposedly groundbreaking cancer research papers published between 2010 and 2012. It was a massive undertaking, a collaboration between the Center for Open Science and Science Exchange. They set out to replicate 193 experiments from fifty three high-impact papers—the cream of the crop, you might say. The results? Dismal.

They could only repeat a measly fifty experiments from a mere twenty three papers.

The reasons? Well, let's just say transparency wasn't exactly a strong suit in cancer research. Many original papers lacked crucial details—the kind of nitty-gritty statistics and methods that are the backbone of good research. Without that, it was like trying to follow a recipe with half the ingredients missing. You could spend hours in the kitchen, but the results would never be what the author intended.

The cancer research fiasco wasn't an isolated case. It was like a bad smell wafting out of a lab, and soon everyone caught a whiff. Researchers at giant pharmaceutical companies like Bayer and Amgen were facing similar struggles. They took a deep dive into sixty seven published studies in the most prestigious journals—*Science, Cell, and Nature*—the holy grail of research publications. Guess what? They couldn't replicate three-quarters of the results!

Even the gold standard of medical research, randomized controlled trials (RCTs), wasn't immune. A group of researchers led by Ioannidis looked at forty nine highly regarded RCTs published between 1999 and 2003. Only eleven had results that nobody questioned. The rest? A whopping seventy six percent couldn't be replicated, or worse, produced the opposite outcome!

Genetic and prognostic studies that were supposed to be lighthouses guiding us through the murky waters of disease were even worse. In seven incredibly promising cancer studies, five turned out to be basically no better than random chance!

The picture was getting bleaker by the minute. A comprehensive analysis of twenty major observational studies with exciting, game-changing results yielded a single, lonely study where the initial findings held true.

It wasn't just a few isolated cases; it was an epidemic. Large-scale studies in psychology, economics, and other fields started sounding the alarm. Learned societies, surveys of researchers, even popular science books—the message was everywhere: reproducibility was in shambles. The cracks in the foundation of science were becoming a gaping chasm, and everyone was starting to take notice.

Consequences of Irreproducibility

The crisis of reproducibility wasn't confined to the sterile walls of research laboratories; it sent shockwaves through the entire scientific ecosystem, creating a ripple effect that impacted everyone from policymakers to patients.

Imagine a world where health policies are based on flimsy research. That's the potential danger of false findings. Policymakers rely on scientific evidence to make informed decisions on public health initiatives, drug regulations, and environmental protections. When that evidence turns out to be shaky, the consequences can be disastrous. Millions of dollars might be wasted on ineffective interventions, or worse, public health might be put at risk by false leads.

The public, too, becomes a casualty in the reproducibility crisis. For years, we've been bombarded with headlines touting scientific breakthroughs, only to find out later that many of them can't be replicated. It's enough to make anyone cynical. The trust we've placed in science—the belief that it holds the key to a healthier, better future—starts to erode. People become hesitant to embrace new medical treatments or change their lifestyles based on research findings, wondering if it's all just a house of cards waiting to collapse.

Perhaps the most concerning impact is on medical research itself. Irreproducibility creates a vicious cycle. We chase down false leads gleaned from flawed studies, wasting valuable time and resources. Promising new avenues of research, based on shaky foundations, often lead nowhere. It's like searching for a cure in a desert filled with mirages—a monumental effort that leads to nothing but disappointment. The patients who stand to benefit from these potential breakthroughs are the ones who truly suffer.

The cracks in reproducibility—the foundation of science—weren't exactly a secret. The news media, those relentless bloodhounds of truth (or at least headlines), had gotten wind of it, and science was facing a public relations nightmare. Prestigious publications—*New York Times, Washington Post,* and the whole A-list—were all running exposés on the "reproducibility crisis." The tone wasn't exactly complimentary. Some journalists, bless their cynical hearts, took a rather mocking approach. "Scientists wasting taxpayer dollars!" they cried.

It wasn't exactly the endorsement we were looking for, but they certainly did have a point. An analysis published in *PLoS Biology* put a number on this frustration: a staggering $28 billion in the U.S. alone, wasted annually due to irreproducibility. That's a billion, with a "B." Billions of dollars were poured into research that couldn't be verified—billions that could be funding genuine breakthroughs. It was enough to make any scientist, myself included, feel a pang of despair.

Why Irreproducibility?

The question of irreproducibility—why so many studies can't be replicated—is a heavy one, and one that gnawed at me for years. From my experience, I see the reasons falling into two camps: bias and statistics. Both contribute to a situation where the results we get may not be what they seem.

Publication bias and the glamour trap. The scientific world thrives on discovery, on groundbreaking studies that push the boundaries of knowledge. And let's be honest, there's a certain glamour that comes with publishing a game-changing paper in a prestigious journal. It's the scientific equivalent of winning the lottery: recognition, acclaim, and a boost to your career. But this allure of positive results creates a dangerous pitfall: publication bias.

Here's the rub: negative results—studies that show no significant effect—rarely get the same fanfare. Journals often view them as uninteresting, lacking the excitement factor that drives readership and citations. Imagine spending years meticulously collecting data, only to have your research languish in the slush pile, gathering dust instead of accolades. This creates a perverse incentive for researchers, a pressure to massage the data or downplay negative findings just to squeeze out a "positive result." It's a pressure that can cloud our judgment and distort the scientific record.

The consequences of publication bias are far-reaching. The scientific literature gradually becomes skewed—a one-sided story in which every study seems to confirm a specific hypothesis, even if reality is far more nuanced. Imagine a detective investigating a crime scene, only focusing on evidence that supports their initial hunch and ignoring anything that contradicts it. The picture they paint might be clear, but it's also incomplete, and potentially misleading.

A 2010 study by Fanelli painted a startling picture of this phenomenon. His analysis revealed that a staggering eighty to ninety percent of published results were positive. It's a statistic that defies logic, a sign that publication bias has become deeply entrenched across all fields of science. This one-sided narrative not only hinders scientific progress but also misleads the public and policymakers who rely on this research to make important decisions about healthcare and public health initiatives.

Addressing publication bias requires a cultural shift in science, a move towards valuing negative results as much as positive ones. Open science initiatives, where data and methodology are shared freely, can help to alleviate the pressure to publish flashy findings. Journals are also starting to play a role by placing greater emphasis on the quality of the research design, not just the outcome. It's a slow shift, but it's a step in the right direction, towards a more balanced and robust scientific record.

When good intentions go awry. The road to scientific discovery is paved with good intentions, but even the most meticulous research can be derailed by the pitfalls of experimental design. Bias—the ever-present gremlin in the scientific lab—isn't just about chasing fame and glory. It can creep in through the cracks in our methodology, leading to subtle yet significant errors.

Picking the wrong participants for a study is like casting the wrong actors in a play. Imagine studying the effects of a new workout program on a group of elite athletes. The results might be impressive, but can they be applied to the average person struggling to get off the couch? The participants we choose can significantly influence the outcome, making it hard to translate findings into real-world applications.

Even seemingly insignificant details, like the gender of the researcher handling lab animals, can have a surprising impact. A study meticulously tracked the activity levels of mice, only to later discover that they were more active when handled by female researchers! This seemingly trivial detail highlights the importance of controlling every variable in an experiment. One unexpected influence can throw the entire study into question, making replication—the cornerstone of scientific progress—nearly impossible.

The pressure cooker: a competitive sport. I already described in the NHM-RC chapter that science is a battlefield, and grant money is the coveted prize. Publishing in top journals is the golden ticket, the key to securing funding and that coveted promotion. But this pressure-cooker environment can lead researchers down a dangerous path, incentivizing them to cut corners and prioritize "positive" results over rigorous methodology.

Imagine a researcher desperately needing to publish a groundbreaking study to secure funding. They might be tempted to massage the data, downplay negative results, or even engage in a practice called "data torture." This involves sifting through mountains of information, looking for any statistically significant pattern, even if it's just a random blip. It's like panning for gold in a river; eventually you might find a glint, but it could just be a fool's gold nugget, devoid of real value. These practices not only undermine the integrity of research but also foster a culture in which the pursuit of novelty overshadows that of truth.

The statistical swamp: numbers can lie. Statistics are supposed to be the beacon guiding us through the murky waters of scientific research. They're the tools we use to analyze the data we collect, to sift the signal from the noise and draw meaningful conclusions. But, like any powerful tool, statistics can be misused, and when they are, we end up wading through a statistical swamp.

Early on in my career, I, like many researchers, fell prey to this very pitfall. Choosing the wrong statistical test is akin to trying to unlock a door with the wrong key. You might wrestle with it for a while, nudge it this way and that, and maybe, just maybe, you'll get lucky and it'll click open. But more often than not, you'll end up frustrated and confused, unsure of what went wrong.

One of the statistical bugbears that loves to trip us up is the p-value. Imagine flipping a coin: heads means the finding we observed is real, tails means it's just due to random chance. A p-value below a certain threshold, typically 0.05, has become a bit of a golden ticket in the world of scientific publishing. A p-value of 0.05 suggests that the odds of getting "heads" by chance are only five percent, making it seem like a slam dunk, a genuine discovery.

But here's the rub: the world of statistics is rarely so black and white. The lower the p-value, the more confident we can be that our finding is real, but even a p-value of 0.05 doesn't guarantee certainty. It just means the odds of seeing this result by random chance are relatively low. Think of it as a spectrum of confidence, not a bright line dividing truth from fiction. A very low p-value, say 0.001, gives us a lot of confidence, but a p-value of 0.05 just tells us the finding is worth investigating further and doesn't guarantee it's real. Misinterpreting p-values can lead researchers to overstate the significance of their findings, mistaking a glimmer in the statistical twilight for the bright light of truth. This is why wading through the statistical swamp requires not just technical expertise but also a healthy dose of skepticism. We need to be cautious, to ensure our results are robust and can be replicated before we celebrate them from the rooftops.

The hydra of multiple tests. There's this concept in statistics called the "Multiplicity," and it's a real monster to contend with. Imagine you're dissecting a complex issue, like the human genome with its billions of genetic variations. You set out to test a specific hypothesis, maybe looking for a link between a particular gene and a disease. But here's the rub: the human body is a complex system, not just a single strand. With so many variables at play, you might be tempted to cast a wider net, to test multiple genes or interactions simultaneously. It seems logical, right? Increase the number of comparisons, increase the odds of finding something interesting.

The problem is this approach is like staring at a giant, intricate fabric and searching for patterns. By pure chance, you're bound to find some kind of shape or some alignment of colors or threads, even if it has no real meaning. In statistics, this translates to "false positives": findings that appear significant due to random noise rather than a genuine underlying connection.

The more comparisons you make, the more likely you are to stumble upon these false positives. In large-scale studies, especially in fields like genomics, where millions of variables are examined, the number of comparisons can explode into the astronomical. It's like rolling a thousand dice at once: the odds of getting a lucky streak—a statistically significant result by sheer coincidence—become overwhelming.

The consequence? A mountain of seemingly groundbreaking findings that crumble under closer scrutiny. Studies that trumpet a breakthrough in gene-disease connection might turn out to be nothing more than statistical mirages. This is why the issue of multiple hypothesis testing is such a hydra—it has many heads, each capable of spewing misleading results that erode the credibility of scientific research.

There was a time, a golden age of science, you might say, where the public held doctors and scientists like me in the highest regard. We were seen as the guardians of truth, the ones wielding the torch of knowledge against the darkness of disease. My own purpose, and I believe the purpose of many in my field, was singular: to alleviate suffering. It was a noble calling, a crusade fueled by a desire to make a tangible difference in people's lives. But then, somewhere along the way, the landscape shifted. Medical research, once a pristine realm of pure inquiry, became entangled with the tentacles of commercial interests. The pursuit of fame and riches began to cast a long shadow, dimming the beacon of truth-seeking that had always guided us. The crisis of reproducibility, with its mountain of unreliable studies, is just a symptom of this larger truth.

The pressure to publish groundbreaking research had become a double-edged sword. Fame and the promise of funding dangled like carrots, urging us to churn out novel findings. But at what cost? As I saw it, the relentless pursuit of novelty was turning research into a frantic race, leaving a trail of shaky results in its wake. We needed a reality check, a return to the rigorous methods that had made science such a powerful tool.

John Ioannidis's paper was a bombshell, a much-needed slap in the face. It wasn't an attack on research itself, but a call for a sturdier foundation. His message echoed with me: even the most exciting findings needed rigorous testing and independent confirmation before we started popping champagne corks. The world of medical research, for all its advancements, could use a healthy dose of skepticism. John Ioannidis, the soft-spoken heretic from Stanford, had become an unlikely hero, serving up a bitter truth on a silver platter. It was a truth we desperately needed to swallow.

The allure of scientific discovery had always captivated me. Yet, as my career in bone health research matured, a disquieting trend began to emerge—a shadow cast over the very foundation of our field: the crisis of irreproducibility. I thought I should do my part to improve the situation. Then came the opportunity to become an Associate Editor of the *Journal of Bone and Mineral Research* (JBMR) and *Osteoporosis and Sarcopenia*. This wasn't just a new position—it felt like a call to arms. Here, I could wield my growing expertise and frustration to effect positive change. Together with editors Fernando Rivadeneira and Roberto Civitelli, we penned an editorial in JBMR in 2019. It wasn't a diatribe, but a rallying cry. We acknowledged the initial consternation in the research community, but also the robust discussions brewing amongst editors, funders, and researchers alike. This was our chance to be part of the solution. We proposed a comprehensive set of new guidelines for data reporting and statistical analysis. My experience as an editor and reviewer for numerous bone and medical journals over the past quarter-century exposed me to the specific pitfalls plaguing bone research. In a separate "perspective article" published in *Osteoporosis and Sarcopenia* in 2020, I delved deeper. I pinpointed the most common issues—study design flaws, shoddy data analysis, and a near-religious adherence to p-values without understanding their limitations. Here, I aimed not just to criticize, but to offer solutions.

These were my initial steps in a long-term battle for a future where bone health research could deliver on its promises. The path wouldn't be easy, but the chance to contribute to a more reliable and trustworthy foundation for scientific progress was a fight worth waging.

Science, in its relentless pursuit of knowledge, can sometimes stumble, but within the lab coat and goggles lies a darker side. My experiences have revealed crucial lessons that transcend the daily grind of research:

The Narcissism Trap. The thirst for recognition can morph into a dangerous foe—scientific narcissism. When self-interest overshadows genuine inquiry, it breeds unethical practices and fosters a toxic environment. This can be countered by promoting a culture of collaboration and open communication within the scientific community.

The Fraudulent Facade. The pressure to publish within the "Publish or Perish" culture can lead some researchers down a dark path—scientific fraud. High-profile cases like Dr. Sato's serve as important reminders of the devastating consequences of such actions. To combat this, we need robust systems for data verification and rigorous peer review processes.

The Quagmire of Predatory Journals. Predatory outlets exploit the Open Access movement, prioritizing profit over quality. These fake journals publish low-grade research and garbage, hindering the dissemination of reliable findings. Early-career researchers are particularly vulnerable. We must promote responsible publication ethics and support initiatives such as "Think. Check. Submit." to guide researchers to legitimate journals.

The Replication Enigma. A troubling trend is the difficulty in replicating published findings. This reproducibility crisis undermines public trust in science. To address this, we need to emphasize robust methodologies, transparency in research design and data analysis, and a willingness to re-evaluate existing findings.

By acknowledging these challenges and implementing solutions, we can strengthen the foundations of scientific research and ensure its continued pursuit of truth and progress.

Throughout my career, I've observed that scientific achievement, or at least its recognition, often relies less on the science itself and more on self-promotion. Scientists need to secure funding, which requires strong communication and networking skills. Landing speaking engagements and attracting mentors hinge on these same abilities. Unfortunately, the scientific world seems to reward a particular personality type—one comfortable with flattery and maneuvering within power structures. This often clashes with the core values of good science, which should prioritize objective truth over social maneuvering.

For me, these skills never held much appeal. I wasn't interested in playing the political game in academia, nor did I believe such tactics were necessary. Unfortunately, these skills weren't included in my scientific training, and, frankly, I wasn't interested in acquiring them.

Chapter Fifteen

Crossing Borders: My American Sojourn

The refugee camp in Thái Lan felt like a different life. Back then, the American flag shimmered like a mirage, a symbol of freedom and a place of endless possibility. Ironically, fate would weave a different path, leading me to Australia for a new beginning. Yet, almost two decades later, the American dream would tap me on the shoulder, whispering its siren song once more.

For years, the annual pilgrimage to the Annual Scientific Meetings of the American Society for Bone and Mineral Research (ASBMR) had become a familiar rhythm. Each city was a fleeting glimpse into the American experience. Cincinnati, Ohio, in 1998 throbbed with the familiar energy of research and professional connections being forged. But during a break, a chance encounter with an American colleague shattered the routine. He introduced himself, Dr. Roger Siervogel, with a warmth in his handshake, confessing he'd known my work for years. His casual invitation to lecture at Wright State University in nearby Dayton felt like the polite gesture it likely was. Yet, a mere two days later, an envelope arrived—a formal invitation and a plane ticket. A part of me, ever the pragmatist, thought, "Why not?"

Dayton unfolded like a travel brochure come to life. My lecture on osteoporosis caught the attention of the medical school dean. His offer to work alongside them caught me completely off guard. Australia was home now, a career carefully cultivated. The thought of uprooting myself was daunting. Yet, the dean's invitation felt more like an invitation to explore, not just a scientific one. He wasn't just offering a job; he was offering an adventure. Intrigued, I promised to consider it.

The following two days were a fast-paced exploration, not only of Wright State, but also of the warmth of American hospitality. Discussions with professors, brimming with intellectual curiosity, felt like a homecoming for the mind. The meticulous planning—a limousine to whisk me back to Cincinnati, a flight back to California—felt more like the treatment reserved for royalty than a visiting scholar. Sitting in that plush car, the vastness of the American Midwest stretched before me like a wrinkled canvas, painted with golden fields and endless horizons. A scientist turned accidental tourist, I fumbled with the touch-screen controls of the minibar, a moment both humorous and surreal. Even the farewell dinner felt like a movie scene: an upscale restaurant, the dean and his colleagues exuding a warmth that defied explanation. Why such generosity from strangers? Was this the American spirit I'd heard so much about?

Back in Australia, the familiar routine reasserted itself. The offer from Wright State became a distant memory amidst the daily grind. But then, at the tail end of 1997, a letter arrived. The dean had created a new professorship, and my name was attached. Guilt, at the thought of their kindness, propelled me forward. A swift application followed and a phone call confirmed the appointment! The American dream, once a fleeting notion, was now a tangible reality. Bypassing the usual bureaucratic hurdles, they'd formed a search committee abroad, showcasing their American pragmatism and eagerness to secure my expertise.

With a mix of trepidation and excitement, I packed my bags, ready to embark on a new journey—a "second exile" from Việt Nam, this time to the land that had once shimmered like a mirage. However, it wouldn't be a mirage but an unexpected oasis—a chance to explore, to collaborate, and perhaps, to finally plant some roots in the fabled Land of Opportunity.

Ohio greeted me in a blaze of autumn glory. As we drove from the airport to my pre-arranged accommodation, the road shimmered with a canvas of fallen leaves—yellow, red, purple, brown—creating a vibrant canvas unlike anything I'd seen before. My new apartment sat nestled on a quiet street, lined with towering trees that mirrored the fiery palette outside my window. Leaves blanketed the ground, untouched, creating a scene straight out of a poem—the rustling symphony Lưu Trọng Lư captured so beautifully in his *Autumn's Sound* poem. Here, in this unexpected pocket of nature, surrounded by the promise of crisp air and changing hues, I felt a surge of affection for this new land. It was as if autumn itself had conspired to welcome me.

That evening, the director hosted a welcome dinner at his sprawling house nestled amidst a lush forest. Guests signed a guestbook, a formality that felt quaintly old-fashioned. Despite the grandeur, the house held an air of quiet solitude—just the director and his wife, their children having flown the coop for careers elsewhere. He greeted me warmly, peppering me with questions about life in Australia, a place he'd visited often. His knowledge of Vietnamese and Asian politics surprised me. Practicality and compassion seemed to coexist within him. He made it clear the university saw me as an investment, one they expected a return on it. Their goal was for me to produce effective research, secure grants, and bolster their reputation. He advised me to take a few weeks off before starting, but truthfully, I yearned to dive in, to finally begin the work I'd dreamt of for so long.

After a week of settling in and addressing administrative issues, I eagerly began my research. The university's generosity stunned me, a cool $25,000 to kickstart my project! This was a striking contrast to the fiercely competitive, underfunded environment I was familiar with in Australia. Here, grants weren't mere scraps to fight over. My colleague even provided a list of agencies eager to support researchers at all levels. This was a true sign of the "Land of Opportunity."

My first day in the lab was a sensory overload. The sheer volume of advanced equipment dwarfed any Australian facility I'd seen. My research team was a compact unit of three: myself, a post-doctoral fellow, and a doctoral student.

Soon, a fourth member joined: Nigel, a bright-eyed fourth-year medical student. Together, our easygoing nature and shared work ethic fueled incredible efficiency.

Days bled into nights as we engaged in passionate debates and discussions that stretched well past midnight. This was a crucible of scientific pursuit, a place where hunger and sleep were secondary concerns in the fervent race to publish before our peers.

Many a night, a sudden burst of inspiration would send me scrambling out of bed and driving to the library, a mere fifteen minutes away, to dive into research papers. Despite the peculiarities of American life, I found myself oddly attuned to this intense, singular focus. Here, in this scientific oasis, I was flourishing.

My first foray into teaching at Wright State proved nerve-wracking. Staring out at a sea of a hundred expectant faces, I felt a surge of self-doubt. Yet, the lecture flowed, peppered with my usual questions to gauge understanding. While pleased to have conveyed the core concepts, I was taken aback by some fifth-year students' basic math skills. Sigma and product symbols? A mystery! Patiently, I unraveled them, and later, a few students lingered, thanking me for my clear explanations. Every beginning is difficult, I thought with a silent smile. This new homeland was already offering a chance to make a difference.

One key difference between American and Australian medical students became readily apparent. The American system, built upon a completed bachelor's degree, seemed to sculpt more mature students with a stronger scientific foundation. However, whispers of the rigorous specialization training systems back in Australia and the UK reassured me—intensity wasn't exclusive to the US.

The student-professor dynamic here also held a certain formality. Gone were the easygoing Aussie first names, replaced by respectful titles like "Professor Nguyen." Despite the formality, the core relationship remained one of equality: professors as guides, growing alongside students, not second parents as in Việt Nam. Both systems held merit, I mused. American professors, particularly, excelled at igniting curiosity and unleashing student potential, a quality I longed to see instilled back home.

My American experience wasn't all sunshine and roses. Public transport, a pale shadow compared to Sydney's, thrust me into the world of car ownership. A used car became my passport to exploration, a constant reminder to hug the right side of the road (a near-miss on a bridge served as a potent lesson!). The freedom of the open road was exhilarating, but exploring a new culture presented its own challenges.

One cultural quirk did raise an eyebrow. While seeking feedback on a paper, I received a critique about my spelling and word usage—*haematology, epidemiological, specialization*—all seemingly incorrect.

"American scientific journals demand adherence to American English," a frustrated professor explained, his body language showing his disapproval.

"When in Rome," I conceded, and from then on, I donned my linguistic chameleon suit.

My first week culminated in a tradition: a talk outlining my research to the department. Afterwards, during a break, a young professor complimented my English fluency.

"Thank you," I replied, "but I'm from Australia!"

His next question left me speechless. "Oh, do people speak English in Australia?"

Here I was, a scholar contributing to a nation leading the scientific discourse, yet a basic fact about a close ally seemed to have eluded this professor.

This encounter sparked a realization. America wasn't a monolith, but a diverse blend of knowledge and experience. Perhaps the professor's geographical isolation in the Midwest limited his worldview. Further interactions across the US painted a more nuanced picture. East and West Coasters seemed more globally aware compared to their Midwestern and Southern counterparts. This newfound awareness fueled a desire to connect and bridge the gaps, not just in scientific knowledge, but also in cultural understanding. In the years to come, I would find myself not just a scientist, but also an ambassador, fostering collaboration and knowledge exchange between my adopted home and my homeland.

The university embraced me with open arms. Research and teaching facilities were top-notch, exceeding expectations. I even enjoyed perks that elicited envy from some colleagues. Remember, they'd made a scientific investment, and the return was evident. Within two years, I'd established a thriving bone research group and secured significant funding for the university. Building bridges extended beyond research. I fostered connections with state health departments and local associations, enriching the university's ecosystem.

A Kindred Spirit in Dayton

Dayton, surprisingly, held a pocket of Vietnamese life—Professor Trần Hữu Dũng, an economist at Wright State. Reserved and private, he rarely spoke of his family, only revealing snippets of his past—his birth year (1945) and his father's roots in Bến Tre, a Mê Kông Delta province not far from my hometown. In 1963, he embarked on an academic journey, studying electronic engineering and physics abroad before returning to Việt Nam to work in Đà Lạt. By 1972, he was drawn overseas once more, this time pursuing a PhD in economics at Syracuse University in 1978. After the war, his visits to Việt Namdwindled.

Our paths crossed during my early, transportation-less days in Dayton. Perhaps sensing the isolation of a fellow Vietnamese in a new land, Dũng reached out. His offer of assistance was impossible to refuse. The next day, his pickup truck became my chariot, ferrying me to buy furniture and essentials. But Dũng surprised me further.

"Forget it," he declared, pushing aside my money for a desk. "Consider it a good omen. No need to spend money." Despite being a decade my senior, he insisted on calling me "sir," a formality that both tickled and humbled me.

His house, nestled in a Dayton suburb, unveiled a world within a world. Stepping into his basement, the "resting place" as he called it, a term particularly apt for the Midwestern love of basements. Entering his basement felt like entering a second home. Spacious, it rivaled Australian houses in size! Here, the scholar reigned supreme. Books, journals, magazines, and newspapers filled every nook. Two large desks housed perpetually lit computers, buzzing with scholarly pursuits. A silent stereo system stood in the corner. This was Dũng's editorial sanctuary—the space where, for over two decades, he'd singlehandedly curated the *Viet-Studies* and *Arts & Letters Daily* pages.

Together, we wrestled the hefty wooden desk into his truck. Unloading and arranging furniture took another half-hour. As we finished, Dũng muttered, "Well, it might be a long time before we meet again." Considering we were colleagues at the same university, I found this puzzling.

True to his word, it was six long months before our paths crossed again. This time, I invited him to see my lab's new equipment and treated him to lunch, a small token of gratitude. When I offered him a bone density scan, he chuckled. "No, let my wife take that one. Your machines might find diseases I don't want to know about."

His wife, Phương Mai, was a force to be reckoned with. A high-ranking university official, I teased them that her authority far surpassed his. Despite her years away from Việt Nam, her Mê Kông Delta accent hadn't wavered, a clear contrast to her husband's English fluency. But where words fell short, her cooking spoke volumes. One evening, Dũng invited me for a taste of home, a delectable Mê Kông Delta feast, prepared with love by Phương Mai. Her braised fish, a symphony of flavors and textures, remains a memory engraved in taste and in time.

That evening marked our third—and sadly, final—encounter. Dũng remained an enigma, a scholar shrouded in quiet dignity, a kindred spirit who offered a lifeline when I needed it most. His kindness, a beacon in a new land, would forever be enthralled in my memory. Years later, I learned that Dũng had passed away. The news arrived as a wave of bittersweet nostalgia, washing over me with the lingering scent of Mrs. Mai's braised fish and the echo of Dũng's gentle voice calling me "sir" in a foreign land. He may have been an economist by profession, but in that moment, he was a compatriot, a bridge between two worlds, and a reminder of the unexpected kindness that can blossom in the most unlikely of places.

My trusty Honda, a cast-off from my friend Dr. Lê Thiết Thành, became my chariot, opening doors to a world beyond the university walls. Ohio, once a lonely expanse, blossomed with friendships. There was the power couple, Nguyễn Văn Toại, an electrical engineering PhD holding a prestigious position, and his wife, a professor of agriculture. Through them, I met Thành, a postdoctoral researcher from England ("Thai Lo people," I'd tease him), and the brilliant minds of

Professor Vũ Quốc Phóng (may he rest in peace) and Professor Phạm Hữu Tiệp, a mathematical prodigy.

But two figures left an indelible mark: Mr. Phong, a former army officer in the Republic of Vietnam Armed Forces, and Mr. Thành, a pilot who soared with American Airlines, the first Vietnamese captain in their ranks. These former officers, though they harbored suspicions about Dũng's political leanings (even accusing me of the same!), held no grudges. Weekends found us driving for miles, not just to visit friends, but to share a drink, as camaraderie transcended political divides. I never mentioned those comments to Dũng, cherishing instead the respect I held for these veterans, men who had borne the weight of a war that continued to cast a long shadow.

Dũng, a man of boundless curiosity, devoured information like a starved man presented with a feast. His articles in Vietnamese publications brimmed with knowledge, not just in his field of economics, but across a broad spectrum. He wasn't just an economist; he was a journalist with an exceptional ability to curate valuable articles, some good, some bad, but all worthy of consideration. "There's humor in the bad ones too," he'd confided with a twinkle in his eye. "A break for the readers."

Online, Dũng meticulously scoured the web, adding his witty, sometimes satirical, commentary to noteworthy articles. Though blocked in Vietnam, *Viet-Studies* and *Arts & Letters Daily* were cherished sources of information for many, including journalists, artists, and even government officials. They read, perhaps not daring to quote openly, but absorbing the knowledge nonetheless. To my friends, I'd often say that these pages were Dũng's greatest contribution to Vietnamese academia. Through them, he shone a light, even from afar, offering a window to the world beyond the government-controlled media. And though not physically present in Việt Nam, I felt a deep debt of gratitude to this quiet scholar who had, in his own way, defied censorship and fostered a more informed citizenry.

My American sojourn opened doors to a world of scientific exchange. Universities across the vast landscape, from the hallowed halls of the Mayo Clinic to the prestigious MD Anderson, welcomed me to share my research. These trips, fully funded oases in the academic desert, were eye-opening experiences. The American scientific community hummed with an energy Australia could only dream of, but beyond the sheer scale, it offered opportunities for collaboration and for building bridges between minds across borders. In academia, as the saying goes, "It's not what you know, but who you know." Heeding the wisdom of those who came before me, I embarked on a quest to expand my network.

The amazing connections I made in my research started with my mentor, but a truly lucky break happened in 1999. I was on a layover in Minneapolis after visiting the lab of the famous Professor Larry Riggs (who later became a friend) at the Mayo Clinic. In the busy airport terminal, I bumped into Professor Clifford Rosen from the University of Maine! He knew my work on osteoporosis and was very complimentary, which I wasn't expecting at all. This chance meeting turned out to be a big opportunity. Professor Rosen was involved with a new scientific journal called the *Journal of Clinical Densitometry* (JCD), and he offered me a great position on its editorial board!

In the scientific world, journals are the lifeblood, the voice of professional societies. A coveted position on their editorial boards becomes a badge of honor, reflecting one's expertise. To serve on an editorial board wasn't just about recognition; it was about service to science and the advancement of knowledge. Having your name on an esteemed journal's masthead was a mark of leadership, a public declaration of your standing in the field. This unexpected windfall left me speechless. Without hesitation, I accepted, even pledging to contribute an article for the journal's very first issue.

The editorial board served as the gatekeepers, meticulously reviewing manuscripts, determining their fate: publication or rejection. This responsibility wasn't to be taken lightly. A rejected paper could derail a career, delay a thesis defense, or shatter promotion hopes. But to accept shoddy research or poorly written articles was to do a disservice to the field and ultimately, to patients who relied on sound science for their well-being. Finding this delicate balance between authorial aspirations and scientific rigor was a constant challenge, usually determined by collective wisdom rather than the whims of a single individual.

As a founding member of the JCD editorial board, I witnessed firsthand the immense effort required to build and sustain a scientific journal. The experience offered a unique window into the inner workings of Western science, laying the foundation for my future endeavors. Today, the JCD, with its distinguished editorial board, enjoys a strong reputation in the field of osteoporosis. And I? I carry a deep sense of pride knowing that I played a small but significant role in its success.

My eight years on the JCD board, a cornerstone of my American experience, opened doors to a cascade of opportunities. The esteemed International Osteoporosis Society invited me to join their *Osteoporosis International* journal... another two terms devoted to advancing bone research. This prestigious invitation was followed by a string of others: *Bone, Current Osteoporosis Reports, Archives of Osteoporosis*, and more. At one point, I juggled a dizzying array of three simultaneous editorial boards, one even within the hallowed halls of endocrinology, the *Journal of Clinical Endocrinology and Metabolism*. These unpaid roles, while demanding, were imbued with a sense of scientific duty, a responsibility to ensure the quality and integrity of published research.

In 2018, a new chapter unfolded. The *Journal of Bone and Mineral Research*, the world leader in its field, was undergoing a leadership shift. The incoming Editor-in-Chief extended an invitation to serve as an Editor, one of four curating specific research areas. Genetics and epidemiology fell under my purview, placing me at the helm of selecting manuscripts and assigning them to esteemed reviewers. This responsibility, with its far-reaching impact on the field, came with a welcome stipend of $5,000 annually (if memory serves me right).

My first act as Associate Editor was a bold one. Scientific reproducibility—the ability to replicate research findings—had become a major concern. Estimates suggested a staggering ninety five percent of medical findings were potentially flawed. To address this crisis, I proposed stricter publication standards for JBMR, a move met with initial apprehension from some board members who feared a decline in published articles and, consequently, revenue. But quality, I argued, trumped quantity. With the Editor-in-Chief's backing, I spearheaded the creation of new editorial guidelines titled, "*New Guidelines for Data Reporting and*

Statistical Analysis: Helping Authors With Transparency and Rigor in Research (2019). The editorial was signed by three of us: Roberto Civitelli, Fernando Rivadeneira, and me. My commitment extended beyond *Journal of Bone and Mineral Research*, leading me to author another article, *Common methodological issues and suggested solutions in bone research* (*Osteoporosis and Sarcopenia* 2020).

The role of Associate Editor held considerable weight. It wasn't just a line on my curriculum vitae; it was a key that unlocked a door to substantial power. Power to shape the conversation in the field of bone and mineral research, power to influence careers, and power to be the gatekeeper of knowledge published in the prestigious *Journal of Bone and Mineral Research*. But this power, I quickly learned, came with a precarious balancing act.

For a PhD student, a rejection from JBMR could be a punch to the gut. Delayed graduation, funding applications gathering dust—the potential consequences weighed heavily. I felt the weight of those dreams with every manuscript I received, a small universe of research waiting for my judgment. Here, the meticulous scientist in me took over. I carefully chose reviewers and experts who could dissect the work with the precision of a jeweler. Their comments, combined with my own assessment, were the compass guiding my decisions.

But wielding that compass wasn't always smooth sailing. The most nightmarish part? Recruiting reviewers. Scientists, me included, were a busy breed. Peer review—the invisible pillar of academic science—was entirely thankless. It was a constant struggle. Ten emails sent, maybe one or two positive responses, the rest a chorus of polite declines or the even more deafening silence of unanswered messages. But I persisted, a knight gathering a (somewhat reluctant) roundtable, because the research deserved that level of scrutiny.

The precariousness of the position really hit home when the politely worded rejections started rolling out. I knew some wouldn't be happy, but the vitriol of some abuse emails was sometimes a shock. My inbox had sometimes become a battleground, filled with accusations of bias, incompetence, and even personal attacks. One email stands out: the author, clearly upset, insisted that his manuscript be published because a US grant funded the work. It was a blatant attempt at pressure, and a reminder that even the most objective decisions could be met with irrationality. This tightrope walk between fairness, safeguarding the journal's prestige, and weathering the potential storms of passionate researchers became painfully clear. The power I held felt more like a double-edged sword than a key in those moments. Yet, with each new week came a fresh manuscript, reigniting my commitment to be the voice of reason, the guardian of good science, even in the face of the storm.

During my tenure as Associate Editor, the journal's impact factor, a measure of its influence, rose by 0.8 points. The acceptance rate, however, dipped slightly, from twenty seven percent to twenty five percent. The board, however, viewed this as a positive trend, a sign of heightened quality control. While other editors maintained acceptance rates between twenty five and thirty percent, mine stood at a lower eleven percent, reflecting the stringent standards I had championed.

These contributions paved the way for leadership roles within both the American Society for Bone and Mineral Research (ASBMR) and the Australian and New Zealand Bone and Mineral Society (ANZBMS). ASBMR, a mid-sized society with a global reach (though with only fifty percent American members), offered a chance to learn the intricacies of running a professional society. As part of the Scientific Publications Committee, my colleagues and I helped shape the future of bone research. From organizing annual conferences that brought together the brightest minds in the field to appointing editorial boards that ensured the highest standards of publication, my work fostered collaboration and accelerated scientific progress. Here, I wasn't just a researcher or an editor; I was a bridge builder, connecting researchers across continents and disciplines. As the sole Vietnamese member in ASBMR leadership, I was proud to contribute to this esteemed committee.

The year was 2017. The ASBMR, by then at forty years old, decided to celebrate its members in a special way. The leadership unveiled a new fellowship award—a recognition for those who, like me, have dedicated themselves to the field of bone and mineral research. It wasn't just about the science, though. The ASBMR valued its members who went the extra mile, who volunteered their time and expertise to the Society, and championed its mission. The general criteria read as follows:

"The Fellow of the American Society for Bone and Mineral Research (ASBMR) program recognizes long-term ASBMR members who have made outstanding contributions to the field of bone and mineral science. The program is committed to recognizing the breadth and diversity of the Society's membership. Preference will be given to individuals who have shown a commitment to ASBMR by having served as a volunteer in the Society or as a Society representative to another organization or initiative. Fellows are nominated by their peers, followed by evaluation and selection by a review committee." (ASBMR as at 2018)

Fast forward to 2018 at the annual ASBMR Scientific Meeting. It was a big occasion, not just for the scientific exchange that always took place, but for the recognition bestowed upon me and eighty six other colleagues. There I stood, alongside my esteemed colleagues like Clifford Rosen (whom I consider a close friend), Jane Cauley, Natalie Sims, Richard Eastell, Graeme Jones (my PhD student fellow in the early 1990s), Douglas Kiel, Rajesh Thakker, and Richard Prince (another Aussie friend). All of us were humbled and honored to be named Fellows of the ASBMR. It was a culmination of years of dedication and a tribute to both our individual pursuits and our collective passion for advancing the field of bone and mineral research.

Beyond the ASBMR, my reach extended to the ANZBMS. Smaller in size but no less impactful, ANZBMS offered a different perspective on bone health research, with a strong focus on the Asia-Pacific region. For two terms, I served as the Chair of their Scientific Committee, a role that placed me at the heart of shaping the society's future. Organizing conferences, devising award policies, and sponsoring research—these responsibilities struck a chord. There was a profound satisfaction in recognizing the achievements of my colleagues, in providing the fuel for their scientific endeavors, and ultimately, in contributing to the greater good.

In the world of science, leadership within professional associations and scientific journals carries significant weight. These contributions become stepping stones on the path to academic advancement. Universities, when evaluating professors and lecturers for promotion, scrutinize these contributions.

I was honored to be among the inaugural fellows of the American Society for Bone and Mineral Research. (2018)

They look at a record of service that speaks volumes about a candidate's impact beyond their own research. This is why, for any aspiring young scientist, I always offer the same advice: volunteer actively for associations. These seemingly small acts of service can blossom into something far greater, a network of connections, a platform for leadership, and ultimately, a pathway to recognition within the scientific community.

Looking back on my path from war-torn Việt Nam to American academia, I'm struck by the unexpected turns life takes, often leading to the most rewarding destinations. The American spirit, with its warmth and generosity exemplified by colleagues and even strangers, has deeply moved me. My time in the US wasn't just about advancing osteoporosis research; it offered a sense of belonging I never imagined in this once-distant land. The vibrant Ohio autumns and the intellectual camaraderie fostered a new perspective on the American Dream—not just a concept, but a lived experience.

Chapter Sixteen

Crossing the Sands of Saudi Arabia

The year was 2009. An email arrived like a desert mirage, shimmering with possibility. It was an invitation from the Royal Society of New Zealand, summoning me to Saudi Arabia, a land of ancient lore and veiled women. My heart quickened. Having never set foot in the Kingdom, the prospect of exploring its enigmatic depths was thrilling.

The email proposed a unique mission: to join a five-member panel tasked with assessing the King Abdulaziz University's Centre of Excellence for Osteoporosis Research (CEOR). My expertise in the field, honed over years of research, felt like a perfect fit. With a sense of honor and intrigue, I accepted the invitation, eager to delve into the heart of Saudi academia.

Bureaucracy, however, loomed like a sandstorm on the horizon. First came the hurdle of Saudi Arabia's Ministry of Education scrutinizing my credentials. Then, the visa application process, a labyrinthine maze navigated through a network of intermediaries who inflated the cost to an eye-watering sum. Yet the weight of my contribution—potentially saving millions for Saudi Arabia—outweighed the financial burden.

My flight to Jeddah, the gateway city, was a revelation. Opting for Singapore Airlines, I found myself cocooned in the plush embrace of business class travel. It felt like an indulgence, yet a necessary one, considering the contribution I was about to make.

Jeddah's airport, however, painted a contrasting picture. Stepping off the plane, I was met with a harsh reality. Disorganization and a lack of amenities characterized the space. Gone was the efficiency of other Asian airports; here, passengers disembarked onto remote tarmacs and shuttled to the terminal.

The customs process was a rigid affair. Stern-faced officials, clad in military attire, scanned passengers with a watchful eye. The air crackled with tension as I joined a sluggish queue that seemed to inch forward at a snail's pace. Each booth was equipped with a camera, ready to capture portraits for the authorities.

A young immigration officer, sporting a beard that hinted at a battle with a dull razor, took my passport. His English, though broken, held a hint of curiosity. "You... from Vietnam?" he inquired, the question hanging in the air.

I confirmed, a touch of amusement bubbling up. "Yes," I replied.

A grin, as wide as his limited vocabulary, stretched across his face. "Vietnam, Ho Chi Minh, huh?" he declared, nodding in approval.

I couldn't help but chuckle. "Actually," I started, "Ho Chi Minh passed away many years ago."

A surprised laugh escaped his lips, as if the news of a communist icon's demise was a delightful revelation. The exchange stretched the tense air of the arrival process, a brief moment of human connection.

Finally, after what felt like an eternity under his watchful gaze, the official stamped my passport with a flourish. With a wave of his hand, he ushered me into the cacophony of the baggage claim area—a chaotic embrace after the sterile formality of immigration.

Smoke hung thick in the air as travelers jostled for their belongings. The air throbbed with a cacophony of shouts and frantic searches. "Oi oi!" echoed through the hall, a celebratory cry upon finding lost luggage.

Emerging from the terminal, I faced another hurdle. My name, a mangled mess on the waiting list, offered little hope. The throngs of waiting figures—mostly men, with women conspicuously absent—seemed oblivious to my predicament. Taxi drivers, their white tunics and beards indistinguishable, swarmed me with offers. Their persistence bordered on harassment, forcing me to retreat for another fruitless search.

Just as despair threatened to set in, a lone figure holding a placard caught my eye. "Welcome Prof. Tuanvan NQUYEN," it read. Relief washed over me. This must be my ride.

The limousine—a well-worn Mercedes—was far removed from the luxurious image I had conjured. Yet, it offered a welcome respite from the airport chaos. The driver, an Indian gentleman who had been working in Saudi Arabia for seven years, launched into a conversation. His scathing critique of the local work ethic and the dominance of expatriates painted a surprising picture of the Kingdom.

The drive to the hotel took us through well-maintained roads, past expansive government housing complexes catering to pilgrims. As we neared the Royal Terminal, the driver pointed out the ubiquitous presence of royalty, their exclusive privileges, a striking contrast to the hustle and bustle of everyday life.

This was Saudi Arabia: a land where ancient traditions met modern ambitions, and where a scientific mission became a cultural odyssey.

A First Night in Jeddah

The Intercontinental in Jeddah, my third in the prestigious chain, unfolded before me. While lacking the captivating elegance of Hà Nội's West Lake branch, it promised a comfortable stay. Security, however, was completely different from what I had encountered before. Here, at the hotel entrance, a fortified barrier guarded by soldiers stood sentinel. My initial confusion, mistaking it for construction, was met with a chuckle from the driver. This was standard procedure.

Inside, the lobby pulsed with a James Bond-esque vibe. Luggage, like passengers at an airport, passed through an imposing X-ray scanner. A knock on my newly settled room's door sent a jolt of surprise. A steward stood with a black briefcase, a "gift" from the Ministry of Education. Filled with documents and an intriguing plaque, it ignited a flurry of questions. Was it merely a thoughtful gift or something deeper?

The Assessment Team takes a commemorative photo with officials from King Abdulaziz University and COER.

The phone buzzed, shattering the comfortable silence in my cozy hotel room. It was Dr. DS, our team leader for the upcoming review. Our little group was a fascinating blend of expertise: Dr. DS, the group head who organized the whole thing; Dr. DF, an Aussie who practically breathed project management; Professor ME, an American geneticist; Professor RF, a Brit with expertise in bone and joint diseases; and me, the Vietnamese Australian researcher who'd dedicated years to understanding osteoporosis. Dr. DS, ever the pragmatist, proposed a working session, not in a sterile conference room, but over a meal at a restaurant. It felt like an interesting twist, a chance to bond beyond the confines of formal meetings.

Dinner was a challenge. The mid-range restaurant, while decent, lacked the vibrancy of flavors I craved. Scanning the menu, I envisioned a symphony of Vietnamese spices—a sharp departure from the sweet, unfamiliar choices before me. A grilled fish and salad, my safest bet, paled in comparison to the culinary adventures I yearned for. My Western colleagues shared my sentiment, while Dr. DS, an old hand in Saudi Arabia, offered a sympathetic smile.

As we ate, we strategized for the coming days. Day one would focus on the CEOR center's self-evaluation, led by directors and department heads. Day two would be ours, dedicated to inspections and assessments. Based on Dr. DS's experience, two roles became clear: he naturally took on the role of team leader, while another served as the spokesperson. My diplomatic demeanor, it seemed, secured my role as the voice of the team, summarizing our findings for both the CEOR and the Ministry of Education.

Jet lag, a frequent companion in my travels, ensured a restless night. The early morning heat, however, promised a refreshing reward—a swim in the pool. To my delight, the mostly-Western crowd at this early hour offered a sense of familiarity.

Breakfast, at least, held a unique twist. The upscale breakfast room offered two distinct sections: one for Arab guests and one for Westerners. Curiosity drew me to a dish labeled "Beef Bacon." Intrigued, I tried it, only to be disappointed. Ultimately, a plate of fruit and coffee offered the only solace for my taste buds. The adventure in Saudi Arabia had just begun, and with it, a cultural dance of expectations and realities.

Crossing Paths at King Abdulaziz University

Our 8:30 am rendezvous point was the hotel lobby, where Dr. AA, our jovial liaison from the Ministry of Education, awaited us. Dressed in the traditional thobe, a striking departure from the Western influences he had absorbed during his studies in Australia and the US, he carried himself with quiet authority. Curiosity piqued, I broached the subject of polygamy, a practice confirmed by Dr. AA. However, financial constraints, he explained, steered most "modern" Saudis towards monogamy. A friendly warning followed—alcohol, a coveted libation back home—was scarce in Jeddah, relegated to whispers of clandestine locations.

With Dr. AA in the lead, we climbed into a car destined for the CEOR center within King Abdulaziz University (KAU). The drive unfolded like a scene from

Việt Nam, marked by a chaotic ballet of cars weaving through traffic. Here, lane markings were nonexistent, replaced by a driving style that mirrored the audacious maneuvers I was accustomed to back home in Việt Nam. Women, confined to the passenger seat by law, were conspicuously absent from behind the wheel.

Towering over the cityscape like an academic beacon, KAU, sprawling across a staggering 150 hectares, resembled a small town. Immaculate roads, complete with traffic lights and stop signs, guided the flow of new, expensive cars. Unlike Việt Nam, motorcycles were absent here. Parking lots stretched out like those at Western supermarkets, but unlike bustling Western streets, these were largely deserted due to the scorching midday temperatures, which reached 45°C.

Dr. Akawi introduces the lab of the Centre of Excellence for Osteoporosis Research at King Abdulaziz University.

Our morning commenced with a courtesy visit to the Vice President. The sheer opulence of his office dwarfed even the Australian Prime Minister's! An expansive hallway adorned with Islamic motifs, led to his imposing, solid-wood door. Three male employees, one presumably the Vice President's secretary, stood guard. The door swung open, revealing a distinguished figure: the Vice President himself.

Clad in a pristine white thobe, he exuded quiet authority. Dr. AA introduced each member of our delegation with utmost respect.

The Vice President's office mirrored the grandeur of its entrance—an expansive space estimated at twenty meters by fifteen meters. His desk, an embodiment of power, sprawled across an impressive four by five meters. Before pleasantries could be exchanged, two attendants materialized, laden with tea, coffee, and an array of refreshments. Conversation flowed effortlessly. The Vice President, a Cambridge-educated scholar with a PhD in Chemistry from the US, spoke impeccable English and possessed refined Western manners. A sense of camaraderie blossomed as we exchanged anecdotes.

Bidding us farewell with warm gratitude, the Vice President acknowledged our long journey and emphasized the value of our feedback in propelling KAU towards even greater heights. Indeed, the hospitality extended by the university was unparalleled, from airfare to luxurious accommodation and lavish meals. A conservative estimate placed their expenditure for our week-long stay at a staggering $10,000 per person. Their generosity was beyond reproach.

Formalities with the Vice President complete, we returned to the CEOR center, eager to delve into the heart of the mission: the inspection. Today was the center's time to shine. The director kicked things off by outlining the CEOR's mission, goals, and organizational structure. This was followed by a parade of presentations from each research program's head, detailing their past achievements, ongoing projects, and future aspirations.

Sitting through a day of PowerPoint presentations, however, proved to be an endurance test. We, the inspection team, felt the presentations meandered, laden with unnecessary details instead of concise summaries. Research programs presented laundry lists of objectives, easily condensed, and boasted about accomplishments that, in all honesty, seemed rather pedestrian. The PowerPoint presentations were far from polished, but crammed with excessive embellishments, distracting animations, and text-heavy slides devoid of graphs. To our astonishment, presenters read verbatim from the slides! Professor ME beside me sighed repeatedly, clearly frustrated, convinced they were deliberately dragging things out. I couldn't help but agree.

The saving grace arrived in the form of the Q&A session. Here, we finally had the opportunity to engage, exchange ideas, and delve deeper. To their credit, the CEOR leadership displayed a refreshing candor in addressing their shortcomings and tackled our probing questions head-on. However, a faint undercurrent of defensiveness peeked through. When I inquired about their foray into stem cell research without an expert on board, the speaker choked back emotion, sharing a story of his father's agonizing death from a fractured femur. This raw vulnerability left me speechless, unsure if further probing was appropriate. Fortunately, DS, the elder statesman of our group, intervened, offering condolences and skillfully steering the conversation back to a scientific plane.

The marathon session, originally scheduled to wrap up by 5 pm, stretched into an exhausting 7 pm. Twenty-hour flights took their toll on everyone. Back at the Intercontinental, we huddled around a dining table, dissecting the 'day's key points and strategizing for tomorrow—our day to take the reins.

The next morning, we addressed the unresolved issues, particularly those concerning finances. Budgetary matters, we learned, were sensitive. When a few team members, particularly DF, the Australian project management expert known for his bluntness, delved into financial capabilities, expenditures, and management practices, the CEOR leadership seemed to retreat behind a veil of polite defensiveness. However, DF's directness, while potentially abrasive, served a purpose: to expose a bureaucratic quagmire disguised as financial management. Surprisingly, though, their research project approval process adhered to rigorous standards, mirroring those of developed nations.

The afternoon saw us finalize the key points for my interim report—the delegation's preliminary assessment of the CEOR's progress. We deliberated carefully, aiming to strike a delicate balance between acknowledging their strengths and offering constructive criticism of their weaknesses. With a clear strategy in hand, we invited the CEOR representatives back in, and it was my turn to deliver the report.

Humor, I thought, might be the perfect icebreaker to ease the tension, so I peppered the initial minutes with anecdotes. The worried expressions on the CEOR leader's faces, however, remained deeply etched. I strategically began by highlighting their strengths and praising their accomplishments. Then, I moved on to their weaknesses, attributing them to time constraints and portraying them as opportunities for growth. Finally, I presented a series of practical recommendations to help them navigate towards achieving their stated goals. The report stretched over two hours, and I remained hyper-aware of their body language, adjusting my tone and pace accordingly. Though they listened intently and took notes, their expressions remained unreadable.

Our report concluded and the floor switched to them. They expressed heartfelt gratitude for our candid feedback and a genuine desire to learn from our experiences with research programs. The discussion closed on a positive note, exceeding both my 'expectations and the team's. As the initial inspection phase came to a close, a sense of accomplishment, tinged with a newfound understanding of the CEOR's realities, settled over us.

Evening Adventure in Jeddah's Old Town

As the day drew to a close, the itinerary offered a welcome change of pace: a guided tour of the historic district followed by dinner. Concerned about our ability to withstand the scorching afternoon sun, the CEOR leaders suggested a late departure, venturing out only after 8 pm.

Despite being dubbed the "Old Town," this area boasted a mere century of history. Narrow, winding streets snaked their way through clusters of lime-built houses. The lanes themselves were quite narrow, some as little as two to three meters wide, practically placing residents face-to-face across the street.

Vendors lined the streets, offering an array of fragrances said to originate from Malaysian and Cambodian forests. These weren't your typical perfumes; rather, small, broken pieces of wood used for incense much like we do back home. Their subtle aromas, while cherished by the Arabs, failed to ignite my sense of wonder. Perhaps it was my unfamiliarity with the scents.

The second most prominent product was perfume, a far cry from the designer brands of the West. Here, the focus was on locally pressed flower essences, notably rose. Not unlike our coconut oil, these "perfumes" promised all-day fragrance with just a dab. Intrigued, I sampled a few varieties and found their scents surprisingly reminiscent of some high-end perfumes. The only difference? These came in miniature bottles.

The market pulsed with life, perhaps because the cooler Sunday evening temperatures drew people out. Africans mingled with the locals, most women shrouded in black abayas, their faces veiled, revealing only their eyes. The eateries, modest and slightly unkempt, emitted a peculiar blend of perfume and...t well, let's just say the allure wasn't culinary. The atmosphere, however, felt strangely familiar—a bustling throng walking through the streets, bumping shoulders without apology, a scene straight out of Việt Nam.

Our market exploration complete, we made our way to Bubbles, a restaurant said to be the city's most opulent. Adorned in Arabian and Islamic motifs, it offered a surprising culinary fusion: Thai, Italian, and Arabic cuisine all under one roof. The menu, frankly, was underwhelming. A Thai spring roll appetizer, followed by Tom Yum soup, and a parade of beef, chicken, and fish main courses (with no pork, of course) left me uninspired. My attempt at the grilled fish ended prematurely, leaving me to seek solace in a simple salad. Alcohol, as expected in Saudi Arabia, was conspicuously absent. The lingering hope was for a swift conclusion to the meal so we could retreat to the comfort of our hotel rooms. Little did I know, conversation would stretch well past midnight before I finally made it back.

After days of intensive work, our report was finalized and submitted to the University Board of Directors for their consideration. While acknowledging CEOR's research efforts despite resource limitations, we presented a series of recommendations to restructure the center to optimize scientific productivity. Six months later, word reached me that King Abdulaziz University had not only decided to retain CEOR but also implement reforms based on our suggestions. A quiet sense of satisfaction settled over me, knowing that my contribution had played a part in ensuring the future of our Saudi Arabian colleagues, at least for a while.

Returning to a Different Jeddah

Three years had elapsed since our initial visit, and here we were —the same five-member team —back at King Abdulaziz University to reassess CEOR's research activities.

On the ride from the airport, the silence from our Filipino driver was initially deafening. But when he discovered I knew about Philippine presidents, a spark ignited. He confided in me about his unused sociology degree back home and the unemployment that forced him to become a VIP driver in Saudi Arabia. Yet, less than a year in, his voice was laced with disappointment. His story echoed my own struggles in the early 1980s. The difference, however, was simple. In Australia, I found the opportunity to thrive, something that seemed to elude him.

The xenophobia and societal disregard for women stood in striking opposition to his expectations. He saw himself as a" foreign worker," working solely to support his family back home. Bitterness tinged his words as he described the harsh realities of being a foreigner here. Lower wages, cramped living conditions, and a justice system seemingly stacked against him—all consequences of his origin. He navigated the chaotic traffic cautiously, determined to avoid any incident that might bring trouble.

The conversation deepened, his voice laced with a sense of humiliation. He viewed working abroad as a national disgrace, a consequence of a homeland rich in resources but controlled by a select few. He spoke of corruption plaguing successive administrations, with only President Estrada earning his favor. His frustration culminated in a question: why couldn't a nation famed for its overseas workforce prosper? His answer: incompetent leadership.

I listened intently, wary of wading into another country's internal affairs. He inquired about my origins, and upon learning I was Vietnamese, a comparison began. He acknowledged Việt Nam's war-torn past but marveled at its rapid development compared to the Philippines. He credited this success to a government that cared for its people, a government, according to his theory, free from corruption.

His words struck a chord of dissonance within me. While his admiration for Việt Nam was heartwarming, it stemmed from a limited perspective, perhaps shaped by propaganda portrayals. The truth was more nuanced. Việt Nam, despite its strides, still lagged behind the Philippines in per capita income. Corruption, too, was a reality we grappled with. Our people, like the Filipinos, sought work abroad, enduring similar hardships.

The memory of Vietnamese women trafficked as brides crossed my mind, sparking a reflection on whether this 'wasn't a manifestation of national shame—women reduced to mere commodities. From this perspective, the plight of the Filipino driver seemed somewhat less dire. Việt Nam had never experienced such a form of humiliation before, leaving me deeply troubled. This realization shattered any sense of privilege, leaving me with a newfound sense of humility. My pride in my nation faded away, replaced by a yearning for a future where our people could attain sustenance and safety within our own borders, where assistance would be provided to detained citizens. It was only then, I pondered, that individuals like the Nguyens could hold their heads a bit higher.

The driver's story reminded me of a news snippet I'd caught earlier: Vietnamese laborers detained in Saudi Arabia, the reason shrouded in mystery. The silence of the labor export company and the embassy's inaction fueled a burning anger within me. Here I was, supposedly a VIP, yet feeling a kinship with my detained compatriots.

My time in Saudi Arabia had become a journey of self-discovery, a humbling realization that national pride often masked deeper complexities. The seeds of empathy had been sown, a shared experience of being foreign workers in a land not quite our own, forging a fragile yet profound connection.

Saudi Arabia's ambitions to join the ranks of research powerhouses were evident. Their strategy: attract global talent and invest heavily in scientific endeavors. King Abdulaziz University, a shining example, ranked 269th in the world university rankings.

The Centers of Excellence initiative exemplified this ambitious plan. Aiming to diversify the Saudi economy beyond oil, the government envisioned these centers as hubs for high-quality research, driving up the quantity and caliber of publications in international journals.

Fourteen such centers were established nationwide, each housing dozens of scientists and research programs. Funded by the Ministry of Higher Education, they operated with financial independence from their affiliated universities. My involvement was with the CEOR. Three years prior, as mentioned above, I, along with a team, had advised them on research strategies and management.

Three years later, the government sought an assessment of the investment's impact. The Royal Society of New Zealand, again commissioned for this task, assembled a review panel—a group of international scientists, including me.

Our intensive three-day visit to CEOR offered valuable insights. Scientists presented detailed reports on research directions, achievements, finances, and a SWOT analysis. Armed with a 300-page document outlining past activities, we focused on active listening and discussion. Closed-door meetings on the third day helped us provide feedback and recommendations for their future trajectory.

The gravity of our decision—whether to recommend closure or continuation—was unmistakable. We had access to all documents, could conduct random checks on scientific data and finances, and inspect labs. This authority, however, came with an unexpected consequence.

The CEOR staff, viewing us with a mix of caution and deference, bent over backwards to accommodate our needs. Witnessing junior colleagues repeatedly address us with titles like "Professor Nguyen" and the constant presence of an attendant even in elevators caused quiet discomfort amongst the team. While accustomed to respect, such an extreme display felt out of place.

CEOR boasted a workforce of over forty scientists and experts across four research programs: basic, clinical, genetics, and dental and bone research. Each program had an assigned leader who reported to a director, a professor serving on the Advisory Board. This board, comprising five local and five renowned international professors, mirrored the organizational structures of research centers abroad, suggesting a deliberate adoption of Western management models.

Their financial resources were substantial. With an average annual government sponsorship of two million dollars (reaching three million dollars in the first year for infrastructure development), they had state-of-the-art equipment comparable to that of any global lab. From advanced bone density measuring machines to on-site biochemical analysis and gene analysis instruments, their facilities had undergone significant upgrades since our initial visit.

Their research focus encompassed genetics, molecular biology, pharmaco-genetics, clinical research, and epidemiology. They had published six scientific papers, with ten in progress, alongside numerous conference presentations and abstracts, and secured three patents within this timeframe. While the volume and quality of publications weren't yet at the forefront, these initial achievements were commendable and earned them a regional reputation. Their future potential for international contributions seemed promising.

Overall, CEOR had demonstrably achieved its stated goals, albeit not at one hundred percent. They had established a well-equipped center with qualified scientists, conducted research, published results, and registered patents. Their progress within three years, especially considering last year's flood that damaged equipment and research animals, was quite encouraging. Compared to other centers at risk of closure, CEOR stood out as a beacon of success.

Our assessment concluded that CEOR had made significant strides. While not without room for growth, particularly in scientific output, their achievements laid a strong foundation for future contributions to the global research land-scape.

A Diplomatic Dinner with Unexpected Turns

The second day of our visit brought an unexpected invitation—a dinner hosted by the esteemed President of KAU. Our initial program focused on independent work and avoiding outside influence. However, their sincerity and the emphasis on "just a scientific discussion" swayed our decision.

The university president, revered as "His Excellency," held a position akin to a government minister, with six vice presidents reporting to him, overseeing key areas such as research and international relations. Understanding the importance of the meeting, we opted for formal attire, despite the British professor's reservations about protocol. While some team members, especially him, disliked formality, I believed it was a matter of courtesy in this cultural context.

The dinner invitation itself held a surprise: a 9 pm start time! This vastly differed from typical dinner hours back home, but as the saying goes, "When in Rome..." We adjusted our expectations for a late night.

The venue, a luxurious Lebanese restaurant by a picturesque lake, confirmed the high regard KAU held us in. Upon arrival, the formality continued with reserved seating and our names displayed, akin to a scientific conference. The president himself sat at the head of the table, surrounded by high-ranking officials. This, it seemed, was their way of fostering connections.

Despite the official atmosphere, the food itself wasn't particularly remarkable. Local specialties pre-ordered alongside a selection of individual choices were offered. While meat dominated the menu (pork being absent, as expected), I opted for a simple grilled fish and salad. The "mandatory" pre-ordered dishes filled me up, and the entire dinner went on until nearly midnight.

Dinners weren't just about the food. They were also opportunities for "mingling," as they called it. While these gatherings lacked the drinks and karaoke of my own culture, the conversations proved surprisingly engaging. The Dean of Medicine, a distinguished middle-aged man, even introduced himself and complimented my intellect. Initially taken aback by his description of me as "frighteningly smart," I later realized it was a term of high praise. He himself embodied the ideal of a global citizen—educated abroad, fluent in English, and deeply informed about current events.

Our conversation flowed from Việt Nam and Asia to education, with a shared distaste for university rankings. He then shared exciting plans: the establishment of fourteen new research centers at the medical school, backed by substantial funding. Enthusiastic for his venture, I used a plethora of positive adjectives to express my admiration.

However, his enthusiasm had an ulterior motive. Midway through the meal, he offered me a glass of orange juice and a proposition: to join KAU. His earlier boasts about resources were a carefully crafted strategy to entice me. He presented several options, including becoming an adjunct professor and spending short periods at KAU each year. This offer was also extended to my colleagues, revealing that the seemingly ordinary dinner was, in fact, a carefully planned recruitment effort.

The Western saying "no free lunch" aptly describes the situation. Their hospitality, undoubtedly genuine, came with the expectation of reciprocity based on Darwinian principles. It served as a reminder of life's interconnectedness, echoing the Vietnamese saying "Living in this world requires kindness to one another." The dinner, originally intended for a scientific exchange, became a fascinating lesson in cultural nuances and strategic maneuvering.

The day after the unexpected dinner, our itinerary shifted to accommodate a meeting with the president of KAU. Reaching the president's office from the CEOR center, though physically close, required a car ride. The ten-minute journey showcased the grandeur of KAU. The president's building, resembling the administrative building of a Vietnamese university but with a hundredfold more opulence, stood tall with a spacious courtyard and a design inspired by both Arabic and Islamic styles. Interestingly, the architect was not Saudi but a distinguished British architect, John Elliot.

Our arrival was met with VIP treatment. Three Mercedes-Benzes transported our group, and we were ushered directly to the main entrance by the president's aides. Stepping inside felt like entering a different world, where cool air, hushed voices, and a sense of solemnity reflected the stature of a leader's workplace.

The president's office occupied the entire top floor, while the vice presidents shared the floor below. Our elevator ride to the fifth floor brought us to a formal boardroom. Name tags were neatly arranged on a table decorated with flowers, further evidence of the visit's meticulous organization. After a brief wait, the president entered, flanked by two vice presidents.

The president, a distinguished gentleman in his sixties with a kingly beard, exuded authority. He greeted each of us warmly with a handshake, a gesture not extended to his Saudi colleagues, perhaps highlighting our guest status.

The meeting, initially conceived as a casual exchange, evolved into a formal affair. The president began by expressing his gratitude for our visit and assistance to KAU and CEOR. He then invited each of us to speak for five minutes.

The director of COER at King Abdulaziz University presents a commemorative plaque to me.

Given the occasion, I opted for a diplomatic approach, focusing on praise. I highlighted KAU's rise in the rankings since his tenure began, crediting scientific research, particularly from the CEOR center, for this achievement. I also mentioned *King Abdullah University of Science and Technology* as an example of how research can elevate a university's stature. While acknowledging their progress, I gently nudged them towards even higher aspirations, such as reaching the top one hundred or even the top fifty in the rankings.

Following our individual remarks, the president expertly summarized the key points and provided fascinating details about KAU. Founded as a private institution in 1967, it transitioned to a public university four years later and earned its current name. By 2017, it secured a respectable ranking of 291st globally, twentieth in Asia, and third amongst Arab nations. He highlighted its vastness, boasting twenty-two faculties, three research institutes, eleven research centers, and its own hospitals. KAU's student body surpassed a staggering 122,000. However, this impressive student population stood in contrast to a noticeably smaller faculty of only 2,719, a detail I found interesting. On a separate note, the president mentioned a notable alumnus of the University—Osama bin Laden.

The president attributed KAU's success to three pillars: people, scientific research, and the American model. He elaborated on their strategy of recruiting renowned scientists from abroad, including Saudis returning from Western institutions. This openness to talent, irrespective of political or religious background, stood out in a nation known for its conservatism. The result? Over thirty percent of KAU's professors hailed from countries like the UK, Canada, and the US.

Scientific research was another cornerstone of their success. KAU dedicated nearly fifty million dollars annually to support students, researchers, and professors, enabling them to pursue research before securing government funding. This impressed me, as I witnessed fourth-year medical students confidently presenting their research alongside their professors. These funds also enabled professors to attend international conferences and remain at the forefront of their fields. The president claimed the university produced nearly 600 research papers annually, a figure that dwarfed Việt Nam's national output.

The final pillar—the American model—provided a framework for departmental autonomy in areas such as personnel selection. However, I suspected another factor: the vast wealth of Saudi Arabia, which they channeled heavily into education and research. What truly impressed me, though, was the emphasis on wise investment. The CEOR center exemplified this; their resources yielded tangible results, not just inflated numbers.

The scheduled half-hour meeting stretched into a full hour. As we wrapped up, the president presented each of us with a hefty, 300-page photo book and a promotional DVD about KAU. Despite the book's impressive size, the image quality fell short of my expectations. The DVD, however, seemed more promising.

The meeting with the president was an insightful peek into the heart of KAU. It served as a reminder of the importance of cultural understanding and strategic approaches within academia. His leadership and vision, along with KAU's dedication to research and openness to global talent, positioned it for a bright future. As our Vietnamese proverb emphasizes, "Every day is a school day," and this interaction at KAU served as a valuable lesson in itself.

Chapter Seventeen

Returning to the Land of Smiles

In 1981, I arrived in Thái Lan, a country that held dark memories for many Vietnamese refugees like me. For most who fled Việt Nam in the 1970s and 1980s, Thái Lan was not associated with fond memories. Countless individuals lost their lives during the perilous journey across the sea, falling prey to ruthless pirates and perceived indifference from the Thai government. Many of my fellow countrymen were among them, and for years I harbored deep resentment. Witnessing the struggle for survival in the refugee camps only deepened this bitterness. By 1982, returning to Thái Lan was unimaginable.

But time, they say, is a relentless sculptor, reshaping even the most hardened emotions. Years later, with a newfound perspective, I began to see things differently. Perhaps, I mused, there was a debt owed to nations like Thái Lan, Malaysia, Indonesia, The Philippines, Singapore, and Hong Kong. Without their willingness to offer temporary refuge, where would we have ended up? Post-war Việt Nam, with its closed borders and communist ideology, wouldn't have welcomed us with open arms. Seen through this lens, Thái Lan's role seemed less callous and more... humane.

The early 2000s ushered in a new era for me and Thái Lan. Scientific conferences became my passport, leading me on a whirlwind tour of Bangkok and exotic places like Chiang Mai, Phuket, and Pattaya. These were fleeting glimpses before returning home. A deeper exploration of the country and its people remained elusive.

Then, in 2004, an invitation arrived: an opportunity to speak at an osteoporosis conference and meet... a princess. This conference, "Strong Bone Asia" (SBA), was a brainchild of Thai colleagues, a regional gathering of osteoporosis experts. They saw me as a founding member, an honor I readily accepted. Over 300 experts from Southeast Asia converged, but none from Việt Nam. Apparently, in their eyes, I still carried the torch for my homeland.

The two-day conference unfolded in Pattaya. Little did I know, the Panatkikhom refugee camp, a place filled with memories of hardship, resided within the same province. The opening ceremony itself was a spectacle, highlighted by the presence of a princess. The organizers, hoping to raise awareness about osteoporosis prevention, had chosen a prominent female figure. While logical, a part of me couldn't help but wonder if a queen, someone well past menopause, might have been a more fitting choice.

Foreigners like myself weren't expected to kneel; a simple bow and handshake would suffice. But preparation reigned supreme. At 5 am, I found myself in a gymnasium, receiving instructions on how to greet royalty. A yellow jacket, a purple ribbon, an SBA logo tie—the uniform for this brief encounter. At 8 am, a convoy emerged—police cars followed by a procession of gleaming black Mercedes. The princess, accompanied by two aides (one holding a bag, the other a parasol), stepped out. Young and vibrant, she exuded intelligence, a recent graduate of Cornell Law School. Western attire adorned her petite frame, and her demeanor radiated warmth as she shook hands with each professor, including me.

Following this exchange, the princess awaited a bone density scan using ultrasound. An elderly female professor and I accompanied her. As the results materialized, perhaps out of respect for the guest, the professor invited me to explain them. Reassuringly, her bone health was excellent. The princess, her curiosity piqued, asked about preventative measures for osteoporosis. It was a reflection of her quick mind, I thought, and I launched into an explanation, though I politely deferred to the professor for additional insights. Our audience with her lasted a mere five minutes before she was whisked away to deliver the opening speech. Briefly emphasizing the importance of bone health and commending the SBA initiative, she wished the conference success before departing for another commitment. Before leaving entirely, however, she made a point of shaking hands with leading professors in the audience.

The conference was a resounding success, generating significant buzz throughout the region. My lecture, focusing on the impact of urbanization on osteoporosis, drew upon my research and that of colleagues from Southeast Asia. This event cemented my role within the SBA initiative, leading to numerous subsequent projects across the region.

Thái Lan is, to me, a land of somewhat contradictions. A place where the vibrant energy of bustling tourist destinations like Pattaya contrasts sharply with the somber memories of the Panatkikhom refugee camp. A place where royalty mingled with academics, united in the pursuit of a common goal: better bone health for all. It was a reminder that bridges can be built, even between the most unexpected of places. And for me, it was the beginning of a deeper connection with a nation that had once been a source of resentment, but was now evolving into a place of respect, collaboration, and scientific progress. This newfound appreciation for Thái Lan wasn't a betrayal of the past; it reflected the healing power of time, the transformative potential of shared goals, and the enduring spirit of scientific inquiry that transcends borders and personal history.

Khon Kaen University

Little did I know that 2013 would bring an unexpected homecoming to Southeast Asia. This time, an invitation arrived from Khon Kaen University (KKU) in Thái Lan, offering a three-month Visiting Professorship. The catalyst behind this exciting opportunity was Dr. Chatlert Pongchaiyakul, a brilliant young Thai doctor I fondly called Gua. Back in 2007, Gua had spent a research year in my lab. His dedication and sharp mind were undeniable, and during his time with us, he co-authored ten scientific papers—a record for any visiting researcher! Returning to Thái Lan, Gua's career soared, driven by his research experience and the skills he gained in Australia. Never one to forget the support he received, Gua stayed in touch, and it was through his warm recommendation that KKU extended the invitation to me.

KKU, a sprawling university in Khon Kaen province (reminiscent of Cần Thơ in my native Việt Nam), bustled with over 40,000 students. While technically on KKU's payroll, the allure of Việt Nam proved irresistible. Several conferences drew me back home during my tenure, but the time spent at KKU remains a cherished memory. It was, in many ways, a homecoming to Southeast Asia, my ancestral land.

L-R: Dr. Åshild Bjørnerem, Tuan Nguyen, and Dr. Chatlert Pongchaiyakul (Gua) at the Annual Meeting of the American Society for Bone and Mineral Research. (Vancouver, Canada, 2023)

But this homecoming wasn't without its surprises. Thái Lan, it seemed, wasn't just economically richer than Việt Nam—a gap of perhaps thirty years—it was also richer in a more profound sense: a richness of emotion and social trust. My arrival at the university-arranged accommodation was the first clue. A spacious, airy room with a beautiful garden view awaited me—a haven for evening relaxation in a hammock, lost in daydreams beneath the vast sky. But a nagging concern flickered in my mind: the absence of a safe. Expressing this to the receptionist, I was met with genuine surprise. "Oh, you don't need that here!" she chirped, gesturing towards the bicycle racks devoid of locks. "No one steals bikes here," she explained, "and no one enters your room." Her words struck a chord, a sharp contrast to the wariness ingrained in me from a less trusting society. A wave of admiration washed over me—reflecting the gentleness and honesty that permeated this place.

Within an hour of my arrival, everything—administrative tasks, computer setup, internet access, even keys—was magically arranged for my temporary office located in a KKU-affiliated hospital. Unlike the sprawling campuses in Việt Nam, KKU's nine million square meters were meticulously planned, boasting university-wide Wi-Fi that rivaled the quality I experienced at UNSW in Australia. The library itself was a marvel, its vastness reminiscent of a small university. All in all, the facilities were exceptional, especially considering KKU's regional status, akin to Cần Thơ University in Việt Nam, yet ranked fourth in Thái Lan.

Thai student discipline left a lasting impression. Despite the 40,000-strong student body and the constant flow of thousands of cars entering and leaving campus daily, not a single car horn blemished the serenity. One evening, standing on the tenth floor, I marvelled at the orderly stream of vehicles, guided by a solitary security guard, reflecting their respect for traffic rules and courtesy toward one another.

A deep respect for hierarchy permeated Thai society. The king, naturally, commanded the highest reverence. Then came the monks, revered figures in this predominantly Buddhist nation. University professors, considered on par with monks, enjoyed particular societal respect. Greetings reflected this order—hands held high above the head for the king, forehead level for monks and teachers, and chin level for others. This respect for educators manifested beautifully in daily interactions. Every time I entered an elevator, a simple ID badge proclaiming my title as "Professor" would prompt both students and doctors to hold the door and let me enter first. It took a few days to overcome my initial hesitation, but eventually, I embraced this privilege bestowed upon faculty.

Sharing knowledge across borders: delivering a lecture at Khon Kaen University.

My days were structured with meetings of all kinds—advising research students, brainstorming with professors, and inspiring young minds. Everyone spoke fluent English, instantly making me feel part of a global intellectual tribe. Weekly meetings with university leadership, from the president to the deans and vice-deans, highlighted their strategic vision and a healthy dose of competition. Bibliometric reports were meticulously tracked, with rivals like Chiang Mai and Songkhla universities closely monitored.

One of the vice-deans, pointing towards charming villas nestled in a forested area, casually inquired if I'd be interested in one. My playful response about potentially turning it into a permanent vacation spot elicited laughter. He explained these were offered as perks to professors. Upon retirement, he suggested, I could return and enjoy a comfortable life here. Thái Lan, it seemed, esteemed professors by offering them not just housing incentives but also preferential enrollment for their children in schools, with research excellence determining the extent of these privileges. The owners of these villas, it was clear, were accomplished individuals still actively contributing to their field.

This warmth extended beyond the university walls. Each evening, I found myself drawn to the local food stalls, savoring mango, papaya salad, and a cool beer. Despite the language barrier, communication flowed through hand gestures and a sense of shared humanity. Vendors treated me with genuine hospitality, never resorting to inflated prices, a pleasant surprise in a foreign land. Their smiles and generous portions spoke volumes about the inherent decency of the people.

Another heartwarming discovery awaited: a community of Vietnamese students pursuing their Master's and PhD degrees at KKU. News of my arrival—a Vietnamese professor gracing their university—spread like wildfire. Many were familiar with my blog and applied the knowledge I shared to navigate their studies. They even had a vibrant Vietnamese student association! Thrilled to connect with compatriots in a distant land, I readily accepted their invitation to speak at a seminar. Sharing my journey—from refugee to returning professor—had a profound impact on them. The seminar was a resounding success, sparking lively discussions and a shared yearning to seek opportunities abroad before returning to contribute to their home country. This impromptu gathering served as a potent reminder that, amidst the unfamiliar, a bond with one's fellow countrymen transcends borders and distance.

Professor Phùng Đắc Cam, an epidemiologist from Hà Nội (Việt Nam), added a delightful thread to the experience. This senior scholar, who graduated from Hà Nội Medical University in the early 60s and earned a PhD in Sweden, brought a wealth of knowledge and a disarming cheerfulness. Despite being our first meeting at KKU, a sense of camaraderie blossomed instantly, fueled by shared stories and a bond forged over countless cups of coffee in Hà Nội upon my return.

Evenings were a time for unwinding with newfound colleagues. Open-air eateries specializing in grilled delights became our haunts. Here, the concept of "all you can eat" took on a whole new meaning. Diners paid a fixed price and then helped themselves to a bounty of seafood, beef, and vegetables, grilling them to perfection. These lively gatherings, initially tinged with their concern about my alcohol tolerance, soon relaxed into comfortable, late-night conversations that stretched until 9 or 10 pm.

Weekend excursions with Gua, my dear colleague, took me beyond the university walls, venturing into the Thai countryside. This, I felt, was where the heart of Thái Lan truly lay, beyond the uniformity of modern cities. The well-maintained highways, built decades ago and bustling with traffic, spoke volumes about the country's progress. Even rural villages, with their meticulously arranged houses and well-maintained roads lined with verdant greenery, exuded a sense of order and prosperity far exceeding anything I'd witnessed back home. This, Gua explained, was largely a result of the reign of King Bhumibol Adulyadej, revered by the people as a saint. His development initiatives, combined with the villagers' own organized traditional occupations, ensured a steady income throughout the year and a comfortable standard of living.

King Bhumibol Adulyadej, a name woven into the very fabric of Thái Lan, transcends mere history. His seventy-year reign, the longest in modern history, speaks volumes about his enduring legacy. But beyond the longevity, it's the story of a king deeply revered by his people—a leader who steered Thái Lan towards the prosperity we see today. His life offers a unique window into Thai history and valuable lessons for our own country.

A quick glance at Thái Lan's prestigious universities reveals a hidden tribute—Mahidol, Chulalongkorn, Mongkut—each bears the name of a king, forming a lineage that ultimately connects to King Bhumibol Adulyadej. Born in Massachusetts in 1927, the youngest son of Prince Mahidol Adulyadej (also known as Prince Songkhla), his story begins far from the throne. His father, a visionary leader who established Mahidol University, was tragically lost when Bhumibol was just two years old. This propelled him, along with his mother and siblings, to Switzerland, where they resided for a significant period.

The reign at that time belonged to King Prajadhipok, who had no heirs. Following a peaceful coup in 1932, a constitutional monarchy was established. The crown passed to Bhumibol's elder brother, Prince Ananda Mahidol, at the tender age of nine. In 1939, he even changed the country's name to "Thailand." However, a tragic and unsolved mystery unfolded in 1946. King Ananda Mahidol was found dead in the royal palace, paving the way for a young Bhumibol, then only eighteen, to ascend the throne.

The king's youth cast a long shadow over his early reign. Fresh out of university, he returned to Thái Lan to a court that viewed him with skepticism. "Your Majesty, you know nothing!" they'd scoff whenever he offered an idea.

He chuckled, a hint of wryness in his voice. "So I kept my mouth shut. I knew things, but..." He trailed off, the unspoken words hanging heavy in the air. But from the very beginning, his heart belonged to his people. His coronation speech wasn't just a declaration; it was a vow. "We shall reign with righteousness," he proclaimed, using the word "we" to weave himself into the fabric of the nation. "For the benefit and happiness of the Siamese people." His voice carried a quiet determination that echoed across the land.

And his actions spoke louder than words. In a move that would define his reign, he embarked on a journey alongside the queen, traversing every corner of Thái Lan's impoverished rural landscape. He wanted to see, with his own eyes, the struggles his people faced. "Your problems," he'd say, his voice thick with empathy, "are my problems too."

The image of him, stripped of royal pomp, sitting on the grass in simple clothes, conversing with farmers, etched itself onto the national consciousness. It was a moment of genuine connection, a king acknowledging the shared humanity that transcended social strata.

These field visits weren't mere photo ops. They were the seeds from which the Royal Development Projects (RDPs) sprouted. The king understood that development couldn't come at the expense of the environment. He delved into research, poring over data on water resources and ecosystems. He wasn't afraid to consult scientists; his thirst for knowledge was unwavering. The culmination of this dedication was the "New Theory on Managing Agricultural Land," a scientific treatise penned by the king himself.

The RDPs themselves reflected his vision for Thái Lan. From the colossal Pa Sak Jolasid Dam to the majestic Rama VIII Bridge, these projects symbolized progress with a human face. But more importantly, they embodied the king's philosophy of sustainable development. These early initiatives, coupled with his commitment to his people, ushered in a new era for Thái Lan. It wasn't an overstatement to say that modern Thái Lan's development bloomed from the king's concern for his rural heartland. And so, the title "Father of the Land" seemed less a moniker and more a heartfelt truth.

Education was a cornerstone of his vision. He himself had diligently pursued knowledge in Switzerland, attending the École Nouvelle and later the University of Lausanne. He strongly encouraged Thais to follow suit, believing in the transformative power of Western education. Scholarships were established to facilitate studies in the US and Europe.

King Bhumibol Adulyadej was a polyglot, fluent in English, French, German, and Thai. He was a skilled photographer and a passionate inventor, even developing rainmaking techniques to combat Thái Lan's droughts. His legacy extends far beyond the political sphere. He was a man of the arts and sciences, a true polymath who inspired his people to excel.

Perhaps the most striking element of King Bhumibol Adulyadej's reign was his ability to bridge tradition and modernity. He embraced Western knowledge and technology while fiercely protecting Thái Lan's unique cultural identity. This delicate balance propelled Thái Lan towards progress without compromising its essence. He wasn't just a king; he was a bridge, a guiding light, a leader who left an indelible mark on his nation's history.

King Bhumibol Adulyadej's reign, spanning an unprecedented seventy years, weathered twenty nine coup attempts, sixteen coups, and sixteen revolutions! Through it all, he remained a constant, a symbol of stability and unity. He wasn't just a revered figure; he was seen as a living saint by his people. His life was free of scandal, standing in clear contrast to the turbulent political landscape. He played a pivotal role in restoring the monarchy to its former position of reverence.

Thái Lan's political landscape has always been a fascinating dance, and King Bhumibol Adulyadej was a masterful choreographer. Unlike the figureheads we were accustomed to back home, the king wasn't content to simply wear a crown. He understood the weight of his position and actively wielded it to maintain stability. The sight of rival generals, locked in a heated dispute, bowing in unison before the king—that was a powerful image. It spoke volumes about the Thai monarchy, not just as a symbol but as a force —an institution with tangible influence.

This institution, from its inception, had chosen a westward path. King Bhumibol, even in the early years of his reign, recognized the threat communism posed to the Thai way of life, to the very fabric of the monarchy. He saw it as an existential threat to the dynasty, and his response was swift and decisive. He aligned himself with America and its allies, a strategic move that ensured Thái Lan's place on the world stage.

But King Bhumibol was far more than just a politician. He was a man of immense creativity, a true artist. He wasn't content to be confined by the gilded cage of royalty. He craved the freedom of expression, and he found it in art. He taught himself to paint, producing works that garnered international acclaim. Photography became an extension of himself, his camera a constant companion, capturing the essence of his kingdom. And then there was music, his love for jazz burning bright. He wasn't just a passionate listener; he was a skilled saxophonist who shared the stage with renowned Thai musicians.

In contrast to the one-dimensional politicians back home, who seemed content with their leisurely pursuits, King Bhumibol was an anomaly. He wasn't a man who merely "rode horses and watched flowers." He was a man who learned, who created, who poured his soul into artistic expression. He was a king who defied expectations, a leader who understood the power of both action and artistry.

A Tale of Two Kingdoms

The lecture tour across Thái Lan was fast-paced, yet a side trip to Laos provided a glimpse into an entirely distinct realm. Stepping off the bus at the border, the contrast hit me like a wave of humid air thick with the scent of unknown spices. Thái Lan, with its bustling markets and gleaming temples, felt positively cosmopolitan compared to Laos' sleepy charm. Here, time seemed to move at a slower pace, the air itself heavy with a quietude that both soothed and unsettled.

The passage across the "Friendship Bridge" turned into a lesson in cultural differences. My Australian passport sailed through Thai immigration efficiently. But on the Laotian side, things ground to a halt. The immigration officer, a man whose uniform bore the marks of countless interactions under the harsh Laotian sun, flipped through my passport with a stoic expression. Minutes ticked by, filled with a silent tension that hung heavy in the air. Finally, the Laotian doctor, a former student who'd arranged the visit, leaned in and murmured a translation. A bribe was being demanded—a flat thirty US dollars, if my memory serves.

The doctor, bless him, was having none of it. He argued for the official fee, a mere five dollars. The exchange, a dance of unspoken rules, stretched on. A phone call, presumably to a superior, finally secured my entry, for a "compromise" of ten dollars. The whole ordeal left a bitter taste in my mouth. It wasn't just the money; it was the echo of a similar experience in Việt Nam, a reminder of a regional struggle against petty corruption that seemed ingrained in the system.

Despite the bumpy roads and lingering poverty, Laos held its own kind of magic. We dined at a renowned Vietnamese restaurant in Vientiane, a sign of the region's interwoven history and of people and cultures moving across porous borders. During the meal, a conversation with the chief medical officer—a woman with a sharp mind and a command of languages that put mine to shame—took an unexpected turn. She posed a series of questions about Laos' future—should they seek partnerships with Western universities, or model their development after Thái Lan or Việt Nam?

My answer, "Choose wherever the light shines the brightest," felt less like a definitive solution and more like a spark. Her laughter, a warm sound that filled the room, told me I'd achieved something more than offering a concrete plan. It was an invitation to think critically, to break free from the shackles of following a pre-defined path.

On the return leg, we stopped in Udon Thani, a province touted as the "heart and soul" of Thái Lan. Scouting for a restaurant, we stumbled upon a gem nestled by a lake. The ambience was a revelation: elegant simplicity that spoke volumes about Thai sophistication, even in a supposedly "remote" area. The service, the food, the very tablecloth—everything whispered a quiet dignity, vastly different from anything I'd ever experienced back home in Rạch Giá. Here, even in a small town, there was a global awareness, a subtle polish that spoke of a country comfortable in its own skin.

Thái Lan, of course, wasn't without its flaws. Corruption, economic inequality, and whispers of political instability all lurked beneath the surface. But when it came to global competitiveness, Việt Nam paled in comparison. Thai rice graced tables in wealthy nations, while Vietnamese exports primarily catered to poorer countries. Even overseas Vietnamese, I realized with a pang, held Thai products in higher regard. It was a sobering reminder of the power of brand recognition and the importance of innovation.

The disparity extended beyond economics. Thai universities, deeply integrated into the international academic sphere, enjoyed a freedom that Vietnamese institutions could only dream about. At Mahidol University, foreign professors outnumbered their local counterparts. Here, knowledge was a global currency, exchanged freely across borders. Thái Lan, it seemed, had embraced a global perspective, while Việt Nam remained hesitant, clinging to a more insular approach.

This trip wasn't just about exchanging knowledge in sterile lecture halls; it was about confronting uncomfortable truths. Thái Lan, a land that had offered me refuge before, served as a comparison to my homeland. The warmth and hospitality of the Thai people, their genuine respect for knowledge, and their adherence to Buddhist values were qualities Việt Nam desperately needed to cultivate. Sure, catching up economically might take time, but mending the moral and cultural fabric would be a generational struggle. Thái Lan, with its flaws and all, served as a reference—a reminder of the potential Việt Nam could achieve through openness, education, and a renewed embrace of its core values. It was a challenge, a call to action that inspired me, a seed of change I hoped to nurture upon my return.

During my three-month tenure at Khon Kaen University, I was immersed in a wealth of intellectual exchanges, cultural immersion, and the formation of deep connections. Leaving KKU was bittersweet. A part of me longed to delve deeper into the rich fabric of Thai life, especially that of farmers, while another yearned to return to Việt Nam and share the knowledge and perspectives I'd gleaned.

Back in Việt Nam, I couldn't help but reflect on the profound differences between the two countries. Thái Lan's orderliness, respect for authority, and visible prosperity stood in relief to the more chaotic, less structured environment of Việt Nam. Yet, beneath the surface, a shared Southeast Asian spirit of resilience and resourcefulness thrummed.

The warmth and hospitality I encountered at KKU had a lasting impression. The impromptu gatherings with colleagues, the students' eagerness to learn, and the genuine camaraderie transcended cultural differences. The respect given to professors, so different from the sometimes-strained relationships back home, was both humbling and inspiring. It affirmed the importance of fostering a nurturing environment that valued intellectual pursuits and mentorship.

The experience also challenged my preconceptions about Thái Lan. While the economic disparity between the two nations remained undeniable, I discovered a hidden richness—a society built on respect, order, and a deep reverence for tradition. King Bhumibol Adulyadej, a revered figure, emerged as a symbol of unity and progress. His development initiatives, particularly in rural areas, had demonstrably improved the lives of countless Thais.

Returning to Việt Nam, I carried a renewed sense of purpose. My experiences at KKU fueled a passion to bridge the gap between the two countries. I actively sought out opportunities to collaborate with Thai researchers, leveraging the connections I'd forged. In my lectures and workshops, I shared my observations about Thai culture and work ethic, hoping to inspire my Vietnamese students to embrace a similar level of discipline and dedication.

KKU wasn't just a professional sojourn; it was a catalyst for personal and professional growth. It fostered a deeper understanding of myself, my heritage, and the diverse cultures of Southeast Asia. The friendships forged, the lessons learned, and the cultural immersion all left an indelible mark on my life.

Chapter Eighteen

Building Bridges in Việt Nam

Việt Nam. The word itself evokes a spectrum of emotions. A mental embroidery woven with threads of childhood memories, the bittersweet ache of leaving, and the uncertainty of a future far away. When I boarded that rickety boat in 1981, escaping the turmoil that engulfed our country, the thought of ever setting foot on Vietnamese soil again seemed a distant dream. The prevailing sentiment back then echoed the melancholic lyrics of Nguyệt Ánh's song: "Once departed, forever separated; once gone, eternally apart." For many Vietnamese refugees, those lyrics rang true, as until now, they have never returned to Việt Nam.

Little did I know that fate, with its unpredictable twists, had other plans. About two decades later, I found myself drawn back to the land of my birth. The return, however, wasn't without its challenges. The bureaucratic process was a labyrinth, evidence of the chasm that had grown between us, the overseas Vietnamese and our homeland. The government viewed us with suspicion, outsiders carrying the invisible baggage of a past we'd all rather forget. Even today, we're categorized as "foreign elements," a term that feels both sterile and distant.

Back then, the mere act of visiting a relative required a lot of paperwork and the watchful gaze of local authorities. Every overnight stay required a stamp of approval, a constant reminder of the limitations placed upon us. Departing felt equally fraught, a passport clutched in sweaty palms, praying a missing document wouldn't trigger a cascade of inconvenience.

Sài Gòn's Tân Sơn Nhứt Airport, now literally renamed as Tân Sơn Nhất Airfield, then a far cry from its modern incarnation, was now a scene of controlled chaos. Immigration was a stern affair, overseen by officials in semi-military garb, their northern accents and curt demeanor adding to the air of intimidation. A "gift" of a few dollars slipped into the passport became the unspoken norm, a way to appease and expedite the process. It was a blatant form of solicitation, a sour note upon arrival.

Customs was another hurdle, manned by men in similar uniforms, their inspections rigorous and their demands opaque. Regulations were wielded like weapons, designed to extract unofficial fees from unsuspecting international visitors, particularly overseas Vietnamese. Luggage was pawed through, a thinly veiled search for opportunities to extort. The cost of leniency was high, stories whispered of travelers forced to part with hundreds of dollars just to retrieve their belongings. This left a particularly bitter taste for overseas Vietnamese returning home, a feeling of exploitation instead of welcome.

In the late nineties, my first trip back to Việt Nam wasn't some grand homecoming tour. It was a simpler reason: to see my ailing father. No lectures, no institutional visits, just a son returning home. Yet, fate, with its uncanny knack for serendipity, intervened. A chance encounter with local colleagues blossomed into something more: concrete plans of action.

Before returning to Australia, I found myself standing in the opulent Windsor Hotel in Sài Gòn, a name echoing from a bygone era. The city itself was a fascinating paradox, reinventing itself brick by brick. There was a palpable buzz in the air as 200 people had registered for my impromptu lecture on osteoporosis (sponsored by a pharmaceutical company), a topic fueled by my research in Australia. By the time I finished, the room overflowed, reflecting a thirst for knowledge and collaboration. The energy was vibrant, electric, and alive.

Gazing into the enthusiastic faces before me, I felt a powerful sense of connection. It was as if I was seeing my own yearning for knowledge mirrored back at me. This eagerness to connect, to bridge the gap between the Việt Nam I remembered and the vibrant nation it was becoming, was palpable. The warmth of the reception and the shared passion for research made everything fall perfectly into place. This wasn't just the place of my birth; it was a place where I could truly belong and contribute. Here, my knowledge and skills could serve as a bridge, fostering understanding between the past and the exciting future unfolding.

Two years later, Việt Nam called me again, this time with the promise of a true vacation. Gone were the hurried days of worry, replaced by the anticipation of a proper holiday. Back then, Việt Nam wasn't a tourist haven yet; its pristine beaches were untouched by sprawling resorts. But its charm revealed itself differently, through the raw beauty of a nation in transformation. It was a country transitioning from its agrarian roots to a vibrant future brimming with potential. Just like my previous visit, I wasn't there for work commitments or official meetings. I simply wanted to immerse myself in the experience and witness firsthand this incredible metamorphosis.

And fate, it seemed, had a serendipitous twist in store. While browsing a charming, old bookstore in Hồ Chí Minh City, searching for a copy of *Eden in the East*, a book I'd proudly introduced, I encountered Dr. Nguyễn Thy Khuê, a prominent endocrinologist in Việt Nam. To her delight, I was a familiar face from past lectures on Southeast Asia, a welcome reminder of a connection made long ago. For me, it was an instant feeling of kinship, a spark of recognition that ignited a warm feeling amidst the bustling city. Little did I know, this unexpected encounter would blossom into a long and fulfilling journey.

Dr. Khuê, a brilliant mind with a keen eye for potential, identified a crucial need in Vietnamese medicine: strengthening research skills among doctors and medical students. Her solution? A summer course on research methods, with me as the instructor! The idea appealed to me. With limited research activity among doctors, the demand, she assured me, mirrored the vast potential of Việt Nam's evolving medical landscape. A seed of possibility was planted, and I knew, with an undeniable certainty, that I would return.

Sowing the Seeds: Building Research Capacity

The first training workshop, though a distant memory in the year 2001, I believe, remains remarkably vivid. The library of Hồ Chí Minh City University of Medicine and Pharmacy transformed into our vibrant learning space. The curriculum focused on equipping participants with data analysis methods and study design, empowering them to make meaningful contributions to the field. Dr. Khuê's dedication was truly inspiring. Despite her busy clinical schedule, she attended every session, her presence motivating the young doctors.

The following years unfolded with a rewarding rhythm of one to two annual training courses, each focusing on a unique theme. However, dealing with Việt Nam's administrative processes presented its own set of challenges. As the Vietnamese saying goes, "hành là chánh" (which literally means admin is a form of torture), established procedures can sometimes turn into obstacles. However, with a bit of ingenuity, they can also be transformed into stepping stones for progress.

One particular instance comes to mind. In the midst of a particularly engaging lecture, Dr. Khuê excused herself to answer a call. Upon her return, her demeanor had shifted—a tinge of worry clouding her usually cheerful face. During the break, I inquired about her well-being, fearing a personal concern. Little did I know, a bureaucratic hurdle had come knocking. To my surprise, Dr. Khuê explained that the course hadn't yet received formal approval. Initially, I was a bit puzzled. After all, the program focused solely on medical education and skill-building. As Dr. Khuê clarified, Vietnamese regulations had specific guidelines: any course featuring a foreign lecturer required authorization from three government departments: Public Security, Health, and Information and Propaganda. While these procedures were in place, obtaining permission for similar seminars involving international participants typically went smoothly.

Dr. Khuê, it turned out, had assumed the previous lecture approvals would carry over. This assumption, however, had almost derailed the entire course. Someone, likely a participant in my workshop, had alerted the Public Security department about my unauthorized teaching activity. Thankfully, the caller, while raising the issue, proved to be understanding and offered guidance on the permission process. As a result, the course proceeded without interruption. I later learned that local public security officials closely monitored every workshop and seminar I conducted in Việt Nam.

This experience served as a steep learning curve for me. Scientific collaboration with "foreign elements" in Việt Nam, I realized, was a dance with a different set of steps compared to neighboring countries. Every class, it seemed, was under a watchful eye, with the potential for monitors disguised as students lurking amongst the participants. Despite the unexpected hurdle, Dr. Khuê's dedication and the students' thirst for knowledge ensured the course's success. It was a small but significant step in building Việt Nam's research capacity, a journey that would continue to unfold in unforeseen ways.

A typical workshop program at Tôn Đức Thắng University.

Partnering with my brilliant student, Dr. Nguyễn Đình Nguyên, and pharmaceutical sponsors, we launched a series of training courses. These intensive sessions, ranging from research design to scientific paper publication, empowered doctors, aspiring researchers, and even future professors with invaluable skills. The curriculum, tailored to specific needs, interested me. Each week-long course attracted a staggering 100-200 participants, many of whom have gone on to become prominent figures in the medical field. Even today, the echo of those early courses organized by Dr. Khuê at the Hồ Chí Minh City University of Medicine and Pharmacy continues to inspire.

News of our endeavors traveled north. Colleagues from famous institutions like Bạch Mai Hospital and Hà Nội Medical University extended invitations. These opportunities not only broadened my reach but also fostered cherished friendships with fellow researchers in the North. The invitations grew, beckoning me to the Central region as well. Soon, I found myself teaching mid-term (one to two weeks) and short-term (one to two days) courses on topics such as evidence-based medicine, osteoporosis and bone health, research methodology, and scientific writing. From Hà Nội to Thái Nguyên, Ninh Bình, and Hải Phòng in the North, to Huế, Đà Nẵng, Nha Trang, and Phú Yên in the Central region, and finally, to Sài Gòn, Vũng Tàu, and countless other southern provinces, I crisscrossed the country. These hundreds of courses touched the lives of over 10,000 individuals, primarily in the medical field.

A typical training workshop at Chợ Rẫy Hospital.

International organizations like the World Bank and the World Health Organization, recognizing the value of our efforts, extended their own invitations. Leveraging my experience as an editor for medical and international journals, I conducted workshops focused on research methods and scientific publishing, not just for the medical field but also for education and social sciences. For over a decade, I participated in over ten such workshops.

While the impact of these lectures was undeniable, a yearning to reach a wider audience grew within me. Books, I realized, offered the potential for a more enduring influence. The first titles, *Entering Scientific Research* and *From Research to Publication: Soft Skills for Scientists*, were met with an overwhelming response, exceeding even the publishers' expectations. These volumes distilled the essence of my years of teaching, offering practical tools and insights for readers.

This initial success spurred the creation of fifteen more books, encompassing research methods, evidence-based medicine, clinical epidemiology, scientific writing, and even university education. The warm reception was humbling—multiple reprints, a "library-ordered" designation by the National Library for "*Handbook of Scientific Research*," and even three Book Excellence Awards.

In 2016, I was confined at home by illness. I found myself restless, my mind yearning for the stimulation of sharing knowledge. One day, on a whim, I stumbled upon a new frontier: YouTube. It felt like uncharted territory, a platform teeming with possibilities. With a playful spirit, I dusted off my old PowerPoint slides and started recording lectures. Data analysis, epidemiology, the intricacies of osteoporosis—I delved into topics that had consumed my research career. Who would be my audience? I didn't know, and honestly, it didn't matter. It was a way to keep my mind sharp, a form of intellectual exercise while I recovered.

I never imagined that these free online lectures would resonate with such a global audience. After delivering over 120 lectures, the view count skyrocketed to a staggering 2.2 million, not just in Việt Nam but worldwide. My voice, once intended for classrooms and lecture halls, had found an unexpected community—a vast, anonymous audience eager to learn. It was a humbling realization, a powerful illustration of the internet's ability to connect people and erase geographical barriers.

Public persona. Never what I envisioned for myself, but those online lectures, a simple act born of confinement, had unintentionally thrust me into the spotlight. Emails flooded my inbox, heartfelt messages from Vietnamese postgraduate students scattered across the globe. They spoke of my lectures, how they'd become lifelines, guiding them through the labyrinthine world of research. Even a decade later, chance encounters in cafes, shopping malls, or bustling streets in

Việt Nam would reveal the ripple effect of those lectures. People, eyes gleaming with gratitude, would share how my books and videos had ignited their research journeys.

These moments were the most rewarding aspect of this whole endeavor. A humbling and constant reminder of the power a single spark can unleash. My online lectures, a mere attempt to stave off boredom, had become a catalyst, igniting a passion for research that continues to illuminate the scientific landscape of Việt Nam. It's an example of the interconnectedness of our world, a beautiful illustration of how knowledge can transcend borders and language barriers to empower others on their own paths to discovery.

Osteoporosis Society

In the early years after returning to Việt Nam, a focus on teaching rekindled my passion for fostering research capabilities. Yet, another passion stirred within me—a deep desire to see Việt Nam confront the rising concern of osteoporosis in a rapidly modernizing society. Neighboring countries boasted vibrant osteoporosis associations, communities that thrived on research and public awareness. Việt Nam, I believed, deserved the same.

Thankfully, colleagues in Việt Nam shared this vision. Dr. Lê Anh Thư, a rheumatologist at Chợ Rẫy Hospital, liked the idea. So did Nicholas Nguyễn, a former refugee in Australia, who had carved a successful path back in Việt Nam as the director of the pharmaceutical company Bridge Healthcare. When Nicholas ventured out on his own to establish Bridge Healthcare, his focus remained firmly on supporting medical associations. The Hồ Chí Minh City Osteoporosis Society, nestled under the umbrella of the city's Medical Association, particularly struck a chord with him.

With Nicholas and his wife's support and the backing of the Medical Association, a pivotal date arrived: August 12th, 2006. The Hồ Chí Minh City Osteoporosis Society (HCMC-OS) was born. Associate Professor Lê Anh Thư became our esteemed president. Her boundless enthusiasm, energy, and innovative spirit were infectious, and for the past two decades, she has led the HCMC-OS with remarkable success.

My involvement with the HCMC-OS has been a constant thread throughout these years. I contribute annually with lectures, ensuring the knowledge base remains fresh. Some years, I take a more active role, helping to organize annual conferences. Building bridges for knowledge exchange became another priority, and I regularly invited colleagues and research fellows from Australia to participate in these events.

The First SBA Conference in Việt Nam

The establishment of the Osteoporosis Society awakened a new passion within me. While already involved with Strong Bone Asia (SBA), an initiative by Thai colleagues to unite Southeast Asian osteoporosis experts, Việt Nam remained conspicuously absent from these discussions. Despite clarifying my Vietnamese-Australian background, colleagues often saw me as a "representative" for the country. This misunderstanding, however, became an unexpected spark. Perhaps, I thought, it was a chance to influence the region from within.

In 2007, I set a daring goal: to bring the SBA Osteoporosis Conference to Việt Nam. My ASEAN colleagues were doubtful. Hosting such an event seemed a stretch for a nation not yet fully integrated into the global osteoporosis community. But I was determined to shatter their skepticism.

Armed with the belief in Việt Nam's potential, I returned home and assembled a dream team. Professor Võ Thanh Phụng, Director of Orthopedic Trauma Hospital, and Professor Dương Quang Trung, President of the Hồ Chí Minh City Medical Association, became my partners. Professor Phụng, with his dedication, even embarked on several trips to Australia to iron out logistics, leaving a lasting impression on our ASEAN partners.

The year 2008 marked a turning point. The Equatorial Hotel in Hồ Chí Minh City thrummed with activity as the first-ever SBA Conference in Việt Nam unfolded. It was a resounding triumph, drawing over 350 attendees from across the globe, including the US, Europe, and even my esteemed mentor, Professor John Eisman, who reveled in his first trip to Việt Nam.

The Strong Bone Asia Conference was first held in Ho Chi Minh City in 2008.

Leading pharmaceutical companies stepped forward as sponsors, a further testimony to the conference's reach and impact. This success story gained significant attention far beyond the conference walls. It became a powerful symbol of Việt Nam's growing presence in the international fight against osteoporosis, a fight I was proud to be a part of.

For me, this SBA conference was an eye-opening experience. Organizing an international scientific conference in Việt Nam for the first time unveiled the intricacies of the administrative landscape. Despite being a formal medical association, obtaining the necessary permissions proved to be an odyssey. From the Ministry of Health to the Police Department, every entity needed to be appeased. Even invited speakers had to go through an extensive paperwork process, submitting their CVs, passports, visas, and conference presentations.

Accustomed to the streamlined Western approach, I watched my Vietnamese colleagues navigate this bureaucratic labyrinth with a mixture of amusement and frustration. Drafting the opening speech for the Minister of Health, Nguyễn Quốc Triệu, became a personal challenge. The pressure to craft a meaningful and dignified speech that wouldn't embarrass the nation was immense.

Borrowing from the "Three-point Rule," I focused on three key issues: the rising burden of osteoporosis in Southeast Asia due to aging populations, the necessity of regional cooperation to tackle this challenge, and the importance of evidence-based medicine in guiding research efforts. The speech, meticulously translated into Vietnamese, went through unexpected revisions.

Professor Trung, upon receiving the Minister's edits, wanted to change the term "Evidence-Based Medicine" to "Medicine Based on Evidence." While the revised phrase captured the essence, it lacked the scientific rigor of the original term. I argued my case, emphasizing the importance of preserving the origin and meaning of "Evidence-Based Medicine," which stemmed from Positivism. Professor Trung, though unconvinced, invoked an adage: "Is he the minister or you're the minister?" Thus, the revised version was included in the speech, which I delivered in English, while the Minister opted to forgo the translated portion altogether.

The seating arrangements offered another glimpse into Vietnamese cultural nuances. The organizing committee was locked in a debate over protocol. With dignitaries such as the Minister of Health, the Chairman of the People's Committee, and university officials all in attendance, assigning seating positions became a delicate dance. My suggestion of randomization was met with a chuckle from Professor Trung. Vertical versus horizontal hierarchies, as well as the Minister representing a centralized ministry versus the Chairman representing a local authority, made ranking a challenge. Thankfully, a solution was reached: placing both dignitaries side by side, a diplomatic compromise was achieved. These bureaucratic hurdles, though tedious, served as valuable lessons in politico-cultural sensitivity.

Five years later, in 2013, Đà Nẵng hosted another successful SBA Conference. These events transcended academic exchange, forging connections between Vietnamese and international counterparts. Furthermore, CME (continuing medical education) osteoporosis classes, organized by invited colleagues, empowered local doctors with the latest knowledge.

In 2016, a heartfelt moment arrived. The Hồ Chí Minh City Osteoporosis Association, celebrating its tenth anniversary, bestowed upon me a medal in recognition of my contributions. The inscription, "In building and developing the osteoporosis field through training, scientific research, and international publications," captured the essence of my journey.

The Asia Pacific Consortium on Osteoporosis

The fight against osteoporosis wasn't confined to Việt Nam. In 2019, my former mentor, Professor John Eisman, reached out with a visionary initiative. He foresaw a looming crisis in Southeast Asia as populations aged rapidly, and osteoporosis was poised to become a significant burden. To combat this, he envisioned a regional association uniting top experts in osteoporosis. John, aware of my efforts in Việt Nam and Southeast Asia, saw me as a crucial piece of this puzzle. He invited me to be a founding member and executive member of the Asia Pacific Consortium on Osteoporosis (APCO). "This is a chance to leave a positive legacy for future generations," he declared.

The inaugural ceremony in Singapore, held in May 2019, marked a momentous occasion. Our founding group, comprising a mere ten executive members, set out with a clear mission: to standardize and improve osteoporosis screening, diagnosis, and management across the Asia-Pacific region. This meant tackling the current mishmash of protocols across different countries, fostering a unified approach to tackle a common enemy.

The impact of APCO was swift. Within five years, the organization blossomed. From a handful of founders, we grew to fifteen executive members and an impressive network of 250 bone health experts from thirty countries in the region. As an executive member, I championed the inclusion of Vietnamese colleagues, ensuring their voices and experiences were represented within APCO.

Founding members of the Asia Pacific Consortium on Osteoporosis.

Key members of the Asian Federation of Osteoporosis Societies.

Meanwhile, my work in the region was gaining recognition beyond Việt Nam. From 2010 onwards, Japanese and South Korean colleagues extended invitations for keynote speeches at national osteoporosis conferences. These visits culminated in a prestigious offer: to join them in establishing the *Osteoporosis and Sarcopenia* journal under the auspices of the Asian Federation of Osteoporosis Societies (AFOS). Excitedly, I took on the role of editor and advisor. The journal, launched in 2015, quickly achieved recognition, earning a coveted listing in the Clarivate index, a mark of its scientific merit.

The 16th AFES Conference

The early 2000s saw a bustle of speaking engagements at endocrinology conferences throughout Asia. These talks not only disseminated knowledge but also forged connections with fellow endocrinology experts in Southeast Asia. An impactful outcome was my introduction to the ASEAN Federation of Endocrine Societies (AFES), a vital organization that advises governments on metabolic diseases and drafts treatment protocols for the region. The Việt Nam Association of Endocrinology and Diabetes (VADE) was a proud member of this esteemed group.

My involvement with AFES extended beyond membership. Prior invitations to speak and even contribute to the establishment of their scientific journal solidified my connection, despite my being "nominally Australian." In 2011, AFES announced a momentous decision—the 16th AFES Conference would be held in Hồ Chí Minh City, Việt Nam. VADE, led by Professor Nguyễn Thy Khuê, would serve as the local host.

This presented a serendipitous opportunity. Professor Khuê, recognizing my experience, invited me to advise on the conference program and manage external affairs. The role thrust me into close collaboration with Professor Khuê and event organizers in Singapore. Numerous trips between Sydney, Việt Nam, and Singapore became routine as we meticulously crafted the conference program. Even years later, at a recent osteoporosis conference in Singapore, the event director still fondly recalled our past discussions—a testament to the lasting impact of such collaborations.

Every conference needs a unifying theme. Professor Khuê and I embarked on brainstorming sessions to find a theme that was both practical and impactful. Leveraging my fluency in English, I proposed to suggest themes in English for Professor Khuê's translation. Drawing on my experience with the SBA conference, we started with keywords: research, science, clinical, application, translation, achievements, and vision. The next step was weaving these keywords into a cohesive statement. After a week of deliberation, we landed on the following theme:

"Translating Endocrinology Research into Clinical Care."

Professor Khuê was particularly drawn to this theme as it emphasized the practical application of research findings in clinical settings. The Vietnamese translation, "Ứng Dụng Nghiên Cứu Nội Tiết Học vào Điều Trị Lâm Sàng," perfectly captured the essence and became the guiding light for organizing research presentations at the conference.

The opening letter also fell under my purview. Confident in my English skills and experience with the ASBMR and ANZBMS, I volunteered to draft the letter. However, this seemingly straightforward task proved to be an exercise in balancing diverse viewpoints. Being Australian offered a distinct advantage, as my proposals were often met with approval from AFES members due to a lack of conflicting interests.

Enhancing the conference's international stature was paramount. My extensive network and long-standing involvement in the field came into play. I proposed inviting renowned experts with a proven track record of supporting Vietnamese colleagues. A list was compiled, featuring luminaries like Dieter Felsenberg, my former mentor John Eisman, Ego Seeman, Elizabeth Barrett-Connor, Steven Cummings, and others. Although not everyone could attend, roughly half accepted the invitation, which significantly elevated the conference's prestige.

The AFES16 conference turned out to be a resounding success. Over 1,300 physicians and experts, not just from Southeast Asia but also from countries like Australia, the US, and Europe, converged in Hồ Chí Minh City. The presence of renowned professors, drawn by the invitation, further bolstered the conference's reputation.

Finally, the crown jewel: the scientific program. With over 200 research papers submitted by regional and international experts, we meticulously divided them into specialized sessions. Osteoporosis, diabetes and foot care, diabetes and neuropathy, vitamin D, and diabetes during pregnancy were just a few of the focused topics.

Dr. Khuê entrusted me with the opening remarks, a challenging responsibility. Professor John Eisman, a dear colleague, offered a playful suggestion: "Imagine yourself as the Minister!" Knowing that wouldn't be genuine, I opted for a more personal approach. My five-minute speech focused on the conference's theme, "Translating Endocrinology Research into Clinical Care," highlighting the practical applications of research for the Vietnamese context. Professor Dương Quang Trung's warm congratulations afterwards, and Associate Professor Thy Khue's quiet praise, filled me with a sense of accomplishment.

Throughout the conference, I had the privilege of presenting on three topics crucial to the region: fracture risk prediction, osteoporosis in Asia, and personalized treatment. AFES16 marked a milestone – Việt Nam's first time hosting such a prestigious event. Skepticism lingered among some attendees regarding Việt Nam's scientific capacity. But the meticulous organization and the caliber of local research presentations shattered those doubts. Professor Khuê's words captivated me: "Transparency and quality are key. They earn respect and appreciation."

The conference served as a powerful symbol of Vietnamese endocrinology's growing maturity. As one attending physician stated, "AFES 2011 offers a chance to assess our healthcare sector and strategize future training. We must keep pace with global advancements, conducting impactful research, not just churning out derivative reports." His words reflected the conference's true victory—not just the exchange of knowledge, but the inspiration to strive for excellence.

My Journey with Tôn Đức Thắng University

The year 2013 brought a serendipitous turn of events. Dr. Lê Văn Út, a familiar face from his doctoral days in Finland, crossed paths with me again. Back in Việt Nam after his studies, he brimmed with ideas to reform the country's scientific research landscape. We'd often debated the merits of scientometrics—a way to measure research impact—back in Australia, and his recent articles advocating for change in Vietnamese newspapers demonstrated his zeal. His arrival at Tôn Đức Thắng University (TDTU), coupled with the visionary leadership of President Lê Vinh Danh at the helm, felt like a unique opportunity to make a real difference.

Dr. Út orchestrated a meeting with President Danh, a Fulbright scholar known for his decisiveness and ambition to reform Vietnamese higher education. As fate would have it, President Danh hailed from Quảng Ngãi, the very hometown of my aunt's husband, creating an unexpected personal connection. His dream? To see Vietnamese universities on the global map, with TDTU leading the charge as a beacon of excellence. When he took over, TDTU was still transitioning from its vocational college roots, but under his visionary leadership, it rapidly transformed into a research powerhouse. He confided in me that TDTU occupied his every waking thought, demonstrating his commitment.

Our discussions culminated in an invitation to serve as an Academic Advisor to both him and TDTU. Between 2015 and 2023, I had the privilege of collaborating with Dr. Út and Professor Danh in this capacity.

My experiences across universities have revealed a fascinating pattern: a mere twenty percent of researchers typically contribute a staggering eighty percent of the scientific output—the 80/20 rule in action. To capitalize on this strength, I proposed the creation of specialized research groups. By establishing a dedicated scientific fund to support their initial endeavors, these groups could develop strong proposals for larger studies and ultimately secure government funding. TDTU embraced this vision wholeheartedly, and within a few years, over twenty research groups were established, demonstrating impressive productivity.

However, my core belief remained unshakeable: a university's true strength lies in its faculty. Prestige comes from renowned professors bringing their expertise and research prowess to the table. As an advisor, I championed the establishment of rigorous faculty appointment and promotion standards, modeled on those employed by leading Australian universities I knew well. We made these transparent criteria readily available online, ensuring everyone was on the same page. Furthermore, we revamped the process itself, introducing a system of peer review by international experts. While this system led to the appointment of several competent professors, it also meant rejecting an Australian candidate who didn't meet TDTU's stringent standards. Ultimately, however, Ministry of Education and Training regulations proved to be an obstacle, and the system couldn't be sustained in its current form.

President Lê Vinh Danh's vision stretched far beyond revamping academics. He approached me with a captivating proposition: to establish a research laboratory dedicated to osteoporosis research at TDTU. The university would provide the infrastructure, a modern facility we could only dream of, but the responsibility for research costs fell entirely on us. The idea stirred a strong passion within me, yet the reality of the distance troubled me: how could I effectively lead a lab across continents?

Dr. Hồ Phạm Thục Lan, a familiar and trusted name from my past collaborations at Hospital 115 and Phạm Ngọc Thạch University of Medicine, immediately came to mind. Her dedication and expertise during our previous osteoporosis research projects had always impressed me. I reached out, proposing the co-directorship of the lab as a way to bridge the geographical gap. Thankfully, Dr. Thục Lan embraced the challenge with the same enthusiasm I felt. And so, the Bone and Muscle Research Lab was born.

The lab itself spoke volumes about TDTU's dedication. Packed with state-of-the-art technology—DXA machines, pQCT machines, sophisticated X-ray systems, and ultrasound—it offered a powerful toolkit for our research. But the lab's true strength resided in the team's volunteer spirit. Dr. Thục Lan and I, along with everyone involved, donated our time and expertise freely. Dr. Thục

Lan's commitment went well beyond her volunteered hours; she even used her own funds to get the lab's initial research off the ground.

The Vietnam Osteoporosis Study

A research lab thrives on the stories it tells through its research. Having witnessed the success of the Dubbo Osteoporosis Epidemiology Study in Australia, I envisioned replicating that impact in Việt Nam. A large-scale, longitudinal study—following thousands of participants over a decade—felt like a groundbreaking opportunity. It would be a significant contribution to Vietnamese research, etching the country's name on the global map of osteoporosis.

However, my esteemed colleague, Dr. Thục Lan, had reservations. The concept of such a long-term study, demanding dedication from both researchers and participants, was uncharted territory in Việt Nam. But my resolve remained firm. Our meetings became a showcase of passionate arguments, driven by presentations brimming with data and motivated by a shared desire to push Vietnamese research forward. I argued that a project of this scale was essential if Việt Nam was to truly etch its mark on the global stage of osteoporosis research. President Lê Vinh Danh's support, along with Dr. Thục Lan's eventual backing after much deliberation, proved to be the turning point. In late 2015, with a shared sense of purpose, we launched the Việt Nam Osteoporosis Study (VOS).

The VOS was audacious in its scope. We aimed to recruit 4,000 men and women from Hồ Chí Minh City, encompassing a broad age range from young adults to seasoned citizens. Ideally, we envisioned following them for a decade, but logistical realities necessitated an eight-year follow-up period. Yet, our core objectives remained firm. The study aimed to assess the true prevalence of bone and joint diseases within the Vietnamese population, identify key risk factors specific to the region's demographics, and ultimately, develop a disease prognosis model tailored explicitly to Vietnamese patients. This, we believed, would be a groundbreaking contribution from Việt Nam to the global medical landscape.

The community response surpassed even our most optimistic expectations. Over 4,200 individuals enrolled, their selfless participation providing an invaluable trove of data that would fuel years of research on skeletal and joint disorders. Dr. Thục Lan's tireless contributions deserve a chapter in the VOS's success story. Along with a dedicated team of resident physicians and medical students from Phạm Ngọc Thạch University of Medicine, we formed the backbone of the project. Their commitment, entirely pro bono, was evident in the early mornings and late nights they poured into the study.

The VOS blossomed into one of the largest bone research projects ever undertaken in Asia. Over its eight-year lifespan, it yielded over fifty published scientific papers, each one a stepping stone towards a deeper understanding of osteoporosis in the Vietnamese population. These publications graced the pages of prestigious journals like *Nature Genetics, PNAS, Bone, Diabetes Care,* and *Journal of Clinical Endocrinology and Metabolism,* propelling the VOS to the forefront of international research. Collaborations with renowned institutions such as Johns Hopkins University and UCSD flourished, fostering a vibrant exchange of knowledge and expertise that transcended borders.

The impact, however, extended far beyond publications. The VOS garnered a staggering ten national and international awards, demonstrating the groundbreaking nature of the research. Recognition poured in from prestigious entities like the Hong Kong International Osteoporosis Symposium, the International Endocrinology Conference in South Korea, and the coveted Alexandre Yersin Award. More importantly, VOS data formed the foundation for the research endeavors of dozens of resident physicians and five doctoral students. These bright minds, nurtured by the project, were poised to become the next generation of Vietnamese researchers, ready to make their own mark on the world stage.

TDTU Distinguished Professorship

Five years in, my work at Tôn Đức Thắng University had become a labor of love. As an advisor and laboratory head, I poured my energy into reshaping the university's research focus and revamping its teaching methods through numerous training workshops. All this, I did without any formal remuneration.

The university, recognizing my contributions, surprised me with the nomination for the Distinguished Professor title. But I had to apply. While initially hesitant, I was persuaded by my colleagues to apply. The application process itself was rigorous—a six-month-long peer review by a distinguished panel of professors from top universities in Western countries.

Crowning a career milestone: appointed Distinguished Professor at Ton Duc Thang University in 2018.

Finally, in late October of 2018, the news arrived. A formal letter, dated October 29th, addressed me as "Professor Tuan" and bore the weight of great recognition: Distinguished Research Professor of Tôn Đức Thắng University:

"Dear Professor Tuan:

Re: Appointment of Distinguished Professor

I am very pleased to advise you that the University Council has approved the recommendation of the Committee of Appointment and Promotion that you will be appointed Distinguished Research Professor of Ton Duc Thang University. The appointment will be effective from August 1st, 2018.

Your application has been examined by 7 eminent scholars from the United States, Australia, Germany, Belgium and our own TDTU professors. All eminent professors have unanimously recommended that you be appointed to the rank of Distinguished Research Professor. This recommendation was based on your distinguished contributions to bone research internationally and your outstanding contributions to the profession in Vietnam. We also acknowledge your continuing services to the University in various leadership roles. The Committee of Appointment and Promotion itself shows the highest regard in which you are held by your peers, and I am happy that this was endorsed by the University Council.

You are the first Distinguished Research Professor of Ton Duc Thang University. The position and title carry a significant social and academic responsibility that I hope you will take it seriously. Please accept my warmest congratulations. I look forward to hearing more of your outstanding achievements in the years ahead.

Yours sincerely,

Le Vinh Danh

President"

The letter spoke volumes. Apparently, all six reviewers, from across the globe—the US, Australia, Germany, Belgium, and even TDTU itself—unanimously endorsed my nomination. My international standing in bone research, coupled with my dedication to elevating Vietnamese science, was convincing to them. They also acknowledged my unofficial leadership roles within the university.

This wasn't just a promotion; it was a pioneering step. The letter itself referred to me as the "first Distinguished Research Professor" of Tôn Đức Thắng University. The weight of expectation settled on my shoulders, a responsibility not just academic, but social as well. Professor Lê Vinh Danh's closing words echoed in my mind: "I look forward to hearing more of your outstanding achievements in the years ahead." It was a challenge I was more than ready to embrace.

Honoring Excellence: The Alexandre Yersin Prize

One source of personal pride stems from my involvement with the Alexandre Yersin Prize for Outstanding Research. In 2017, the Swiss-Vietnamese Medical Association (HELVIETMED) established this award, named after the distinguished Swiss-Vietnamese scientist Alexandre Yersin (1863-1943). The "Alexandre Yersin Prize for Outstanding Publication" aimed to ignite a passion for international publication among Vietnamese medical researchers, recognizing and celebrating remarkable scientific achievements.

Dr. Nguyễn Quan Vinh, HELVIETMED's president and a former "boat people" like me, shared a unique background with me—both of us, former seafarers, harbored a common desire to support young Vietnamese colleagues. His invitation to chair the evaluation committee for research and award presentations resonated deeply. My experience chairing osteoporosis research award committees in the United States and Australia made the decision an easy one.

My first order of business was crafting a robust evaluation criterion, designed to empower and elevate Vietnamese research. While a growing number of Vietnamese research papers found their way into international medical journals, a concerning trend emerged—most were led by foreign researchers. To address this, I outlined four clear criteria for the award:

1. Publication in a medical journal within the past two years of the award date.

2. Consideration for "original articles" or "case reports" with original data.

3. Research conducted entirely within Việt Nam.

4. Authorship: the candidate must be the first, corresponding, or a significantly contributing author acknowledged in the publication.

To further refine the selection process, I established five key evaluation benchmarks:

1. Scientific quality (maximum 40 points)

2. Research significance (maximum 20 points)

3. Innovation (maximum 20 points)

4. Impact (maximum 10 points)

5. Journal Prestige (maximum 10 points)

Next came the formation of the Scientific Council, a distinguished body of seven independent experts. For the inaugural term (2017-2018), the council boasted an impressive roster:

- Myself, serving as chair.
- Emeritus Professor Vũ Việt Nữ, University of Geneva, Switzerland.
- Professor Anh-Tuấn Đinh-Xuân, Hôpitaux Universitaires Paris Centre, France.
- Emeritus Professor Ezio Giacobini , University of Geneva, Switzerland.
- Emeritus Professor Jean-Pierre Kraehenbuhl, CEO of the Health Sciences eTraining Foundation, Lausanne, Switzerland.
- Professor Huỳnh Đỗ Uyên, Bern University Hospital, Switzerland.
- Dr. Vincent Vinh-Hung, University Hospital of Martinique, France.
- Dr. Nguyễn Quan-Vinh, Fribourg, Switzerland.

A press release announcing the award and inviting applications was met with an enthusiastic response. Within three months, over sixty applications poured in. The Scientific Council undertook a meticulous independent evaluation process, eventually shortlisting four exceptional studies for the coveted award.

Dr. Vương Thị Ngọc Lan and Colleagues: Their research compared the efficacy of fresh and frozen embryo transfer in In Vitro Fertilization (IVF). Their findings, published in the prestigious *New England Journal of Medicine*, demonstrated that both methods were equally effective, paving the way for more flexible and potentially safer IVF protocols.

Dr. Hà Tấn Đức and Colleagues: Focusing on emergency patient care, their study identified key factors related to mortality and subsequently developed a prognostic model. This groundbreaking work, published in *Scientific Reports* (a *Nature* group journal), offered valuable tools for Vietnamese hospitals to prioritize treatment and reduce mortality rates.

Dr. Hồ Phạm Thục Lan and Colleagues: Their research, published in the *Journal of Clinical Endocrinology and Metabolism*, tackled the long-standing question of which factor—muscle mass or fat mass—has a greater impact on bone density. The answer? Muscle mass. This discovery provided valuable insights for preventing osteoporosis through physical activity.

Dr. Ngô Tất Trung and Colleagues: Their focus was on streamlining blood infection diagnosis. They developed an innovative PCR method that significantly reduced turnaround time and improved the accuracy of pathogen identification. Published in *BMC Infectious Diseases*, this research offered a groundbreaking solution for a life-threatening condition.

The award ceremony, held at the Saigon Prince Hotel in Hồ Chí Minh City, was a momentous occasion. Officials from the Swiss Embassy, hospital directors, university representatives, and a throng of journalists converged to celebrate Vietnamese excellence in medical research.

The Alexandre Yersin Prize continues to flourish. Every two years, new calls for submissions are issued, and outstanding research receives its well-deserved recognition. Since its inception in 2017, over twenty Vietnamese researchers have been honored, solidifying the award's place as a beacon of scientific achievement and fostering a generation of passionate Vietnamese medical researchers who are making a global impact.

A Dream Realized: The Birth of a Research Institute

Over two decades ago, the seeds of a dream were sown during a mentorship with Dr. Nguyễn Thanh Hương, a graduate student in Hà Nội. Việt Nam, I saw, was fertile ground for medical research, a landscape bursting with questions begging to be explored. Back then, I'd occasionally share a fantastical vision—a world-class research institute, Việt Nam's answer to Australia's Garvan Institute, where I'd spent over two decades. But it remained just that—a dream veiled by financial constraints and a healthy dose of skepticism about its feasibility.

Time, as it tends to do, marched on. Retirement plans were coming together as my second fellowship with the National Health and Medical Research Council (NHMRC) in Australia drew to a close. Then, fate intervened. A chance encounter with a former research student, Dr. Trần Minh Giang, led me to Mr. Ngô Chí Dũng, a man with a captivating enthusiasm for research institutes.

Initial conversations made me hesitant. Was this simply another well-meaning pipe dream? But fate, it seemed, wasn't finished playing its hand. An invitation to join the Tâm Anh group landed in my lap.

My role was to establish a private medical research institute, the first of its kind in Việt Nam. I embraced the mission with love and enthusiasm. The first task was to determine the name for the institution. After days of consideration and discussions with colleagues, I proposed the name "*Tâm Anh Medical Research Institute*" (TAMRI). After further deliberation, we decided to drop "Medical" from the name, thus becoming the *Tâm Anh Research Institute*, but we retained the abbreviation TAMRI. This name reflected our commitment to both medical and non-medical research.

Then, the logo for the institute. Nights turned into weeks as I scoured the logos of famous medical research institutes around the world—the Garvan Institute, a constant companion on my screen. Simplicity and a touch of gravitas, that's what I craved for. My vision took shape: a backdrop of regal purple, the color of medicine itself, cradling four sturdy columns—a visual representation of the BCDE pillars that grounded our research. And then, the name. I insisted on a slight alteration—"*Tâm Anh*" with a diacritical mark over the "â." It wasn't just a name; it was a promise, a "bright soul" embarking on a journey of discovery.

Little did I know, the PR team at Tâm Anh Hospital was on a similar quest. A flurry of logo designs landed on my desk, each sparking spirited debates. Finally, after countless rounds of back-and-forth, a winner emerged. Minimalist and elegant, it was perfect. Two intertwined lines, forming the letters "ta," their ends morphing into four distinct lines, a subtle nod to the BCDE pillars. Nestled beneath, "mri" in a deep purple, a discreet acronym for "medical research institute." And crowning it all, the full name, "Tâm Anh Research Institute," standing proud and resolute. It wasn't just a logo; it was a declaration. We were ready.

Next, I focused on the institute's scientific structure. I spent weeks researching the organizational frameworks of renowned research institutes worldwide. Armed with this new information and drawing on my leadership experience at the Garvan Institute in Australia, I devised the "BCDE structure": *B* for Basic Science, *C* for Clinical Science, *D* for Data Science, and *E* for Education and Training. Thus, TAMRI would be built on four pillars: Basic Science for fundamental research, Clinical Science for clinical studies and randomized controlled trials, Data Science for AI, big data, and bioinformatics, and Education & Training.

These pillars, I envisioned, would provide the specialized skills needed to support dedicated research groups, each focusing on a specific disease or even a particular aspect of a disease. We would actively encourage the formation of these research groups, welcoming both internal and external talent. Collaboration with leading international centers would further enhance TAMRI's scientific prowess.

TAMRI logo

At the launch event in May 2023, I unveiled TAMRI's vision. We aspired to become a force to be reckoned with, a "serious player," as we'd say in English, in Southeast Asia's medical research landscape. High-quality research, coupled with a timely translation of those findings into practical clinical applications, would be our guiding light.

Our research strategy encompasses both the short-term and long-term perspectives. In the short term, we'd focus on a mix of clinical trials, observational studies, and fundamental research. Existing clinical research projects and epidemiological studies would serve as a springboard, with the addition of a basic research component. Long-term aspirations leaned towards precision medicine and digital health. A bold dream danced in my head: a study utilizing Internet of Things (IoT) technology to prevent chronic diseases for millions of Vietnamese citizens. This, I yearned, would become TAMRI's signature achievement.

Scientific integrity, a pressing concern not just in Việt Nam but globally, was another area demanding attention. The specter of scientific misconduct in recent years has eroded public trust in science. Recognizing this, drafting research regulations, scientific integrity protocols, and research conduct guidelines based on established Australian and American models became a top priority. Regular training sessions would be an ongoing commitment, ensuring that all collaborators and colleagues at TAMRI not only produce high-quality research but also conduct themselves with integrity.

TAMRI's vision, a concise yet potent statement, captured our essence: "Become a leading medical research center in Asia through internationally significant research and through collaboration, translating discoveries into clinical applications to improve patients' quality of life." Discovery, translation, and collaboration—these were the three pillars upon which TAMRI would be built. We would delve into fundamental research, conduct rigorous clinical trials, and, through collaboration with key partners, transform research breakthroughs into tangible applications that would improve the lives of countless patients. The journey had begun, and the future of TAMRI, much like the research landscape of Việt Nam, brimmed with exciting possibilities.

Holding the establishment certificate for Tâm Anh Research Institute (TAMRI) at its inauguration on May 28, 2023.

But TAMRI wouldn't simply be a research powerhouse. It aspired to be a beacon of scientific excellence, fostering the next generation of Vietnamese researchers. A dedicated training department would offer programs on Good Clinical Practice (GCP), Continuing Medical Education (CME), ethics, and scientific integrity, creating a well-rounded foundation for all researchers.

Furthermore, TAMRI would become a haven for foreign postdoctoral researchers. Recognizing the importance of this crucial stage in a researcher's career, we aimed to provide opportunities beyond the PhD, a bridge between their academic achievements and independent research. For many Vietnamese-origin researchers who completed their PhDs abroad, the path back home often led to a dead end—a lack of infrastructure and opportunities for continued research. We envisioned TAMRI as a fertile ground where these returning researchers could flourish. I said the following on the inauguration of TAMRI:

"It is truly an honor for me to stand before you today to inaugurate the Tâm Anh Research Institute. First and foremost, I express my gratitude to all of you for being present at this moment to witness the birth of a scientific institution in Vietnam. Today marks the beginning of a new era in medical research in Vietnam.

I extend my sincere thanks to the leadership of Tâm Anh Hospital for entrusting me with the responsibilities I have accepted with full awareness of the responsibilities and vision they entail. I never underestimate the role of the Institute and my own responsibilities.

We are living in an era where medical research in Vietnam must confront numerous significant challenges. One of these challenges is to chart a course for the coming decades so that Vietnam can attain a deserving position within the international medical community.

Therefore, the Tâm Anh Research Institute will strive to become a leading medical research center in Asia. It's as simple as that. We will achieve this goal through internationally significant research endeavors and through collaboration, transferring discoveries to clinical applications to enhance the quality of life for patients. That is the vision of the Institute.

Over the past 30 years, university and research institute systems worldwide have undergone significant transformations. In the past, research institutes and univer-

sities were seen as 'ivory towers,' engaging in detached research with little relevance to the public or as 'talking in the clouds.' Those days are long gone. Today, these research institutes must bear responsibilities to the community, and their research must be meaningful and beneficial to the community and patients. This requirement is even more pressing for Vietnam. Therefore, the vision of the Tâm Anh Research Institute emphasizes translational research and endeavors to accelerate the translation of research results into clinical practice.

Medicine is an environment where change is a constant law, and the need for discoveries and innovations is paramount. Continuous change in medicine demands quick adaptation, and to adapt, the Institute will strive to attract scientists with new skills and fresh perspectives. They will collaborate to delve into disease mechanisms and seek therapies to enhance the quality of life for patients. Therefore, the mission of the Tâm Anh Research Institute is: to improve the health of patients in Vietnam and the world. We will accomplish this mission through scientific research, transferring discoveries, and implementing evidence-based medical practices.

The Tâm Anh Research Institute will create an environment for experts from various medical disciplines, from basic research to clinical research and data science. Through collaboration between these disciplines, we will expedite the translation of research outcomes into clinical practice. And, I emphasize once again that everything the Institute will do in the future aims to alleviate suffering and improve the quality of life for the community.

As you can see, the Tâm Anh Research Institute harbors great ambitions and benevolence. To realize these ambitions requires the efforts of all of us here, from nurses, doctors, scientists, directors, to local and national-level managers.

I invite you and our colleagues to embark on a new journey together. We will expand the horizons of medicine, challenge the status quo, and unlock the potential of the Vietnamese people to establish a new position for Vietnam in the international medical arena.

With profound gratitude to all of you and our fellow scientists!"

Tâm Anh Research Institute blossomed with surprising speed. Within six short months, we'd conducted over ten clinical trials and launched a series of observational studies. Collaboration was key, and we forged a strong bond with

Stanford University, tackling the thorny issues of epidemic prevention, infectious diseases, and cancer research. Stanford, a familiar stomping ground from my years abroad, beckoned me back several times as we fleshed out our action plan and reconnected with old friends.

For fourteen months, I poured my heart and soul into TAMRI. I envisioned it as a beacon of excellence in medical research, a place where new insights would be discovered, contributing meaningfully to global medical literature and benefiting patients. Building it from the ground up was exhilarating. I recruited a talented team of postdoctoral scientists from overseas and clinical researchers from Việt Nam, shaped a comprehensive research agenda, and laid the foundation for what I hoped would be a lasting contribution.

But along the way, new developments emerged. My vision for TAMRI began to diverge from the leadership's thinking. These weren't insurmountable differences, but they were significant enough to make me question my place at the helm. Ultimately, the decision to leave TAMRI was difficult, but I knew it was the right one. Leaving TAMRI wasn't an ending, but a new beginning. It was a chance to reflect on the challenges and triumphs of that chapter, and to use those experiences to guide me on the next one.

A Clash of Cultures: Lessons Learned

Returning to Việt Nam, a nation brimming with potential, I felt a surge of optimism. My years abroad, steeped in the scientific rigor and respectful work cultures of Australia and the United States, fueled my desire to "import" these values. Universities, hospitals, and research institutes each held the promise of a fair and transparent environment where talented minds could flourish.

One aspect that particularly appealed to me was mandatory training for new hires. Courses on bullying, discrimination, and workplace etiquette seemed like an excellent foundation for fostering a respectful atmosphere. Beyond the practical knowledge, I saw these programs fostering personal growth, a crucial step in building a strong scientific community.

However, my idealistic vision soon collided with the harsh realities of some Vietnamese workplaces. Here, in contrast, toxicity seemed to fester. It wasn't a subtle disharmony; it was a jarring discord. I witnessed a university dean, his office adorned in a manner that felt more Arabian than Eastern, behave like a feudal lord. Visitors were expected to bow and remove their shoes, while underlings, even doctors and professors, faced verbal tirades that bordered on abuse. It was a scene straight out of a bygone era, a chilling reminder of the power dynamics that could still exist. In Australia, such behavior would have resulted in swift disciplinary action, even termination.

My observations extended beyond isolated incidents. Conversations with colleagues revealed a disturbing pattern. Public agencies and hospitals often housed individuals who wielded their authority like blunt instruments, resorting to public humiliation and verbal abuse. One such encounter involved a nurse, berated to the point of tears for simply inquiring about a testing method. The perpetrator, later revealed to be someone with questionable qualifications and an inflated sense of self-importance, wielded power gained through connections rather than merit. I learned that his case wasn't unique.

This pervasive disrespect extended even to the realm of scientific discourse. Meetings devolved into arenas for uncultured remarks, with individuals in positions of authority making unfounded accusations about colleagues' integrity. The lack of professional courtesy and the victims' stoic acceptance left me bewildered. Here, in a country with such intellectual potential, dissent seemed stifled, replaced by a culture of quiet endurance.

The rationales behind this behavior were even more perplexing. When questioned, victims cited financial constraints as a reason to endure the abuse. It was a stark contrast to the workplaces I had known, environments where open communication and respect for peers formed the foundation of a productive work environment.

My experiences in Việt Nam were a powerful reminder of the complexities of cultural exchange. While I yearned to see the values I held dear take root, I learned a valuable lesson in respecting existing dynamics. I realized, however, that change wouldn't be achieved through a simple transplant of foreign practices. It would be a gradual process, one fueled by education and a shift in societal expectations. And for myself, it meant fostering a different kind of leadership—one based on guidance and encouragement, rather than a rigid imposition of a foreign ideal. The journey to a more respectful and productive work culture in Việt Nam, I realized, would be a shared one.

Therefore, I endeavored to establish a civilized working environment for the Tâm Anh Research Institute. To prevent unfortunate incidents, I drafted and implemented a Code of Conduct based on the code of conduct established by the Australian National Health and Medical Research Council.

As I embarked on my journey in Việt Nam, these principles became my compass. It wasn't about imposing Western ideals; it was about bridging cultural divides and building common ground based on mutual respect and shared values. The path wouldn't be easy, but with open communication and a sincere desire to learn from each other, the potential for a thriving research environment—one fueled by professionalism in all its aspects—seemed within reach.

In the West, it was a well-oiled machine. Punctuality was paramount, promises kept with resolve. A simple email could be a binding contract, a missed meeting, a social faux pas that demands an apology. Dress code mattered; a crisp suit wasn't just attire, it was a silent declaration of respect for the occasion and those involved.

Việt Nam, I discovered, embraced a different rhythm. Emails often arrived stripped of formalities, penned in a way more casual than expected. Deadlines were met with a relaxed approach; the urgency of the West was a foreign concept. Appointments held a certain looseness, the concept of time seemingly more fluid. At an international conference, I found myself chairing a session where scheduled presenters simply vanished, leaving empty slots and a gaping sense of bewilderment.

This cultural dissonance extended beyond scheduling. Feedback often took a harsh, condescending tone, aimed at belittling rather than building up. Finding the positives in a student's work seemed a lost art, replaced by a relentless focus on the flaws. Even attire became a point of contrast. High-ranking officials, in a bid to be seen as "of the people," donned casual wear that felt incongruent with the solemnity of scientific discourse.

Yet, amidst these initial observations, glimmers of hope emerged. Hospitality staff, trained under foreign management, exuded a level of professionalism that was truly remarkable. Their crisp uniforms, warm greetings, and genuine helpfulness were a refreshing contrast to some academic circles. Perhaps, I thought, a new generation was emerging, one that valued professionalism as a cornerstone of success.

Over the years, my commitment to Việt Nam has never wavered. I've poured myself into education, conferences, research, and anything that could contribute to the burgeoning scientific landscape. My Australian colleagues often expressed surprise at my continued involvement. But for me, it was never a question of choice. As a Vietnamese citizen, it felt like a responsibility —a way to give back to the land that had nurtured me. Thankfully, I wasn't alone. Kind and dedicated individuals like Dr. Thy Khuê, Prof. Dương Quang Trung, Prof. Võ Thành Phụng, Prof. Lê Vinh Danh, Dr. Lê Văn Út, and Prof. Nguyễn Thanh Bình welcomed my efforts and helped make my contributions meaningful.

Building a robust research culture in Việt Nam wouldn't be about transplanting Western ideals wholesale. It would be about fostering mutual understanding, respecting local customs while instilling the values of professionalism so critical in the global scientific arena. It wouldn't be a quick transformation, but a slow, patient process, one that built bridges of respect between cultures. It was a future I fervently believed in, one where Vietnamese research could truly shine on the world stage.

Chapter Nineteen

Two Homes, One Heart

The year 2025 marked a significant milestone: fifty years of the Vietnamese diaspora. My adopted home has become a haven for a thriving Vietnamese community, now boasting nearly 335,000 members, making it one of the nation's largest ethnic groups. Vietnamese boat people exemplify more than survival; they are architects of cultural vibrancy within their adopted countries.

Australia Day 1982 was when I arrived in the country seeking refuge. Exactly four decades later, another significant event unfolded on that same national holiday: Australia Day 2022, when Queen Elizabeth II bestowed upon me the Order of Australia. This honor was profoundly meaningful to me, recognizing my "significant contributions to medical research, to osteoporosis and fracture prevention, and to university education."

This wasn't just about personal honor; it was a validation of the field of osteoporosis research itself. For over three decades, I'd dedicated myself to reducing fracture risk and extending patient lifespans. Osteoporosis, impacting millions globally, was an area ripe for "precision medicine"—a field that leverages genetic and environmental factors to personalize diagnosis and treatment. Through a series of fortunate opportunities, we'd achieved significant milestones: redefining osteoporosis, rewriting textbook segments, discovering osteoporosis-linked genes, creating genetic signatures, and developing the world's first fracture prognosis model. These were just a few steps on a journey towards managing osteoporosis more effectively.

This honor also highlighted the strength of Australian medical research. Despite a population of only twenty-five million, Australia stood as a scientific powerhouse, particularly in the medical field. Eight of its sixteen Nobel laureates were medical scientists. This success stemmed from a potent combination: coherent government strategies, substantial investments, and a carefully nurtured scientific workforce.

Yet, a sobering reality lay beneath the surface. The daily struggles of my fellow researchers, myself included, were often unseen. From newly minted doctors to established professors, securing a stable career path was a constant challenge. Postdoctoral positions, crucial to career development, were limited by fluctuating funding. Even professors faced the pressure of securing research grants, with success rates hovering around a meager nine percent, a significant drop from a decade ago. Adding insult to injury, even successful grants often covered only sixty percent of research expenses, leaving the remaining forty percent dependent on philanthropists and university support.

But amidst these challenges, a burning passion for science persevered. Many researchers, including myself, pursued research even without guaranteed funding. Some even dug into their own pockets to fuel their scientific endeavors. The immediate impact of our work might not always be obvious. Who could have predicted the use of mRNA technology in developing COVID-19 vaccines? Or the application of gaming principles in economic science? The value often lay in the long term, in the foundational knowledge that led to rapid development of COVID-19 drugs and vaccines. For this reason, I saw my colleagues as "silent heroes," their dedication paving the way for future breakthroughs.

Echoing this sentiment was Australian Health Minister Greg Hunt's vision for Australian medical research to become a global leader. In the field of osteoporosis, Australia has indeed set the bar high. However, to truly achieve global leadership, Minister Hunt's words needed to be translated into action. A robust system that nurtured and empowered talented scientists was vital.

The Order of Australia held special significance for another reason as well. It transcended personal recognition, acknowledging the contributions of the Vietnamese community to Australia. It was a point of pride, not just for myself, but for all Vietnamese Australians. The Order wasn't just an individual distinction; it was another "Nguyen" inscribed onto the map of achievements in my adopted homeland.

Leaving Vietnam, I'd never dreamt of awards or accolades. Those early years were a relentless struggle—working long hours to support myself and send money back home. Education followed, then the fierce competition of academia. Life presented its twists and turns at every corner, leaving little time for thoughts of recognition.

Yet, just like a fruit grower, the seeds of dedication sown with care eventually yield sweet rewards. The act of giving, of offering one's knowledge and expertise, eventually finds a way of reciprocating. And in that reciprocity, I found a deep sense of fulfillment, a connection that bridged the miles between my two homes, Australia and Việt Nam. The journey continues, underscoring the enduring power of knowledge, collaboration, and a shared passion for science.

Echoes of Recognition

The weight of the Order of Australia settled upon me with a profound sense of responsibility. Little did I expect the outpouring of congratulations that followed. Letters arrived from esteemed figures: the Governor and Premier of New South Wales, the Prime Minister himself, and a chorus of ministers, legislators, and university heads. Even CEOs from the corporate world extended their well-wishes. From colleagues across the globe, messages of warmth and admiration flowed in. Such widespread recognition left me humbled, a feeling that only deepened with a series of unexpected honors.

Following the announcement on January 26, 2022, most local and national newspapers extensively reported and featured images of me. *The Torch*, our local newspaper, went a step further by dedicating its entire front page to celebrate two members of the community, myself and Professor Ross Jeffree, who were honored with the award.

News

Pair honoured to be recognised

February 1, 2022

☐ *Professor Ross Jeffree.*   ☐ *Professor Tuan Van Nguyen.*

The Torch recognizes Professors Ross Jeffree and Tuan Nguyen. (February 1, 2022)

Following the announcement on January 26, 2022, Fiona McGill from the University of Technology Sydney interviewed me to explore the journey that led to this prestigious award. The article, titled "Anniversary honour for a life's work on osteoporosis," delved into the research, motivations, and impact of my efforts in this crucial field. Here is the link to the article: https://www.uts.edu.au/new s/tech-design/anniversary-honour-lifes-work-osteoporosis

One day, a call from the office of Member of Parliament Tania Mihailuk pierced the quiet rhythm of my day. Her secretary informed me that Ms. Mihailuk had delivered a "Statement of Recognition" in the New South Wales Parliament, lauding my contributions to Australian healthcare and higher education. A certificate of recognition, she mentioned, was on its way. Gratitude welled up within me as this heartfelt gesture transcended any personal achievement.

The following day, another wave of emotion washed over me. An assistant from Member of Parliament Wendy Lindsay's office contacted me. Ms. Lindsay, too, had presented a statement in the Legislative Assembly, etching my name into the official record, the Australian "Hansard." These pronouncements, delivered within the hallowed halls of Parliament, truly touched me. It wasn't just about individual recognition; it was about the validation of a life dedicated to research and education.

The news of the "Statements of Recognition" delivered by Tania Mihailuk and Wendy Lindsay, two Members of Parliament, came as a complete surprise. While I hadn't personally met either woman, their reputations preceded them. Ms. Mihailuk, a stalwart of the Labor Party, was a strong supporter of the Vietnamese community during challenging times. Ms. Lindsay, from the opposing Liberal Party, was equally renowned for her social activism. A cynical mind might suspect political motives, a calculated move in the lead-up to the next election. But I chose to believe in the genuineness of their gestures. Within the Vietnamese community, their actions truly touched the hearts of many people. Here were two figures, on opposite sides of the political spectrum, united in their recognition of an immigrant's journey.

The Investiture Ceremony

Months later, on a cool May 13th, the weight of that dream solidified at Government House in Sydney. The investiture ceremony, simple yet imbued with quiet reverence, left an indelible mark on my soul.

Each honoree was allowed two guests. Accompanying me were my wife, a constant source of love and support, and my elder brother, the brave soul who'd taken that leap across the ocean with me all those years ago in 1981. My sister, Kim Vui, the one who shared that daring escape, and Nga, my sister from Việt Nam, couldn't be physically present but joined us through a video stream outside the Government House.

We were twenty eight individuals that day who received recognition. The meticulousness of the organizers was a subtle symphony—individual invitations for every guest and a controlled flow into the ceremony hall. Inside, a thoughtful gesture awaited us. Families were ushered to the front, a silent acknowledgment of the invisible threads woven into our achievements.

Detailed instructions followed, including a choreography of greetings, movements, and the proper way to address the Governor. Even our attire received a final, discerning eye, a reminder of the momentous occasion. As a hand adjusted my clothes, a fleeting thought danced in my mind: Meeting the Governor—a big deal indeed. Yet, amidst the formality, a sense of surrender took hold. I was ready to receive the honor.

The preparation and rehearsals concluded, and the ceremony commenced. The master of ceremonies, Mr. Michael Miller, an assistant to the governor, called the guests to stand for the governor's entrance. Her opening remarks impressed me. In the indigenous language, she acknowledged the traditional owners of the land before delving into the history of the Order of Australia. Established in 1975, a mere three months before the tumultuous events that unfolded in Vietnam, it marked a turning point. Prior to this, Australian honors originated solely from the UK. Prime Minister Gough Whitlam of the Labor Party, envisioned a system to celebrate Australians for their achievements and service. His vision was clear: an honor that would be highly esteemed by the nation, hence the title "Order of Australia." However, a nod to tradition remained, as Queen Elizabeth II, the head of state, still held the power of approval.

The governor's words were a reminder of the complex interplay of history, politics, and personal journeys. The ceremony unfolded, etching this momentous day into my memory. But as I stood there, the weight of the honor wasn't just about individual recognition; it was a culmination of years dedicated to research and education, a bridge built between my adopted home and the land of my birth. This wasn't an ending; it was a new chapter, a springboard for continued contributions to both Australia and Việt Nam.

On January 26, 2022, exactly forty years after settling in Australia, I was awarded the Order of Australia. In the picture is Governor Margaret Beazley AC on the day of the award ceremony at Government House, New South Wales, on May 13, 2022.

After pinning the medal, the governor would exchange pleasantries with each recipient. These conversations, seemingly beyond the reach of microphones, remained private whispers between the two. In my case, she acknowledged my work in osteoporosis research and my contributions to the university.

"There's still much to be done in reducing mortality among osteoporosis patients," I replied.

With a shift in theme, she jokingly asked, "Do you think I need to run every day?"

The playful spirit continued in my response. "You seem to be doing quite well, but with these beautiful gardens surrounding you, why not take a stroll each morning and afternoon?"

On January 26, 2022, exactly 40 years after settling in Australia, I was awarded the Order of Australia. In the picture is Governor Margaret Beazley AC on the day of the award ceremony at Government House, New South Wales. (May 13, 2022)

Laughter filled the air before she requested a commemorative photo, forever capturing that moment. Following the ceremony, a light banquet hosted by the governor brought together all the honorees and their families, roughly a hundred people in total. The menu was a celebration of Australian delicacies, particularly those from New South Wales, paired with fine wines.

During the banquet, the governor sought me out for a more personal conversation. She inquired about my arrival in Australia: a large boat or a small one? My answer—a small boat—elicited a chuckle. "So you're a boat person?" she asked.

Pride welled up within me as I responded, "Yes, I am."

She confided that her work as a lawyer in the 1980s had brought the plight of Vietnamese asylum seekers and boat people to her attention. Stories of child refugees arriving with no English, who later thrived, some even becoming lawyers like herself, inspired her. Meeting a boat person like me, established in academia, was a first for her.

The governor revealed that an Australian ambassador in Vietnam had previously commented on the infrequent return of boat people to Việt Nam. My return and contributions seemed to be a refreshing counterpoint. I explained the complexities behind the phenomenon: missing families, political anxieties, and the harsh realities of departure.

However, for me, the return was driven by collaborative research opportunities and scientific exchange, all of which were layered on top of a forty-year journey as an Australian citizen. My identity and my reasons for being here were crystal clear.

The governor's testimonial for the Order of Australia, I later learned, was written in a style that felt both intricate and dated. But the personal interaction and the exchange on that day transcended formalities. It was a human connection, a recognition that was significant to me. The testimonial read as follows:

"*Whereas with the approval of Her Majesty Queen Elizabeth The Second, Queen of Australia and Sovereign of the Order of Australia, I have been pleased to appoint you to be a Member in the General Division of the Order of Australia.*

I DO by these Presents appoint you to be a Member in the General Division of the said Order and authorize you to hold and enjoy privileges thereunto appertaining.

Given at Government House, Canberra under the seal of the Order of Australia this twenty-sixth day of January 2022.

By His Excellency's Command Secretary of the Order of Australia"

The Order of Australia was a culmination of my journey, one shaped by countless interactions, collaborations, and the support of many. I am deeply grateful to the research fellows in labs across Australia and Việt Namwhose tireless efforts contributed to my work. While it's impossible to acknowledge everyone, I would like to express my sincere gratitude to a few individuals who have had a particularly significant impact on my career.

Professors John Eisman and Philip Sambrook, my mentors, have been instrumental in my development. Professor Eisman's intellectual brilliance and belief in my abilities have been invaluable. Dr. Sambrook, a renowned figure in the field, provided invaluable guidance throughout his lifetime, and his legacy continues to inspire me. I am also indebted to Dr. Paul Kelly, a former colleague who has become a close friend and confidant.

A particular debt of gratitude goes out to my colleagues and friends in Việt Nam. Their support was integral to this recognition. The Order of Australia Council acknowledged my work at universities such as Tôn Đức Thắng, Đà Nẵng, Hà Nội University of Pharmacy, and Hà Nội Medical University.

The Governor-General's Office, I later learned, had meticulously contacted all my past workplaces: research institutions in Australia, the United States, Switzerland, the UK, Thailand, Singapore, Việt Nam, and beyond. While I never saw the letters of support from colleagues scattered around the globe, the very knowledge of their existence filled me with warmth. Many, bound by confidentiality, celebrated my nomination before I even knew it was happening. This outpouring of support, unseen yet deeply felt, underscored the interconnectedness of the global research community.

Finally, a heartfelt thank you to the anonymous "good Samaritan" who nominated me for the award. Your belief in my work fueled the embers that led to this recognition. And to the Order of Australia Council, my deepest gratitude for your meticulous consideration over the past two years. Their rigorous process guaranteed the award was based on genuine merit.

On this occasion, I wrote to my friends and colleagues in Australia, sharing my thoughts on the honor and the medical research landscape in the country:

I am obviously a happy scientist at this moment, but my thoughts are with the majority of my colleagues in the medical research community. Why I am thinking of them? Because I am part of the research community that constantly struggles to survive. The lack of career structure and lack of funding have put us in a very precarious position. Each of us literally survives for only 1 year. We don't know whether we will receive a grant in the coming year to support our position and our team. Even if we succeed in getting a grant, it covers only 60% of our salary costs, and the gap is dependent on the mercy of the university or philanthropy. Nevertheless, we have passion, we have a clear goal, and we believe in excellence, and that is why some of us even work without salaries.

Some of us spend many decades silently pursuing an idea that may not have an immediate impact, but brick by brick, we build solid knowledge bases for others to improve health care for the community. The rapid development of Covid-19 vaccines is a good case in point. I would like to take this opportunity to tell the public at large that the Australian medical research community is a group of highly devoted scientists who are striving to improve the health status of each and everyone in the general community. They are our unsung heroes.

Our Minister for Health, Mr. Greg Hunt, said that the medical research community had 'a golden opportunity to be a global leader'. I totally agree with his view, but we need to do more: we need to create a sustainable system to nurture the best researchers to realize that potential.

Today is also a very special day for me. Exactly 40 years ago on this day (26/1/1982) I arrived in Australia as a refugee from Vietnam. Australia has given me (and many other Vietnamese refugees in the 1980s) a chance to start a new life and to make meaningful contributions to this beautiful country. Like many refugees in my generation, I started my life in Australia with a shirt on my back, and not a penny in my pocket. Needless to say, over the past 40 years I have faced many challenges; however, each challenge has only strengthened me to make me the person I am today.

Australia is a small country, but we have disproportionately contributed to the protection of refugees worldwide through several humanitarian programs. That is something we can be proud of. However, at present, Australia ranked 30th in terms of refugee protection, with the rate of protection or resettlement being ~23 refugees per 100,000 people, a 70% drop from the pre-pandemic years. I therefore believe that we as a country can do more to help refugees. They, just like me of 40 years ago, want to have a chance, and we should give them a chance.

I would not be where I am today without the help of my family and my colleagues, who are equally worthy of the honor. I sincerely thank each one of my colleagues in Australia, the United States, Europe, and Asia, especially Vietnam, for helping me reach a stage where I can proudly hold up this honor as a mark of my progress and achievement. This honor is an encouragement for me to do more work to relieve the consequence of osteoporosis globally.

Two lands call me home, each with a distinct claim upon my heart. Australia, the compassionate haven that opened its doors to boat people like me, offered refuge and the promise of a new life. It is a debt I can never fully repay. Yet, Việt Nam, the land of my birth, the soil from which my roots draw sustenance, remains the very fabric of my being. While I am deeply grateful to Australia (and the United States) for their generosity and the opportunities they have afforded me, a deep and abiding love for Việt Nam always echoes within me. It is a love born of shared history, culture, and the unbreakable bonds of family. I am bound to Australia by the formal ties of citizenship, a commitment I honor with pride and dedication. But to Việt Nam, I am bound by something far deeper: the enduring ties of kinship, a filial duty that compels me to contribute to her well-being, to honor her past, and to hope for her future.

Chapter Twenty

Reflections

The Vietnam War cast a long shadow, uprooting millions of Vietnamese from their homes. This mass exodus, unlike anything the country had ever witnessed, forced families to make unimaginable choices. I was caught up in a tumultuous period of history and was forced to leave my homeland. Looking back on my life and the lives of my friends, I realize that every Vietnamese person, especially those who sought refuge abroad, carries a unique story. Each refugee bears a piece of a turbulent past—a personal narrative of overcoming adversity and finding hope in unfamiliar lands. They departed, carrying with them their homeland and a rich cultural heritage. In their adopted societies, they have made significant contributions, enriching these communities with diverse perspectives, skills, and talents.

Each refugee's story is a chapter in the broader history of our world. This memoir is written to help the world, and especially younger generations of Vietnamese, understand and appreciate these stories, to foster empathy, and to build a more harmonious and prosperous community.

I consider myself a lucky individual. My first stroke of fortune was growing up and benefiting from South Việt Nam's educational system before 1975, which integrated Humanism, Nationalism, and Liberal.

Humanist education prioritizes human life and well-being, treating individuals as ends in themselves rather than means to an end. It promotes equality and provides equitable educational opportunities for all. Nationalistic education respects traditional values, customs, and the nation's cultural heritage, preserving and promoting the best aspects of our cultural identity. Liberal education emphasizes open-mindedness and forward-thinking, embracing democratic values, social progress, and global cultural values to contribute to national and societal modernization. I am grateful to our predecessors for creating such an advanced educational system, which shaped who I am today and empowered me to pursue further studies in Australia.

This educational system exposed me to new ideas from abroad and the works of Northern Vietnamese authors. The Vietnamese literature curriculum included works by Nguyễn Tuân, Xuân Diệu, Huy Cận, Tế Hanh, Lưu Trọng Lư, Phạm Huy Thông, Thanh Tịnh, Văn Cao, Hữu Loan, and others, regardless of their political affiliations. Philosophy courses covered communism and sparked lively debates.

The education system I experienced was a sacred institution. Politics and the military did not influence examinations. The story of Ngô Đình Nhu's eldest daughter, who was denied admission to medical school due to insufficient scores, is a testament to this. No one, not even those close to President Ngô Đình Diệm, dared to intervene. General Cao Văn Viên, then a highly educated military officer, was allowed to pursue a Bachelor of Arts degree. He even failed an oral exam conducted by a young conscript, but no one interfered. This demonstrates the academic freedom enjoyed by the education system at that time.

Nelson Mandela once said, "Destroying any nation does not require the use of atomic bombs or the use of long-range missiles. It only requires lowering the quality of education and allowing cheating in the examinations by the students." This statement serves as a timely warning for Việt Nam today.

My second stroke of luck was settling in Australia. As a refugee, I never imagined ending up in Australia, a country I knew little about beyond kangaroos. Fate led me to this "Lucky Country," and I have never regretted my decision. Australia supported me during my most difficult times and provided me with opportunities that would have been impossible to achieve in Việt Nam. Both Australia and the United States offered me equal opportunities, including access to world-class institutions that took centuries to build. They celebrated my successes and were patient with my stubbornness and cultural differences. After graduating, I was encouraged and supported in pursuing a career in academia and research at leading institutions worldwide. I experienced opportunities that I could never have dreamed of in my homeland.

There's a saying, "Geography is destiny," and I believe it's true. I am convinced that any Vietnamese person, given the proper education and opportunities, could excel in the global scientific community. Just as plants need a suitable environment to flourish, refugees like us would not have achieved our current stability and success without the hospitality of countries like the United States, Australia, and Canada. Many refugees, who were once high school dropouts, manual laborers, or farmers, have achieved remarkable accomplishments in various fields, including science, education, business, and the military. The world's most prestigious scientific journals feature Vietnamese names, and there are Vietnamese-American generals in the US military. These accomplishments would have been unlikely to occur in Việt Nam. Indeed, geography can shape destiny.

This realization deepens my appreciation for the Vietnamese proverb, "Remember the planter when eating the fruit." While the United States and Australia are not perfect, and no place is truly perfect, refugees like me owe a debt of gratitude to these countries and their people.

My third stroke of luck was encountering good people. These individuals—whether mentors, colleagues, or students—have guided and inspired me. The first was Professor John Eisman, a former mentor and lifelong friend. We collaborated for thirty years, and many people wondered how we could work together for so long, given his demanding personality. I believe our shared goals and mutual respect were key. Of course, we had our disagreements and periods of silence, but we always managed to find a way to reconcile. Through Professor Eisman, I was introduced to renowned scholars in my field, including B.L. Riggs, Joseph Melton III, Steven Cummings, Elizabeth Barrett-Connor, Pierre Delmas, Clifford Rosen, T.J. Martin, John Kanis, Juliet Compston, John Wark, Ian Reid, and Ego Seeman. They supported my academic career, helping me secure leadership positions in professional societies and serve on the editorial boards of top-tier journals. Without their guidance, I would not be where I am today.

I believe that every individual is shaped by their interactions with others and their environment. Our relationships with friends, colleagues, family, and students, as well as our experiences in different settings, from rural villages to international stages, contribute to our unique identities. These interactions are irreplaceable and create a one-of-a-kind tapestry. As Hermann Hesse suggested, our encounters, both in person and online, are not random but serve specific purposes and life lessons. With that in mind, I would like to express my sincere gratitude to all those who have touched my life.

I believe in the principle of "what goes around comes around." I'm a survivor. Surviving a perilous sea voyage was almost miraculous. In the mid-1990s, I survived another car accident on the Sydney Harbour Bridge. It was a foggy day, and I couldn't see clearly. My brand-new Ford Telstar flipped over, with all four wheels in the air. I was hanging upside down as the car continued to slide and hit a bridge pylon. I saw the sparks from the car's undercarriage against the road and thought I was going to burn to death. Miraculously, several cars behind me managed to stop in time and helped me out. The accident caused a traffic jam for hours and became national news. When I got home, my mother-in-law lit incense and said, "It's thanks to the blessings of our ancestors." I believe that. My parents were very charitable during their lifetimes, helping many people. I think that their good deeds have brought me good fortune. Therefore, I believe that if I do good deeds today, I will reap the benefits in the future.

In my generation, I strongly believe in the advice to share two things: knowledge and kindness. Knowledge can open doors and change lives for the better. But it's our integrity, kindness, and how we treat others that truly define us. Therefore, I always prioritize sharing knowledge and treating everyone with kindness.

However, I'm not perfect. I've made many mistakes. In the past, I'm sure I've said things that I would say differently if given a second chance. I could blame it on my Western upbringing (where people are more direct), but I think it's partly because I was young, competitive, and didn't think things through. I hope you won't repeat my mistakes and will apply a three-step filter before speaking. Before expressing an opinion, ask yourself three questions: Is what I'm going to say true? If it's true, is it necessary? And if it's necessary, will it offend or harm anyone? It wasn't until I was in my 50s that I fully understood these questions. If the answer is "yes" to all of these questions, perhaps we should consider staying silent.

Many people who meet me often comment that I look younger than my age. I think this is partly because I try to keep my mind active by constantly reading and writing. Additionally, I believe in forgetting two things: painful memories and grudges. In fact, this has always been my natural inclination. Throughout my life, I've faced unfair and hostile criticism, even from people I have helped enthusiastically. I never held grudges against them, simply because I forgot.

When I first returned to Việt Nam for short-term courses, some people speculated that I was losing my job abroad and returning home to make a living. Others, seeing my enthusiasm for teaching with Dr. Nguyễn Đình Nguyên, spread rumors about our ulterior motives. But I didn't blame anyone and believed that my actions would speak louder than words.

Life journey is by default, never smooth. Just like driving on a highway, there are occasional traffic jams and potholes. The path to scientific success is no different. There are periods of frustration and uncertainty about the future. Practical concerns, such as navigating a competitive environment, can consume our energy and distract us from our long-term goals. Additionally, we always have to deal with those who envy us and try to bring us down. In Western culture, there's a distinction between competition and envy. Competition is a positive trait, as it drives individuals to strive for excellence. Envy, on the other hand, is destructive and only drains energy.

Readers of this memoir may only see my successes, but that's not the whole picture. Behind the awards and accolades is a long list of failures. I failed three times before receiving a fellowship from the National Health and Medical Research Council. Multiple failures preceded every successful research grant. I faced countless rejections before publishing articles in prestigious journals. These failures, invisible to the public, could fill a "resume of failures."

I am sure that we all have a "resume of failures." It helps us redefine success. Most of us equate success with achieving our desired goals, whether it's wealth, status, or fame. However, the original meaning of "'success," dating back to the 16th century, comes from the Latin word "succedere," which means "to come after," "to advance," or "to follow." In this sense, success is simply about making an effort. The musician Vũ Thành An once wrote a line that I deeply appreciate: "Only after enduring the hardships of winter can we truly appreciate the warmth of summer." We must experience failures and setbacks to truly savor the sweetness of success.

Failures often force us to change, both ourselves and our perspectives. In today's language, we call this "self-transformation." It means constantly renewing ourselves and our thinking. Our understanding is never static, but rather evolves over time and with new experiences. The renowned physicist Richard Feynman once said, "You are under no obligation to remain the same person you were a year ago, a month ago, or even a day ago. You are here to create yourself, continuously." This aligns with the Buddhist concept of impermanence.

Life is a continuous learning journey, not just from our failures but also from those around us. Having lived in the West for over 40 years, I've learned many valuable lessons. Here are ten things I've learned from my experiences in Western society:

Tolerance: Contrary to the stereotype of selfish and cunning Westerners, I've found them to be incredibly generous and tolerant. Americans, Australians, and Canadians have generously supported Vietnamese refugees, even those they didn't know personally. Western countries have opened their doors to millions of refugees from Eastern Europe, Africa, and other regions, welcoming them with open hearts. Even smaller countries like Switzerland and Nordic nations, with little historical connection to Việt Nam, have welcomed tens of thousands of Vietnamese refugees.

Social Ethics: I used to hear that Westerners were immoral and hedonistic. This is a grave misconception. Westerners are highly moral, perhaps even more so than Easterners. They prioritize human life and base their decisions on human values. They also place great importance on etiquette and social norms. Westerners, like us, respect their elders and younger generations. They have long-standing traditions of etiquette, as seen in British royal ceremonies and university graduations.

Westerners also care deeply about animals. Their treatment of livestock and pets may come as a surprise to many Easterners. This is not mere showmanship but a genuine respect for life. Scientific experiments involving animals must undergo rigorous ethical review.

Moreover, Westerners are deeply concerned about the environment. Countries like those in Northern Europe and Australia have strict environmental regulations and educate their young about the importance of ecological conservation.

Respect for Women: A significant difference between Việt Nam and the West is how society treats women. In Việt Nam, there's a tradition of male dominance and sexism, leading to unequal treatment of women. While Western societies have historically treated women poorly, they have learned from their mistakes and made significant progress. Today, women in Western societies are treated with respect.

Western governments actively promote gender equality in all aspects of society, from political representation to academic and corporate leadership. They implement practical policies and regulations to achieve gender parity. I've made a conscious effort to promote gender equality in my own lab, ensuring equal representation of women and men. While I've occasionally faced criticism for favoring women, I've never compromised on this principle.

Respect for Individuality: Vietnamese and Asian people tend to be very personal, often inquiring about a person's background, social status, and political views. They judge others based on these personal details. In contrast, Westerners tend to be less concerned with personal details. They focus on a person's ideas and knowledge, regardless of their background or political affiliation. I've worked on a scientific committee for ten years without revealing my refugee status. My supervisor only learned about my past as a hospital kitchen worker a decade after I started working there. Westerners value privacy and avoid prying into personal matters.

Americans don't judge individuals based on their political beliefs or religious affiliations. They evaluate people based on their work and its quality. As a scientific assessor, I've never considered a person's background or social status. This approach is both fair and objective. We should learn from Westerners and respect individual privacy.

Kindness and Gratitude: Western kindness is evident in their frequent use of the phrase "thank you." Saying "thank you" is a common practice, not just for receiving help but also for helping others. It's a form of acknowledgment and gratitude. Psychological studies have shown that expressing gratitude is a positive behavior that promotes happiness. Saying "thank you" can create positive energy within a community.

During my academic career, my supervisor reminded us to thank pharmaceutical companies for sponsoring conferences and to acknowledge contributions in our research presentations. I've continued this practice with my own students. Expressing gratitude is a simple yet powerful way to cultivate positive relationships. We should learn from Westerners and practice gratitude more often.

Respect for Diversity: Western societies are multicultural, multi-ethnic, and multi-party. From a young age, children are taught to respect differing opinions. They learn to live in a diverse society. Therefore, there's no discrimination based on political affiliation in the workplace.

In his memoir, Professor Clive Hamilton recounts how a right-wing economics department hired him despite his left-wing political views. The department head explained that she wanted to foster diversity of thought. Hamilton found this experience to be one of the most valuable in his life. This example illustrates how embracing ideological differences can enrich professional environments and personal growth.

Humor: When I was in Việt Nam, I admired the comedic talent of Charlie Chaplin. Later, in Australia, I became a fan of Benny Hill's witty and humorous sketches. Westerners possess a keen sense of humor, which is comparable to that of the Vietnamese.

Mark Twain once said, "Humor is mankind's greatest blessing." Humor is a positive trait that helps us cope with life's challenges and difficulties. Perhaps this is why Westerners have such a strong sense of humor.

Give and Take: This principle is about fairness and reciprocity. Westerners highly value "give and take" as it ensures equity. Fairness is a cornerstone of Western societies, underpinning many policies and initiatives.

Some young Vietnamese people nowadays often prioritize self-interest, asking, "What's in it for me?" This narrow-minded thinking neglects the needs of others. In contrast, Westerners consider the benefits for both themselves and others, embodying a sense of fairness and reciprocity.

Quality over Speed: Vietnamese people often pride themselves on their efficiency and speed. They compare the rapid construction of infrastructure projects in Việt Namto slower-paced projects in Western countries. While this may be true in some cases, Westerners prioritize quality and long-term sustainability. They consult with experts from various fields and consider the environmental impact of projects. They even involve patients in the design of medical equipment. This methodical approach may seem slow, but it ensures high-quality and durable outcomes. We should learn from their commitment to quality and long-term vision.

Innovation: Eastern cultures tend to value tradition and stability, while Western cultures emphasize innovation and progress. Western institutions, such as my research institute and universities, regularly hold retreats to discuss current challenges and brainstorm new solutions. This culture of innovation encourages creativity and keeps organizations at the forefront.

In today's competitive scientific and technological landscape, innovation is crucial for staying ahead. Emerging Asian countries often invite Western experts to share their knowledge and insights, and are willing to pay substantial fees for innovative ideas.

I hope this memoir, though lengthy, offers valuable insights and reflections. I am not comfortable talking about myself, as it can come across as self-aggrandizing. I am aware that constantly referring to myself can be self-centered, but these are genuine experiences, both joyful and painful, successes and failures. I want to emphasize that these are personal experiences and observations, not generalizations.

I believe that we are tied to specific places. Despite spending many years abroad and adopting Australia and the U.S. as second homes, I still feel a deep connection to my homeland. In my early years away, I doubted if I would ever return. As time passed, I felt increasingly distant from my roots. However, over the years, I've come to realize that my departure wasn't a rejection of my homeland, but rather a preparation for a better return. Through brief visits, I've contributed to my homeland in meaningful ways. It's through these experiences that I've truly understood my identity and my connection to Việt Nam.

Epilogue: A Circle Completed

In 1982, I set foot in Australia alongside my brother and sister, carrying nothing but hope and the weight of an uncertain future. We were young, single, and strangers in a foreign land, yet bound by the silent promise to rebuild our lives in this place of newfound possibility. The years have unfolded like the turning pages of a book, filling our lives with love, growth, and the warmth of family. Together, we have been blessed with three sons (or nephews) and five nieces. They have flourished, completing their university education and carving out their own careers, with four choosing the medical path. Unlike us, whose hearts still echo with memories of Việt Nam—its sorrows, its beauty, its losses—they are wholly Australian. This is the only home they have ever known, and the land we once called our own is, to them, little more than a distant story.

My brother, through four decades of tireless dedication, built a life from the ground up, shaping metal with his hands as he shaped a future for his family, before finally laying down his tools in well-earned retirement. My sister, steadfast and determined, still carries on with her business, embracing each new day with the same spirit that brought us here. And as for me, my journey has taken me deep into the world of bone science, where my work in osteoporosis research continues to bridge two lands—Australia, where I have found purpose, and Việt Nam, where my heart still lingers. Through it all, I remain committed to giving back, weaving together the threads of knowledge and compassion, and honoring the journey that has shaped us into who we are today.

Looking back, my life unfolds like a complex, intricate pattern, each thread woven with resilience, determination, and a belief in the power of human potential. From the harrowing escape from Việt Nam, I landed in refugee camps that etched indelible marks on my soul. They were years of deprivation, yet they also forged a spirit of indomitable hope. Australia, a land of opportunity, welcomed me with open arms. It was here that I laid the foundation for my academic pursuits, discovering a passion for the intricacies of bone health. The challenges were immense, but they fueled my determination to succeed. With each research breakthrough, each award bestowed, I felt a profound sense of fulfillment, a validation of the arduous path I had traversed.

Returning to Việt Nam was a homecoming of a different kind. The country had transformed, yet the echoes of the past reverberated. It was an opportunity to give back, to share the knowledge and expertise I had acquired. To witness the impact of our research on the lives of countless individuals and to inspire a new generation of scientists is a privilege beyond measure. Vietnamese boat people exemplify more than survival; they are architects of cultural vibrancy within their adopted nations.

As I stand at this juncture, looking back and forward, I am filled with gratitude. Gratitude for the strength to endure, the courage to dream, and the resilience to rebuild. Gratitude for the life I have built, for the challenges that shaped me, and for the opportunities that continue to unfold. My story is a reflection of the human spirit's capacity for transformation. It is a story of Việt Nam, of Australia, and of the interconnectedness of our world. It is a story that, I believe, transcends borders and cultures, inspiring others to find their own paths to achievement.

The journey may not be over, but the destination is clear: a world where knowledge is shared, where compassion prevails, and where the human spirit knows no bounds.

Praise From Colleagues

"Professor Nguyen is recognised internationally for his scientific expertise, particularly in epidemiology, biostatistics, and genetics. It is clear that he is highly regarded in many countries across the region and worldwide. I cannot consider another scientist in this area who would be more highly regarded. One example of this is his invitation to serve as Associate Editor of the most highly ranked bound journal internationally, the Journal of Bone and Mineral Research, the official Journal of the American Society for Bone and Mineral Research.

Professor Nguyen has demonstrated an amazing commitment to improving medical education and research in Vietnam. He has established a number of highly sought-after research contributions to these activities. His commitment has translated to numbers of Vietnamese scientists and scientists from other countries in the region being exposed to the highest levels of scientific expertise in bone science, in particular. There are few people who have demonstrated such engagement and leadership to student learning and development."
—**Professor John Eisman**, AO, FAHMS, MBBS, PhD, FRACP, former President of the Australian and New Zealand Bone and Mineral Society (ANZBMS), former Editor in Chief of Journal of Bone and Mineral Research, Professor of Medicine, UNSW Sydney and University of Notre Dame

"Dr. Nguyen and I have begun and developed our professional journeys concurrently, even though at geographical antipodes, and share a passionate attraction to bone and mineral research. Throughout my 40-year career, Tuan's research activity and publications have always been at the cutting-edge of our knowledge of genetics and epidemiology of osteoporosis and metabolic bone disorders. As such, I am quite familiar with his work, and have followed him since the earliest stages of my career. Therefore, I can say that I have known Dr. Nguyen primarily by fame throughout my entire career, and interacted with him directly, when I asked him to serve as Associate Editor of the Journal of Bone and Mineral Research, which I led as Editor-in-Chief, between 2018 and 2022.

Dr. Tuan Nguyen is a world-renowned clinical scientist whose activity during his 30-year-long career has contributed to transform our understanding of how genetic traits affect bone homeostasis. Since the early 1990s, at the time of his post-graduate training with Drs. Eisman and Sambrook, at the Garvan Institute in Sydney, Australia, his name has been associated with the then budding area of genetics of osteoporosis. He was part of the investigative group led by Dr. Eisman that, for the first time, reported an association between a variant of the vitamin D receptor gene and bone mass, a milestone paper that sparked an entirely new area of research. He has continued to push the boundaries of our understanding of genetic factors in the pathogenesis of osteoporosis throughout his entire career and remains very active to date."
—**Roberto Civitelli**, MD, Sydney M & Stella H Schoenberg Chair in Medicine, Former Chief, Division of Bone and Mineral Diseases and Musculoskeletal Research Center, Washington University in St Louis, Missouri, USA

"I know Prof. Nguyen as a colleague working in similar fields of research. We have never formally collaborated in our research. Professor Nguyen has been an outstanding contributor for many years to research in the fields of epidemiology and genetic epidemiology of osteoporosis. Among other contributions, he has led major developments in the understanding of low-trauma fracture risk and the prediction of fractures for clinical application (e.g., the Garvan Fracture Risk

Calculator, which is widely used in research and clinical practice). He has guided and supported the development of osteoporosis research programs at multiple institutions in Australia and internationally. He also plays important consultancy roles for government bodies and industry.

In terms of scholarly activities, Prof. Nguyen is very active and highly-regarded as a reviewer of research proposals, student theses and works submitted for publication; these activities include service to many academic institutions, funding bodies, scientific journals and major conference program committees. He has successfully supervised a substantial number of higher-degree students. He has delivered a large number of invited lectures at prestigious conferences and institutions.

Prof. Nguyen has developed and conducted an impressively large number of teaching and training courses in Vietnam over many years, including several at Ton Duc Thang University. I note that he holds the positions of Deputy Chair of the Council for Scientific and Training Affairs and Director of Laboratory of Bone and Muscle Research at Ton Duc Thang University. These and numerous other roles/appointments in Vietnam are ample demonstration of his commitment to teaching, training, and research in Vietnam. As Prof. Nguyen's CV also demonstrates, he has and continues to hold numerous leadership positions in Australia and internationally.

I would rank Professor Nguyen's standing among the top 5% of international researchers of professorial or equivalent position and active in epidemiological/clinical research in the bone and mineral field."
—**Professor John Wark**, MBBS, PhD, FRACP, AM, Emeritus Professor of Medicine, University of Melbourne; Emeritus Honorary Consultant, Department of Diabetes & Endocrinology and Bone & Mineral Medicine, Royal Melbourne Hospital

"Tuan is a humble man. He is a lover of the scientific method and a lover of rigorous study design, execution, and interpretation. He is an educator and mentor whose words are softly spoken, graceful, and so true. Collaborating with Tuan in writing a scientific paper, and listening to him at the microphone at national and international meetings is an honour, privilege, and a journey of freedom in critical thinking, reading, writing, and speech—a journey of courage in striving for excellence, a metaphor of his journey through the heart of darkness to the light of a life in science."

—**Professor Ego Seeman**, MBBS, MD, FRACP, AM, FAHMS, Professor of Medicine, University of Melbourne, former President of ANZBMS, one of the world's most influential and most-cited researchers in the field of osteoporosis

"Dr. Tuan V. Nguyen, a refugee to Australia 35 years ago, has become one of the most influential epidemiologists in the study of bone. His long-standing interest in genetic and epidemiological risk factors for fracture in the individual led to his important contribution to osteoporosis: his concept of individualized fracture risk assessment. His research insights contributed to the widely used Garvan Fracture Risk Calculator, which is more predictive of fracture than the WHO model. Clearly, he is more than just an eminent epidemiologist. Dr. Nguyen has conceptualized novel ways of understanding and integrating data, using statistical techniques to better understand biological processes and consequences. His interests also include the use of genetic profiling in fracture risk assessment; he has conducted simulation studies demonstrating its effectiveness.

As a result of his multi-disciplinary approaches, Dr. Nguyen has been part of and led numerous studies that have helped refine our understanding of bone loss, the significance of osteoporosis in men, and premature mortality post fracture. Dr. Nguyen's research has contributed to a paradigm shift in our understanding of individual risk assessment in the course and management of osteoporosis. His statistical knowledge is unparalleled; his visionary use of applying statistics to understanding the biology of bone health and disease has had profound clinical impacts. His insights are paralleled by his generosity as a mentor, colleague, and professor."

—**Professor Elizabeth Barrett-Connor** (now deceased), MD, Distinguished Professor, Division of Epidemiology, the University of California at San Diego, School of Medicine, one of the eminent researchers in women's health and osteoporosis

Acknowledgements

I am profoundly grateful to the many individuals who played a vital role in bringing this memoir to life. Dr. Lê Anh Nguyệt's artistic vision shaped the book's first impression with her exquisite cover design. Dr. Quan-Vinh Nguyen, President of Helvietmed, provided invaluable suggestions that significantly improved the narrative. The insightful edits from my colleagues, Dr. Trần Sơn Thạch and Associate Professor Nhâm Trần, were instrumental in refining the manuscript. I extend my heartfelt thanks to Mr. John Launder, whose powerful photographs from his time as an Australian volunteer in Thai refugee camps during the 1980s provide a poignant and essential visual record of the Vietnamese refugee experience.

My research would not have been possible without the dedication and support of my students and colleagues to whom I am deeply grateful: Dr. Nguyễn Đình Nguyên, Dr. Trần Sơn Thạch, Dr. Trần Hoàng Ngọc Bích, Mai Thị Hà, Dr. Huỳnh Bảo Ngọc (Josie), Dr. Nguyễn Gia Huy, Dr. Hoàng Khương Duy, Dr. Krisel de Dios, Dr. Nguyễn Đình Tân (Tommy), Dr. Steve Frost, Dr. Mei Chan, Dr. Hồ Lê Phương Thảo, Dr. Phạm Thị Mỹ Hạnh, Dr. Trần Minh Giang, Dr. Lê Thị Thuý An, Dr. Lê Minh Thuận, Dr. Hà Tấn Đức, Dr. Nguyễn Thái Hoà, Dr. Thái Viết Tặng, Dr. Nguyễn Thị Thanh Hương, Dr. Phạm Nữ Hạnh Vân, Professor Shuman Yang, Professor Chatlert Pongchaiyakul, and Professor Henrik Ahlborg.

References to the Vietnam Osteoporosis Study and the Osteoporosis Society in Hồ Chí Minh City spoke volumes of the collaborative efforts that had yielded significant results. Here, a special thank you goes out to Professor Nguyễn Thy Khuê, Professor Nguyễn Thị Hùng, Dr. Hồ Phạm Thục Lan, Dr. Phạm Văn Đởm (may he rest in peace), Professor Nguyễn Thanh Bình (may he rest in peace), Dr. Lê Văn Út, and Professor Lê Vinh Danh. For over twenty years, they placed their trust in me, entrusting me with the critical task of building scientific capacity in Việt Nam. Their belief in the power of knowledge-sharing fostered a collaborative spirit that transcended borders and languages.

I extend my gratitude to Amy M. Le, the brilliant editor at Quill Hawk Publishing. With her keen insight, patience, and unwavering vision, Amy guided me through every page, transforming my memoir into something clearer, deeper, and more resonant. Thank you, Amy, for believing in this story, for challenging me to go further, and for turning a raw manuscript into a work I'm truly proud to call my own.

About the Author

Tuan V. Nguyen arrived in Australia as a Vietnamese refugee on January 26, 1982, after fleeing Vietnam in a rickety boat in April 1981 and spending a year in refugee camps in Thailand. He started his new life in Australia working as a kitchen hand at St Vincent's Hospital, returning a decade later to pursue his doctorate there. His groundbreaking research on the genetics and epidemiology of osteoporosis has gained international recognition.

Currently, he serves as Distinguished Professor of Predictive Medicine at the University of Technology Sydney and Adjunct Professor of Epidemiology at the University of New South Wales. He is also an Elected Fellow of the Australian Academy of Health and Medical Sciences, the Royal Society of New South Wales, and the American Society for Bone and Mineral Research. On January 26, 2022, marking 40 years in Australia, he was awarded the Order of Australia, the nation's highest honor, for his significant contributions to medical research, osteoporosis prevention, and higher education.

Kangaroo Dreams is Professor Nguyen's memoir. From fleeing Vietnam by boat to washing dishes in Sydney, Australia, Nguyen rose to become a leading scientist and global expert in bone health. With unwavering determination, he earned two doctorates, returned to the hospital he once cleaned—this time as a research leader—and was awarded the Order of Australia for his impact on global health. This inspiring memoir is a testament to resilience, curiosity, and the power of dreams against all odds.

Bibliography

In this section, I provide sources for key statements in the book. The bolded texts are excerpts from the book, followed by their sources indicated after the colon.

Chapter 1: The Mekong Flows Through Me

The United Nations estimated that from 1975 to 1995, close to a million Vietnamese embarked on perilous sea journeys:
The State of The World's Refugees 2000: Fifty Years of Humanitarian Action - Chapter 4: Flight from Indochina. https://www.unhcr.org/media/state-worlds-refugees-2000-fifty-years-humanitarian-action-chapter-4-flight-indochina

A staggering 200,000 to 400,000 vanished: Associated Press, ngày 23 tháng 6 năm 1979, San Diego Union, ngày 20 tháng 7 năm 1986. See generally Nghia M. Vo, The Vietnamese Boat People (2006), 1954 and 1975-1992, McFarland. and Rummel, Rudolph (1997), Statistics of Vietnamese Democide, in his Statistics of Democide, Table 6.1B, lines 730, 749-751.

Chapter 2: Unforgettable Days

According to Vietnamese authorities' own admissions to Amnesty International, by 1980, over 100 re-education camps dotted the landscape. Report of an AI Mission to the Socialist Republic of Vietnam, 1/6/1981. https://www.amnesty.org/en/documents/asa41/005/1981/en/?ref=luatkhoa.com

By 1988, a Vietnamese deputy foreign minister acknowledged the imprisonment of 100,000 former RVN personnel: Law Magazine https://www.newspapers.com/image/692864443/?match=1&terms=re-education+camp%2C+vietnam&ref=luatkhoa.com

Chapter 7: Building Bones Career

Dubbo Osteoporosis Epidemiology Study: https://researchdata.edu.au/dubbo-osteoporosis-epidemiology-study/96809.

The Garvan Institute's genesis can be traced back to 1963: https://www.garvan.org.au/about-us/history

A twin bone density study ignited a new flame in my curiosity: Nguyen TV, Howard GM, Kelly PJ, Eisman JA. Bone mass, lean mass and fat mass: same genes or same environments. *Am J Epidemiol* 1998; 147:3-16.

The vitamin D receptor gene: Morrison NA, Qi JC, Tokita A, Kelly P, Nguyen TV, Croft L, Sambrook PN, Eisman JA. Prediction of bone density by vitamin D receptor alleles. *Nature* 1994; 367:284-287.

The link between fractures and mortality, as well as the accelerated bone loss in the elderly: Center JR, Nguyen TV, Schneider D, Sambrook PN, Eisman

JA. Mortality after all major types of osteoporotic fracture in men and women: an observational study. *Lancet* 1999; 353:878-82.

Explore the often-overlooked issue of osteoporosis in men: Nguyen TV, Eisman JA, Kelly PJ, Sambrook PN (1996). Risk factors for osteoporotic fractures in men. *Am J Epidemiol*; 144:255-263.

Chapter 8: Crafting Prediction

Professor Richard Wasnich (then at the Hawaii Osteoporosis Center, Hawaii, USA), penned a critical piece in a leading journal: Wasnich R. Consensus and the T-score fallacy. Clinical Rheumatology 1997; 16:337-339.

However, my analysis of the Dubbo data revealed a significantly higher lifetime fracture risk: Nguyen ND, Ahlborg HG, Center JR, Eisman JA, Nguyen TV (2007). Residual lifetime risk of fractures in women and men. *J Bone Miner Res*;22(6):781-8.

These findings, published in two important papers in *Osteoporosis International* (2007 and 2008): Nguyen ND, Frost SA, Center JR, Eisman JA, Nguyen TV (2008). Development of prognostic nomograms for individualizing 5-year and 10-year fracture risks. *Osteoporos Int*; 19(10):1431-44. Nguyen ND, Frost SA, Center JR, Eisman JA, Nguyen TV (2007). Development of a nomogram for individualizing hip fracture risk in men and women. *Osteoporos Int*;18(8):1109-17.

One prominent professor even penned an editorial in a leading journal, hailing the arrival of fracture risk prediction models as a "revolution" and a "major advance": Aspray TJ. New horizons in fracture risk assessment. Age and Ageing 2013; 42: 548–554.

Chapter 9: Earning Doctorates

Inspired by this model, I spearheaded a study involving over 200 pairs of MZ and DZ twins: Nguyen TV, Howard GM, Kelly PJ, Eisman JA. Bone mass, lean mass and fat mass: same genes or same environments. *Am J Epidemiol* 1998; 147:3-16.

The University of New South Wales, my academic home, outlined the criteria for this prestigious honor: https://legacy.handbook.unsw.edu.au/general/2009/SSAPO/AwardRulesDSc.html.

DSc graduation ceremony:
https://www.youtube.com/watch?v=X0F6ekEiqhc

"I just needed a chance": from refugee to the heights of Australian medical research: Article by Ben Doherty, Guardian 19/6/2017.

Chapter 10: Striving for Recognition

The NHMRC fellowship became more than an award: https://www.nhmrc.gov.au/funding/statements-expectations.

A recent survey by the University of Melbourne painted a concerning picture: a mere 16% of faculty and professors in Australia's top universities were Asian: Nana Oishi: Workforce Diversity in Higher Education. The Experiences of Asian Academics in Australian Universities. Asia Institute of the The University of Melbourne, 2017.

Chapter 11: Climbing the Academic Ladder

The Australian Academy of Health and Medical Sciences:
https://aahms.org/about.

The Royal Society of New South Wales: https://www.royalsoc.org.au.

Chapter 12: Transformative Years

"BONEcheck": https://bonecheck.org

We christened it the "osteogenomic profile," a reflection of the interplay of genes and bone health: Ho-Le TP, Pham HM, Center JR, Eisman JA, Nguyen HT, Nguyen TV (2018). Prediction of changes in bone mineral density in the elderly: contribution of "osteogenomic profile". *Arch Osteoporos.* 2018;13(1):68.

Unveiling Skeletal Age: Tran TS, Ho-Le TP, Bliuc D, Abrahamsen B, Hansen L, Vestergaard P, et al. "Skeletal Age" for mapping the impact of fracture on mortality. *eLife.* 2023.

The appointment of Distinguished Professor: https://www.uts.edu.au/about/uts-governance/policies/uts-policy/appointment-distinguished-professors-procedure

A Eureka Moment in the Fight Against Hip Fractures: Tran, T. S., Ho-Le, T. P., Bliuc, D., Center, J. R., Blank, R. D., & Nguyen, T. V. (2023). Prevention of hip fractures: Trade-off between minor benefits to individuals and large benefits to the community. Journal of Bone and Mineral Research. https://doi.org/10.1002/jbmr.4907.

Chapter 14: Unmasking Science

"An Essay on Science and Narcissism":
Professor Bruno Lemaitre. https://www.amazon.com/Essay-Science-Narcissism-high-ego-personalities-ebook/dp/B01DS47AN4

It wasn't until a team of New Zealand and UK scientists, Drs. Mark Bolland, Alison Avenell, and Greg Gamble: Mark J. Bolland, Alison Avenell, Greg D. Gamble, and Andrew Grey. Systematic review and statistical analysis of the integrity of 33 randomized controlled trials. *Neurology* 6/12/2016.

While reviewing COVID-19 research, I came across a paper by Professor Didier Raoult: Gautret P, et al. Hydroxychloroquine and azithromycin as a treatment of COVID-19: results of an open-label non-randomized clinical trial. Int J Antimicrob Agents 2020 Jul;56(1):105949.

He mentioned Raoult's prolific publication record – a staggering 2,053 papers between 1979 and 2018: https://theconversation.com/why-the-h-index-is-a-bogus-measure-of-academic-impact-141684.

Consider Mrs. Tu Youyou: Xiao Zhai, Qijin Wang, Ming Li. Tu Youyou's Nobel Prize and the academic evaluation system in China. Lancet 23/4/2016.

Back in the 1960s, Eugene Garfield: Paul Wouters. Eugene Garfield (1925-2017). Nature 23/3/2017.

In 2005, the American physicist Jorge Hirsch introduced this new metric: J. E. Hirsch. An index to quantify an individual's scientific research output. Proc Natl Acad Sci 2005;102(46):16569-16572.

In 2008, librarian Jeffrey Beall of the University of Colorado emerged as a champion against this trend: Beall, J. (2017). What I learned from predatory publishers. *Biochemia Medica 2017;27*(2), 273-9.

It truly touched me when Richard Smith:
BMJ Blog 5/12/2017.
https://blogs.bmj.com/bmj/2017/12/05/richard-smith-strong-evidence-of-bias-against-research-from-low-income-countries.

"Most published research findings are false": John P. A. Ioannidis. Why Most Published Research Findings Are False. PLoS Medicine 30/8/2005. https://journals.plos.org/plosmedicine/article?id=10.1371/journal.pmed.0020124

Take for example the Reproducible Project in Cancer Biology: Reproducibility Project - Cancer Biology. Link: https://elifesciences.org/collections/9b1e83d1/reproducibility-project-cancer-biology

A group of researchers led by Ioannidis looked at 49 highly regarded RCTs: John P A Ioannidis. Contradicted and initially stronger effects in highly cited clinical research. JAMA 2005;294(2):218-28

An analysis published in *PLoS Biology* put a number on this frustration: Leonard P. Freedman, Iain M. Cockburn, Timothy S. Simcoe. The Economics of Reproducibility in Preclinical Research. PLoS Biology 9/6/2015. https://journals.plos.org/plosbiology/articleid=10.1371/journal.pbio.1002165.

A 2010 study by Fanelli painted a startling picture: Daniele Fanelli. "Positive" Results Increase Down the Hierarchy of the Sciences. PLoS ONE 7/4/2010.

Together with editors Fernando Rivadeneira and Roberto Civitelli: Nguyen TV, Rivadeneira F, Civitelli R (2019). New Guidelines for Data Reporting and Statistical Analysis: Helping Authors With Transparency and Rigor in Research. *J Bone Miner Res*;34(11):1981-1984.

In a separate "perspective article" published in *Osteoporosis and Sarcopenia* in 2020: Nguyen TV (2020). Common methodological issues and suggested solutions in bone research. Osteoporos Sarcopenia;6(4):161-167.

Chapter 15: Crossing Borders: My American Sojourn

Professor Tran Huu Dung, an economist at Wright State: https://en.wikipedia.org/wiki/TranHuuDung

With the Editor-in-Chief's backing, I spearheaded the creation of new editorial guidelines titled *New Guidelines for Data Reporting and Statistical Analysis: Helping Authors With Transparency and Rigor in Research*: Nguyen TV, Rivadeneira F, Civitelli R (2019). New Guidelines for Data Reporting and Statistical Analysis: Helping Authors With Transparency and Rigor in Research. *J Bone Miner Res*;34(11):1981-1984.

The general criteria for fellowship of the American Society for Bone and Mineral Research: https://www.asbmr.org/award-grants/recognition-awards/fellows-of-the-asbmr.

Chapter 17: Returning to the Land of Smiles

Dr. Chatlert Pongchaiyakul, a brilliant young Thai doctor I fondly called Gua: https://scholar.kku.ac.th/researchers/342.

KKU, a sprawling university in Khon Kaen province: https://www.kku.ac.th.

Chapter 18: Building Bridges in Việt Nam

The Asia Pacific Consortium on Osteoporosis: https://apcobonehealth.org/about

The 16th AFES Conference: https://endocrinology.dk/PDF/AFES2011First%20Announcement.pdf

The Vietnam Osteoporosis Study: Ho-Pham LT, Nguyen TV (2017). The Vietnam Osteoporosis Study: Rationale and design. *Osteoporosis and Sarcopenia*; 2:90-97

The Alexandre Yersin Prize:
https://helvietmed.org/alexandre-yersin-prize-for-outstanding-medical-publications

Tâm Anh Research Institute (TAMRI): https://tamri.vn/en

Chapter 19: Two Homes, One Heart

Ms Tania Mihailuk MP:
https://www.parliament.nsw.gov.au/Hansard/Pages/HansardFull.aspx#/DateDisplay/HANSARD-1323879322-121970/HANSARD-1323879322-122088

Ms Wendy Lindsay MP:
https://www.parliament.nsw.gov.au/Hansard/Pages/HansardResult.aspx#/docid/HANSARD-1323879322-122929

Index